# Words
*and*
# Images

*Edited & Translated by*
ANTHONY WALL

UNIVERSITY OF
CALGARY
PRESS

# WORDS
*and*
# IMAGES

*A French Rendez-vous*

University of Calgary Press
2500 University Drive NW
Calgary, Alberta
Canada T2N 1N4
www.uofcpress.com

LIBRARY AND ARCHIVES CANADA CATALOGUING IN PUBLICATION

Words and images : a French rendez-vous / edited and translated by Anthony Wall.

Includes bibliographical references and index.
ISBN 978-1-55238-259-2

1. Visual communication.  2. Written communication.  3. Words in art.
4. Art and literature.  I. Wall, Anthony, 1956-

P93.5.W66 2010           302.2           C2009-907187-8

The University of Calgary Press acknowledges the support of the Alberta Foundation for the Arts for our publications. We acknowledge the financial support of the Government of Canada through the Book Publishing Industry Development Program (BPIDP) for our publishing activities. We acknowledge the financial support of the Canada Council for the Arts for our publishing program.

Printed and bound in Canada by Marquis
∞ This book is printed on FSC Silva Edition & FSC Flo Dull paper

Cover design by Melina Cusano
Page design and typesetting by Melina Cusano

# Table of Contents

List of Illustrations vii

List of Tables xi

Acknowledgments xiii

Preface xv

Introduction xvii

1. Obscure Objects of Depiction and Description:
The Example of Alechinsky's and Bonnefoy's Painted
Wall (Rue Descartes, Paris)
*(Marie-Dominique Popelard)* 1

2. Mary Magdalene in the Village of Emmaus:
Notes on Two Paintings by Laurent de La Hyre
*(Bruno Nassim Aboudrar)* 25

3. Painting the Readers of the Eighteenth Century
*(Anthony Wall)* 61

4. The Decisive Moment
*(Stéphane Lojkine)* 93

5. On the Strategies of Portraiture in the Images
and Texts of Seventeenth-Century Spain
*(Pierre Civil)* 139

6. The Invention of Prehistoric Rock Art:
A Visual Experience
*(Béatrice Fraenkel)* 171

7. Word-and-Image Studies in France:
   A Bibliographical Essay                              201

8. Other Cited (but unillustrated) Works of Art         233

Colour Plates                                           239

Index                                                   249

# List of Illustrations

*Boldface page numbers refer to colour reproductions.*

1a.  The Alechinsky-Bonnefoy Wall, 40 rue Descartes, Paris (close-up).  6, **239**

1b.  The Alechinsky-Bonnefoy Wall, 40 rue Descartes, Paris (with an advertisement).  17

2.  Laurent La Hyre, *Noli me tangere*, 1656, oil on canvas, Grenoble, Musée de Grenoble, 162 x 175 cm.  43, **240**

3.  Laurent La Hyre, *The Appearance of Christ at Emmaus*, 1656, oil on canvas, Grenoble, Musée de Grenoble, 162 x 165 cm.  44, **240**

4.  Nicolas Poussin, *Noli me tangere*, 1653, oil on wood panel, Madrid, Museo del Prado, 47 x 39 cm.  48

5.  Lavinia Fontana, *Noli me tangere*, 1581, oil on canvas, Florence, Galleria degli Uffizi, 80 x 65.1 cm.  49

6.  Titian, *Noli me tangere*, ca. 1512–1514, oil on canvas, © London, National Gallery, 110.5 x 91.9 cm.  51

7.  Hans Holbein the Younger, *Noli me tangere*, ca. 1524, oil on oak panel, Hampton Court (England), The Royal Collection (© 2010, Her Majesty Queen Elizabeth II), 76.7 x 95.8 cm.  53, **241**

8.  Lancret, Nicolas, *La Malice*, first half of the 18th century, oil on canvas, Dublin, National Gallery of Ireland, 36 x 29 cm.  62

9.  Jean-Baptiste Deshays, *Portrait of a Young Woman Holding a Book* (*Presumed Portrait of Madame Deshays*), ca. 1760, oil on canvas, private collection, 51 x 43 cm. (Foto Marburg/Art Resource, NY).  64

10.  François Boucher, *Rest during the Flight into Egypt*, 1737, oil on canvas, Saint Petersburg, The State Hermitage Museum, 139.5 x 148.5 cm.  67

11. Sir Joshua Reynolds, *Portrait of Giuseppe Baretti*, 1773–1774, oil on canvas, private collection, 73.7 x 62.2 cm.  68

12. Pierre Subleyras, *Presumed Portrait of Giuseppe Baretti*, ca. 1745, oil on canvas, Paris, Louvre, 74 x 61 cm. (Eric Lessing/Art Resource, NY).  69, **242**

13. Michel-Barthélemy Ollivier, *Thé à l'anglaise chez le Prince de Conti dans le Salon des Quatre-Glaces*, 1766, oil on canvas, Versailles, Musée national du Château et de Trianon, 53 x 68 cm. (Réunion des Musées nationaux/Art Resource, NY).  75

14. Jean-François Gilles Colson, *Portrait of a Young Girl Reading*, second half of the eighteenth century, oil on canvas, Morlanne (Pyrénées-Atlantiques, France), Musée du Château, 58 x 48 cm (photograph by Jean-Marc Decompte, Conseil général des Pyrénées-Atlantiques).  77, **243**

15. Louis Tocqué, *Portrait of Arnoldus van Rijneveld*, ca. 1730–1739, oil on canvas, Amsterdam, Rijksmuseum, 91.5 x 72 cm.  79

16. Jean-Baptiste-Siméon Chardin, *Le Singe antiquaire*, 1740, oil on canvas, Chartres, Musée des Beaux-Arts, 28.5 x 23.5 cm. (cliché Musée des Beaux-Arts de Chartres).  81

17. Pierre-Louis Dumesnil the Younger, *The Attending Physician* (*Presumed Portrait of Nicolas Beauton*), 18th century, oil on canvas, Bordeaux, Musée des Beaux-Arts, 32.3 x 44.1 cm. (Eric Lessing/Art Resource, NY).  85

18. Nicolas Poussin, *Israelites Gathering Manna*, 1639, oil on canvas, Paris, Louvre, 149 x 200 cm.  96

19. Timanthes, *The Sacrifice of Iphigenia*, according to a fresco found in Pompei, 1st century A.D., Naples, National Museum of Archaeology, 138 x 140 cm.    110

20. Annibale Carracci, *Hercules at the Crossroads*, ca. 1595–1596, oil on canvas, Naples, Museo e Galleria nazionali di Capodimonte, 237 x 167 cm.    114, **244**

21. Pieter Pauwel Rubens, *The Birth of Louis XIII*, ca. 1621–1625, oil on canvas, Paris, Louvre, 394 x 295 cm.    119

22. Jean-Baptiste Greuze, *Portrait of Madame Greuze (The Well-Loved Mother)*, 1765, pastel with red, black, and white chalks and stumping on laid paper, Washington, National Gallery of Art, 44 x 32.2 cm (image courtesy of the Board of Trustees, National Gallery of Art).    121

23. Jean-Baptiste Greuze, *The Well-Loved Mother*, 1769, oil on canvas, Madrid, Collection of the Marquee Laborde, 99 x 131 cm.    122

24. Charles Michel-Ange Challe, *The Death of Cleopatra*, 1761, according to the engraving by Jean-Baptiste Michel (ca. 1770–1778), Lisbon, Biblioteca Nacional de Portugal, 40.6 x 28.7 cm.    125

25. Jean-Baptiste Greuze, *Filial Piety (The Paralytic)*, 1761, oil on canvas, Saint Petersburg, The State Hermitage Museum, 115 x 146 cm.    128

26. Juan de Courbes, *Lope de Vega*, engraving, 1630. In *Laurel de Apolo con otras rimas*, by Lope de Vega, Madrid: Juan Ganzález, 1630.    144

27. Juan de Courbes, *Luis de Góngora*, engraving, 1630. In *Lecciones solemnes a las obras de Don Luis de Góngora*, by José Pellicer de Salas y Tovar, Madrid: Imprenta del Reino, 1630.    146

28. Francisco Pacheco, *Retrato de fray Luis de León*, engraving. In Francisco Pacheco, *Libro de descripción de verdaderos retratos de ilustres y memorables varones*, edited with an introduction by Pedro M. Piñero Ramírez and Rogelio Reyes Cano (Seville: Diputación Provincial de Sevilla, 1985), 67.    149

29. El Greco (Domenikos Theotokopoulos), *Fray Hortensio Felix Paravicino*, 1609, oil on canvas, Boston, Museum of Fine Arts, 112.1 x 86.1 cm (photograph © 2010, Museum of Fine Arts, Boston).    152, **245**

30. Juan de Valdés Leal, *Don Miguel de Mañara Reading the Rule of the Holy Charity*, 1681, oil on canvas, Seville, Hospital de la Caridad, Chapter House, 196 x 225 cm.    155, **246**

31. José de Ribera, *Teresa Writing with the Inspiration of the Holy Spirit*, 1644, oil on canvas, Valencia, Museo de bellas artes de Valencia, 129.5 x 104.4 cm.    158

32. Francisco de Zurbarán, *Saint Serapion*, 1628, oil on canvas, Hartford (Connecticut), Wadsworth Atheneum Museum of Art, 120 x 103 cm (The Ella Gallup Sumner and Mary Catlin Sumner Collection Fund).    161, **246**

33. Panel of negative hands in the Gargas cave, photograph by Béatrice Fraenkel.    172

34. Incomplete negative hands in the Gargas cave, photograph by Béatrice Fraenkel.    172

35. Photograph from in front of the La Mouthe cave, during an excursion organized for the Congress of the French Association for the Advancement of Science held at Montauban, August 4, 1902. From left to right: Félix Regnault (4th person), Émile Cartailhac (5th person), François Daleau (7th person, seated), Henri Breuil (13th person), Émile Rivière (14th person), Saint-Germain-en-Laye, Archives of the Musée d'archéologie nationale (fonds Breuil, Album #1).    186

36. Drawings by Breuil from the Altimara cave, 1902–1903, pencil, sanguine and pastel on paper, 36.5 x 54 cm, Paris, Musée national d'histoire naturelle, Main Library (fonds iconographique Breuil, no. 54 1933bis).    190

37. A page from the notebooks of François Daleau, reproduced in Marc Groenen, *Pour une histoire de la préhistoire*, Grenoble: Jérôme Million, 1994.    192

## List of Tables

Table 1: Discoveries and Announcements    32

Table 2: Appearances of Jesus    32

Table 3: Misrecognition    38

Table 4: Recognition    38

Table 5: Number of sites discovered per year    187

# Acknowledgments

The original French-language version of Béatrice Fraenkel's article was published in *Gradhiva* 6 (2007): 18–31, a journal published by the Musée du Quai Branly in Paris. The editor and translator gratefully acknowledges the kind permission of the journal to publish an English-language version of this article.

Every effort has been made to secure the rights of all the images produced in this volume wherever such permission is required. For permission to reproduce the images contained herein, we gratefully acknowledge:

The Biblioteca nacional de Portugal, Lisbon, Portugal
The Conseil général of the Département des Pyrénées-Atlantiques,
    Pau, France
The Musée de Grenoble, Grenoble, France
The State Hermitage Museum, Saint Petersburg, Russia
The National Gallery, London, United Kingdom
The Musée national d'histoire naturelle, Paris, France
The Musée d'archéologie nationale, Saint-Germain-en-Laye, France
The Louvre, Paris, France
The Rijksmuseum, Amsterdam, Netherlands
The Collection of the Marquee Laborde, Madrid, Spain
The Hospital de la Caridad, Seville, Spain
The Board of Trustees, National Gallery of Art, Washington, U.S.A.
The Galleria degli Uffizi, Florence, Italy
The Museum of Fine Arts, Boston, U.S.A. (Isaac Sweetser Fund, 04.234).
The Musée des Beaux-Arts, Bordeaux, France
The Musée des Beaux-Arts, Chartres, France
The Musée national du Château et de Trianon, Versailles, France
The Museo de Bellas Artes, Valencia, Spain
The Museo del Prado, Madrid, Spain
The Museo e Galleria nazionali di Capodimonte, Naples, Italy
The National Gallery of Ireland, Dublin, Ireland

The National Museum of Archaeology, Naples, Italy
The Royal Collection, United Kingdom
The Wadsworth Atheneum Museum of Art, Hartford, Connecticut,
U.S.A. (The Ella Gallup Sumner and Mary Catlin Sumner
Collection Fund).
Art Resource, New York, U.S.A.

# PREFACE

Ce livre cherche à diffuser des travaux écrits en français dans un domaine de recherche particulièrement vivant qui explore les multiples relations entre les mots et les images à la fois dans la vie de tous les jours et dans les arts. En France, depuis plus d'une quinzaine d'années, les recherches dans ce champ ont connu un essor remarquable.

De nature interdisciplinaire, publiées en français et faisant l'objet de nombreuses recherches à travers toute la France et dans plusieurs autres villes de la francophonie internationale, ces travaux sur les relations entre parole et image ne sont pas bien connus dans le monde anglophone. Le présent livre, consacré à la diffusion d'une branche de la pensée française, s'offre à la lecture des chercheurs et étudiants intéressés qui ne lisent pas le français. Ainsi propose-t-il au lecteur anglophone une porte d'entrée vers un monde d'une grande richesse intellectuelle.

Pour son appui généreux et constant, à la fois pour le premier colloque tenu en français à Calgary au printemps 2007 et pour la production de ce livre en anglais, nous tenons à remercier le Centre Français de l'Université de Calgary.

This book aims to disseminate a number of French-language works belonging to a field of study which is particularly vibrant at the present time. This field concerns the multiple relationships and connections obtaining between words and images, both in everyday life and in the arts. In France, for the past fifteen years or more, research in this line of inquiry has been remarkably active.

Interdisciplinary by their very nature, French-language publications dealing with this nexus have appeared in virtually every corner of France and in several important cities in the French-speaking world outside of France. Unfortunately, they are not very well known to the English-speaking community of scholars. The present book has thus been conceived with the idea of making this important branch of French-language research known to English-speaking researchers and students who do not read French. It is hoped that the book will open a window for them unto a world that is of great intellectual worth.

The editor and translator of this volume wishes to express a sincere word of thanks to the French Centre at the University of Calgary for its constant and generous support not only for the organization of the original study days held in Calgary in the spring of 2007, which are at the heart of this project, but also for the material production of the present book in English.

# INTRODUCTION

The present collection of essays deals with the multifarious ways in which the words and images of art and everyday life interact with one another. They stem for the most part from an international symposium held at the University of Calgary in March–April 2007, a meeting which was attended by researchers associated with the Research Group APPLA & CO ("Approches pragmatiques en philosophie du langage et en communication") from the Université de la Sorbonne Nouvelle-Paris III and with the "Texts and Images Research Group" at the University of Calgary. The topics studied during the symposium also interested participants from the Université de Provence (France) and the École des Hautes Études en Sciences Sociales in Paris. Following the symposium, several of the papers presented were reworked and subsequently translated from French to English, before being edited for inclusion in the present volume.

The reader will immediately notice the interdisciplinary nature of the essays included here. The range of subjects represented is indicative of the wide variety of disciplines present at the symposium, just as the latter are all part of the broad field of inquiry we choose to call "word-and-image studies." A prominent part of the intellectual scene in many countries around the world, "word-and-image studies" are particularly active in France at the current time. Amongst the disciplines present here – philosophy, literary studies, art history, anthropology – it is hoped that, through this representative selection of essays, the main thrusts of research initiatives, currently unfolding within the French-speaking world, will become discernable for the English-speaking reader. It is also hoped that some of the originality of the research currently being published in France will become evident for the reader despite the fact that these studies appear in translation (never an utterly reliable tool of communication).

As is well-known, "French theory" was a fashionable phrase used for designating the vibrant humanistic research which occurred in France from the late 1960s to the early 1980s. Originating in the disciplines of anthropology and linguistics, French theory spread – first in the forms of structuralism and then of post-structuralism – into other disciplines such as literary studies, philosophy and psychology, and eventually permeated virtually every corner of the French academy. On the western side of the Atlantic, both in North and South America, semiotic approaches to the study of culture, largely based on the work of the French structuralists, and the subdiscipline later known as "Literary Theory" enjoyed tremendous prestige both in the eyes of students and of researchers. This was all part of what has since been described as the "linguistic turn" of the human sciences; in France, by the late 1990s and in the first decade of the new millennium, the earlier furor of the linguistic turn has all but abated, and cognitivism in the disciplines of philosophy and psychology has achieved new prominence. Linguistics and the philosophy of language no longer appear to be the "master" disciplines that they once were.

Alongside the rise and fall of French Theory and its various strands, there developed in France another combination of interdisciplinary interests around the various ways and possibilities in which words and images work together. Definite advances had been achieved during the structuralist period, particularly in visual semiotics, psychology, and in the philosophy of images. At the same time, the traditional discipline of art history no longer seemed so adamant to defend its hitherto impregnable fortress along with all its closely guarded disciplinary walls. The advances in computer technology, which gave new possibilities for collecting, storing, and sharing images, also had a key role to play in allowing researchers other than art historians to gather and to study images in new and exciting ways. In all this, the seminal work written by two towers of intellectual strength and curiosity in France, Louis Marin and Daniel Arasse, was instrumental in initiating unexplored avenues of interdisciplinary research, ones that were destined to lead to a better understanding of the ways in which images and words speak to us either together or separately. Several active foyers of research activity – for example in Toulouse around Arnaud Rykner and Philippe Ortel, in Paris around Mireille Gagnebin, in Poitiers around Liliane Louvel and

Henri Scepti, in Leuven (Belgium) around Myriam Watthée-Delmotte, in Montreal with the Figura Research Group and the Centre de recherche sur l'intermédialité, began to spring up and to flourish. There were, and still are, many other research centres and university departments throughout the French-speaking world where word-and-image studies play an important role. Given the liveliness of this interdisciplinary field, the present collection of essays can in no way be inclusive of all the important developments of word-and-image studies in France and elsewhere in French-speaking universities. It can, however, be claimed that each of the essays published here is representative of a major thrust in this field of inquiry.

Marie-Dominique Popelard is a professor of aesthetics and the philosophy of language at the University of the Sorbonne Nouvelle-Paris III where she teaches courses in the philosophy of communication and leads the research group APPLA & CO (Approches pragmatiques en philosophie du langage et de la communication). Her article on a large painted wall situated along the Rue Descartes in Paris describes how the perception of the painted surface of the wall along with that of the painted poem both influence and support one another. The wall is a fine example of a cultural artefact which disallows talk of one medium being subordinated to the other, be that either the words or the images. As such, it poses serious problems for much current thinking in the philosophy of mind, ways of thinking which still have not come to grips with some of the major issues explored here concerning the intertwining of words and images in human understanding. The essay also suggests, in the strongest of terms, that the temptation to understand the reading of the wall's words independently of the images, and vice-versa, is inevitably doomed to failure, as both the structure and content of the verbal language as well as the shapes and colours of the images clearly show. This text has been placed at the beginning of the collection the reader is about to read precisely because it puts several central theoretical issues on the table. In particular, the article delineates several crucial problems concerning depiction and description within various types of human language and how the same philosophical issues concerning human expression take various forms according to the specific medium in which they are concretized.

Bruno-Nassim Aboudrar is a professor of Art History teaching in the Department of Cultural Mediation at the Université de la Sorbonne Nouvelle-Paris III. The article translated here deals with the invisibility of the Christ figure after his Resurrection; it studies in particular two evangelical scenes which solicited much interest among painters in the sixteenth and seventeenth centuries, first the meeting between Christ and Mary Magdalene outside the tomb on Easter Sunday morning and, second, the supper at Emmaus, which occurred later on during the same day (a scene which included Christ, two apostles, and several other persons). For both of these scenes, Aboudrar brings into focus the intricate interplay between the paintings studied and relevant evangelical and mystical texts, all of which deal with the same topic of seeing the invisible. He especially highlights the role of several mystical thinkers in this context, including authors working more or less at the same time as the painters featured here. The art historian thus throws much-needed light on many profound connections between the issues broached by painters and those mystical texts of their time which underpinned much of what they were thinking in pictorial terms. To this extent, this article represents another way of showing the interconnection of texts and images and it does so for a very painterly artist such as Laurent de La Hyre.

University Professor of French at the University of Calgary, Anthony Wall presents a panorama of the rich and relatively unknown corpus of French paintings from the eighteenth century that portray someone in the act of reading. Scenes of readers present an outstanding locus with which to study the interaction between literary and pictorial traditions. The corpus of eighteenth-century readers, representing both major and minor painters of the Enlightenment, allows us to see painting as commenting in a variety of ways upon literary activity. These paintings also give us an invaluable glimpse into the historical movement in Europe that led us from a view of reading seen as a public activity to one that saw it as a private one. This historical movement is anything but a smooth passage, and the study presented here purports to point out the exceptional nature of Joshua Reynolds's portrait of Giuseppe Baretti when seen in the context of European Enlightenment thinking. Although English and French painters often approach the iconography of reading in different ways, one sees here an amazing convergence of issues between the issues explored by Reynolds and those by several French painters of the same period.

Stéphane Lojkine is a professor of eighteenth-century French literature at the Université de Provence, where he specializes in the works of the writer-philosopher Denis Diderot. In the study presented here, Lojkine concentrates on Diderot's conception of the "decisive moment" as it appeared both in Diderot's monumental *Salons* – a virtual encyclopaedia of French art from the eighteenth century – and as it relates to the nascent philosophy of art and aesthetics in the European Enlightenment, with particular emphasis on Lessing's work. Lojkine traces Diderot's thinking to that of the founding French Academician Charles Le Brun from the mid-seventeenth century, which he discusses in relation to the analysis Diderot made of two French artists from his own time, one great and one small, namely Jean-Baptiste Greuze and Charles Michel-Ange Challe. The latter paintings are also discussed in relation to Diderot's theory of time as applicable to painting. Here, Diderot's philosophy of time takes on particular significance in the context of his vast knowledge of seventeenth-century painting and theory, most notably of Nicolas Poussin and Annibale Carracci.

Pierre Civil is a professor of Spanish literature of the Renaissance and the early modern period. Currently Vice-President (Research) at the Université de la Sorbonne Nouvelle in Paris and professor of Spanish in the Department of Hispanic Studies of the same university, he presents here a study of portraiture as it was practised in the particular socio-historical circumstances of the Spanish court during the late 16th and early 17th centuries. It is of course impossible to understand this special brand of portraiture without the involvement of theological teaching and the wider aesthetic practices that were prevalent at the time, in particular Jesuit theology with all its Spanish quirks. It is furthermore necessary to take into account the important role that written words played within the very frame of the portraits themselves, both in engravings and in oil paintings. With all its power, wealth, and influence, Spain can be seen as an important crucible in the birth of Early Modern European culture. One quickly realizes that it is impossible to understand Spanish portraits of this period in the absence of the various verbal discourses that accompanied them, whether they be poetic, theological, or philosophical. In this context, one is able to see the particular place portraiture achieved both within the artistic practices of Spain at the time and in relation to several important poetic traditions. This is not surprising, in light of the fact that the philosophical aesthetics of the day theorized the rivalry, if not the fraternity, between poetry and painting in their respective propensities for portraits. The painting of portraits is therefore not just a question of using colours and composition in an increasingly sophisticated manner; it is especially a profoundly philosophical and poetic art.

Béatrice Fraenkel is a Director of Research at the prestigious École des Hautes Études en Sciences Sociales in Paris, where she gives graduate seminars related to her topic of predilection: the anthropological history and semiotics of writing. In the study published here, she inquires into the strange history of the many hand-paintings that were, and still are, an integral part of several prehistoric caves, discovered both in France and in Spain, that had been sites for archaeological digs in the nineteenth and early twentieth centuries. What is amazing about these caves is that, for decades, in these same sites, the hand-paintings situated on the walls and ceilings of the caves went either completely unnoticed or, when they had been seen by accident, were inevitably misunderstood either as fakes or as belonging to relatively recent cultures. They were virtually never seen by archaeologists for what they were: signs of human artistic activity from over thirty thousand years ago. Using a Foucaldian framework informed by phenomenological philosophy, Fraenkel explores the reasons why it was literally impossible for earlier researchers to see these hands for what they were, that is until an epistemological shift had occurred within the discipline of archaeology. Fraenkel is thus enabled to show the strong links between, on the one hand, what the researcher actually sees when on a dig and, on the other, what the researcher currently believes according to the readings he or she has made within his or her discipline. The wall paintings at issue are testimony to the fact that human language was probably born within a curious mixture of language and painting.

The rewriting of the papers included in this volume was greatly facilitated by the friendly and comfortable environment that the University of Calgary was able to provide to the participants of the Calgary symposium during the spring of 2007. The original papers delivered lasted approximately forty minutes and each was followed by a lively period of discussion, which sometimes lasted up to an hour. Discussions continued unabated during meals and several outings. They later led to a second conference, held in Paris, in November 2008, and will culminate in a major international conference to be held at the Centre international de Cerisy-La-Salle in Normandy, France, in June 2010.

Each of the contributions printed here closes with a short bibliography containing the titles quoted in that particular study. It also gives the English translations of these titles, when available. The exception to this last rule is the bibliographical essay to be found at the end of the volume. Here, the appended bibliography purports to give a detailed picture of virtually all the major strands of contemporary "word-and-image" research in France. The works listed at the end of this essay should therefore be seen as supplementary to the three important currents of research that are discussed in the essay itself, even in those instances where they have not been mentioned explicitly, either in the six preceding essays included in this volume or in the pages of the essay. The final bibliography includes French-language publications, printed mainly in France, more or less since the beginning of the current flurry of works, that is, since 1993. It has been assembled with a view to giving the reader an overall picture of both the scope and the vibrancy of this particular interdisciplinary field of studies at the current moment.

The Faculty of Humanities, the French Centre, and the Department of French, Italian and Spanish, all at the University of Calgary, contributed both moral and exceptionally generous material support for this international endeavour. May these printed words of thanks show the high level of gratitude we all felt during the privileged days we spent in Calgary during the final days of March and the early days of April 2007, feelings which all of us still share today along with the many fine memories created by fruitful exchange. As editor and translator of this volume, I wish to dedicate these pages to the memory of Dr. Rowland Smith, Dean of the Faculty of Humanities from 2004 to 2008. He gracefully opened our colloquium in French on the first day.

# Obscure Objects of Depiction and Description: The Example of Alechinsky's and Bonnefoy's Painted Wall (Rue Descartes, Paris)

*Marie-Dominique Popelard*

> According to its Greek, Oriental and Roman traditions, Byzantium had always believed that there existed a natural equivalence, or complementarity, between words and images. Describing, writing, tracing, engraving, painting, all these activities were most often expressed by a single word: *graphein*. – Gilbert Dagron

When speaking of texts and images, the least one can say is that there is a wide choice of relevant objects available for study as well as many approaches for studying them. The methodological choice adopted here will consist in placing myself, quite purposely, in a zone that straddles both texts and images, a zone that also transgresses the boundaries of several academic disciplines. While some disciplines start with a text and work toward an image, others concentrate on the image in order to take the presence of a text into account. Dialogic pragmatics offers a most appropriate way of dealing with these multiple points of view; it is an approach that puts all the relationships it can discover at the fore-ground of its study, relationships between, on the one hand, questions concerning the elaboration of expressive material in all its concreteness and, on the other, the human activities that lead to such productions.

Let us state, from the start, that while we shall be discussing a paint-ing that enters into a dialogue with a poem, i.e., one that shows the poet Yves Bonnefoy in artistic dialogue with the painter Pierre Alechinsky, the overarching aim of our discussion is not exactly an aesthetic one. This example has been chosen mainly because it provides a paradigmatic case of certain generic relationships that obtain between a text and an image, relationships that poetry and painting are able to illustrate in such outstanding ways. The generic relationship broached here has to do with the referential relations established between Yves Bonnefoy's poem and Pierre Alechinsky's drawing. We begin with two trivial questions: (1) does the one depict what the other describes? and (2) is the relation-ship between the two a symmetrical one? In reply to these questions, we begin by noting that relationships can also be of reciprocal complemen-tarity and that, as such, they may well represent the type of relationships we need to consider. If, as people often say, words are lacking in the face of images, let us assume that images are also lacking in the face of words. Do texts and images accomplish the same communicative tasks in such a way that it is possible to consider poetry and painting as if they were quietly walking together hand in hand? When considered together, both textual and iconic productions describe and depict, and they do this by making the object of their respective description or depiction present in our minds.

It nevertheless appears difficult to deny, from the very outset, that reciprocal limitations obtain between verbal and pictorial language. Consequently it would be unwise to place words and images in separ-ate realms, especially when we realize that, whenever we are faced with an iconic emptiness, we are tempted to find appropriate words to fill the space,[1] just as when we are faced with verbal silence we are equally tempted to find appropriate images.[2] Even when carefully distinguished according to their respective powers, texts and images can nonetheless

MARIE-DOMINIQUE POPELARD

complement one another. In certain instances, at least, it seems as if it were possible to *show* what we could not *say*, or even to *say* what we were unable to *show*. All this leads us to believe in the possibility of liberating the adage contained in Ludwig Wittgenstein's *Tractatus* concerning language and silence – "Whereof one cannot speak, thereof one must be silent"[3] – from interpretations claiming that it refers solely to the impossibility of metalanguage *within* language. Can we not read it as suggesting that words and images call out to one another through the very insufficiency of their respective autonomies? Or we can perhaps read it as suggesting that, once a break has been clearly established between the verbal and imagistic modes of human communication, there still remains the possibility of inserting the one into the other.

It also seems clear that images and words are able to take pragmatic advantage of certain moments, that is, when their respective communicative aims either come close together or even merge, moments when their paths either cross one another or follow parallel trajectories;[4] the meanings and semiotic practices at play both in the case of words and in that of images communicate with one another in the same way that we can speak of communicating vessels. The same is true when they are used in aesthetic productions, which is not entirely surprising when we consider that no real proof has ever been adduced for any definitive break between images and verbal language, ever since theoretical approaches were devised to deal with the one or the other (let us not forget that visual semiotics first worked on the bases established by linguistics).[5]

The mere fact that we are dealing with words that speak and images that demonstrate can now be used to consider the idea that images can also speak and words can also demonstrate. Could it be that in such instances words and images are merely attempting to imitate one another? On the wall of a building on the Rue Descartes in the Fifth District of Paris, words written by a poet accompany a coloured drawing made by a painter. What, if any, are the particular expressive powers that are gained by the juxtaposition of drawing and poem? Part of the interest in asking this question lies in seeing what happens to the semiotic realm when it is placed in an aesthetic context. Further, it prompts us to ask what happens to an object – in this instance a tree – when it is constructed simultaneously by description and by depiction.

## THE SAME INSCRUTABILITY OF REFERENCE?

Let us postulate, for a moment, that description and depiction are characteristic of two different modes of "speaking about" the world, in other words two types of reference, respectively the one employed by poetry and the one employed by painting. Now, if such were the case, our query would then become part of a project destined, first, to find all the possible ways in which these modes apply to the world and, second, to define what each mode is able to teach us about the world. Without adopting any firm ontological position concerning the fact that a painter decides to show (or not to show) certain objects in the world or that an author has the binary choice either of making objects exist, or not, through his words, an agreement is at the very least possible concerning the metaphorical capacity of painting: painters present certain apparent beings about which, even if nothing else can be said about them, we can affirm that the nature of their being consists in being visible. And it is in this ability to make things visible that the painting's fictive abilities also lie, fiction understood here in the sense that the visible beings constructed within the artwork are make-believe, since they only exist insofar as they are part of an artwork.

Things are no different in the case of literary works. As is true of painting, writers only retain for their created beings those elements that are relevant for the work as a whole. In this instance we have a clear example of a criterion that is wholly "pragmatic," i.e., that of relevance, one which must be understood in terms of the relevance for an author, relevance for the reader, or even relevance for the story being told. Concerning the literary being thus constructed, we can thus postulate that the nature of its being consists in being readable.

Constructed in order to be visible or readable, the beings presented by the painter and the writer depend on the abilities possessed by the viewer-reader to see or to read them. In other words, they depend on a critical ability to understand them and to identify what has been made visible-readable.[6] Let us call these beings "objects," following here in the tradition established by Peirce, and also respecting the linguistic usage established by Goethe. Goethe is precisely concerned with this same question of "objects" when, paragraph by paragraph, he quotes from and comments upon Diderot's *Notes on Painting*, and even going further than Diderot himself who was careful to distinguish his own work as a writer from that accomplished by a painter. In particular, Goethe stresses a distinction between rhetoric – in German expressed as *Redekunst* – and painting according the relationships they entertain vis-à-vis the singular nature of the object they present:

> Painting is very distant indeed from rhetoric [*Redekunst*], and even if one could also admit that the visual artist sees objects in the same way that the orator does, one would nevertheless see that a very different force is awakened in the one as compared to the other. The orator races from one object to another, from one artwork to another: for him it is a matter of reflecting on them, of apprehending them, of gaining an overall view of them, of classifying them and of addressing their characteristics. The artist, on the other hand, relies directly on the object, he unites with this object in love, he shares the best part of his mind and his heart with it, he reconstructs it.[7]

We notice that Goethe follows Diderot in his attempt to understand the particularities of literary and pictorial creation: of interest here are the similar ways in which Goethe and Diderot conceptualize the work of a writer in terms of a universal ideal, and that they do this within a philosophical framework whose rational character is rather obvious. In contrast to the universal ideals of the writer, the painter pursues a much more empathetic enterprise. If these analyses are true, we could consequently imagine that every viewer-reader – and we shall not forget that

IA.  THE ALECHINSKY-BONNEFOY WALL, 40 RUE DESCARTES, PARIS (CLOSE-UP).
(SEE ALSO P. 239 FOR COLOUR REPRODUCTION.)

Goethe and Diderot are also viewers-readers – is able to recognize that the difference between the writer's work and that of the painter should be discernable in the differences between the results of their respective works. If Goethe and Diderot are right, we should be able to find some trace of the singularity of the object of which they speak within the tree painted by Alechinsky, the painted object with which every viewer would enter into an empathetic relationship, while the poet Bonnefoy would have us travel from tree to tree in a much more rational relationship.

The coexistence of a poem and a coloured drawing on a single exterior wall in Paris compels us to believe that, in this case at least, different modes of reference are coupled together within a single work . In reading the poem, one immediately notices the relevance of their collaboration.

Passer-by,
look at this large tree
        and through it
it may suffice.

For even ripped, sullied,
        the tree of the streets,
'tis the whole of nature,
        the whole sky,
the bird lands there,
        the wind moves there, the sun
tells the same hope there despite
        death.

Philosopher,
does chance let you have the tree
        in your street
your thoughts will be less arduous
        your eyes more free,
your hands more desirous
        of less night.[8]

For indeed, already on the second line of the painted poem, we encounter an instance of indexicality. As soon as I, the passer-by, hear my name called out in the first line of the poem as the relevant "passant" [passer-by] named by the text, I am immediately invited to proceed to the second line of the poem where I am told to "look at this large tree" ["regarde ce grand arbre"], the indexical expression clearly referring to the tree that is painted to the left of the poem itself.

In our study of this special wall, we shall begin with the poem for three reasons: first, because resemblance constitutes the mode through which we have the easiest access to the represented world; second, because *eikonismos* or *eikon* (words normally translated from the Greek as "description") have, as their first meaning, the idea of "icons in words," and therefore resemblance is first of all presented by a verbal description;[9] and third, because verbal language is able to create "identifying portraits" or "iconic portraits," verbal objects about which Gilbert Dagron underscores the relative paucity of their vocabulary. For these reasons related to the historical precedence of verbal descriptions, a context where painted descriptions come after the verbal ones, I propose to start my analysis with Bonnefoy's poem, rather than with Alechinsky's image.

After having called out to the passer-by, the written text immediately refers to the image, thus confirming a process that, in Diderot's *Salons*, virtually functioned like an adage: it is in reference to an image that the text is constructed.[10] The poem refers to the drawing by means of a demonstrative – "*ce* grand arbre" [*this* large tree].[11] In this instance at least, the referent of a demonstrative is clearly established, and without the slightest hesitation. For, indeed, next to the wall, there is no other tree available to do the semantic work called for. As the tree is drawn next the poem, it functions perfectly well for assuming the role of referent. In accordance with the observable simplicity of the drawing – "and through the tree/ it may suffice" ["et à travers lui/ il peut suffire"] – the text now becomes clearer about its mention of a tree. This is because just any old tree will not do, only the one that has been drawn on the wall by the painter. And by designating this particular tree, the poem acquires a certain precision about its "object" that only the drawing is able to bestow upon it. The poet would not in any way travel "from object to object," despite what Goethe had to say. Just like the painter, he would be able to designate an object in a rigid fashion, that is, refer to a singular identifiable object, or at least to a singular painted object. Under these circumstances, why is it that the poem should continue any longer, and why is it that the drawing does not immediately cease to solicit our attention?

The poet answers the latter question by presenting an argument which begins with the conjunction "car" [for]: "Car même... / c'est toute la nature/ tout le ciel" [For even... / 'tis the whole of nature/ the whole sky]. How is it possible for a singular object thus depicted, and designated by a demonstrative particle, to embrace the universal nature of such a quantifier – "the whole"? This is something the passer-by will soon want to understand. The tree, that is to say *this particular* tree that the word "tree" points to, is endowed, as a "tree of the streets" ["arbre des rues"], with the ability to represent. Yes, the passer-by is thus reassured, what is meant here is that drawing of a tree, "even ripped, even sullied" ["même déchiré, même souillé"]. That "arbre des rues" is the tree drawn on the wall and this tree has now acquired a special ability: despite its singularity it is able to refer to "the whole of nature," and through it one gains access to the whole sky. Once drawn, "a" tree would have the ability to represent the entire species in its natural context. In this way, the drawing enables such a commutation from the singular to the universal, something to which the "philosopher" will refer in the third verse when he speaks of "the" tree. A principle of semantic substitutability is guaranteed by the drawing at the very moment when the words of the poem hesitate between the "I" as passer-by looking at the large tree and the "I" as philosopher who has enough luck to have the tree in his street. From a gaze always capturing singularity, how shall I manage to gain possession of a universal tree? The freedom of my eyes is at stake here, and my hope is a violent one, as another poet, Apollinaire, once said.[12]

Let us further agree that indexicality (that mode of reference linking a sign with that to which it refers by means of an existential relationship) characterizes the poem on the wall. Like all instances of an indexical expression, the one contained in the poem does not in itself designate any singular object.[13] If we recall how Gottlob Frege characterizes meaning as a mode of establishing reference, and if we compare this characterization with other modes of reference established by Charles Sanders Peirce, then we can admit without any great difficulty that there is more than one way of establishing reference with iconic, as well as with symbolic, means. Such is the case even when the tree painted on the wall is said to represent a singular object, that is, in this instance, the Alechinsky-tree (with a hyphen). And this is because the theme of the tree is much too common in the painter's work for us to admit to any singularity in the case of a painted tree. Will it however be possible to find singularity somewhere else?

The third part of the poem appears quite accommodating in the face of this universalizing power inherent in verbal language. One might wish to compare the tree as described in the poem with the tree depicted in the drawing; one might further wish to examine how it is that the painted tree does not represent any tree in particular but refers to the concept of trees, that is to say, not to a general concept, but rather to a visual concept, such as Rudolf Arnheim describes it in his work on *visual thinking* where, in one particular chapter, he explicitly compares verbal concepts with pictorial ones. Let us look for a moment at this possibility.[14] We can surmise that Arnheim believes it necessary to oppose the visual with the verbal by removing from verbal language all those expressive powers he sees as more properly belonging to the realm of visual language. Thus he writes that "language attributes individual signs to individual concepts and describes thoughts and experiences as sequential events. [...] Therefore, it does most of its work by assigning labels to facts of experience. These labels are arbitrary, in the sense in which a red light is an arbitrary traffic sign for stopping."[15]

It is on this basis that Arnheim proceeds to distinguish between those expressive forms in which modes of reference are isomorphic and those where they are not. Whereas, in his view, an image would present an example of isomorphism between the semiotic elements that do the work of representing and the "object" represented, a verbal text is by definition non-isomorphic. At this point in his argument – and this is precisely where Arnheim is useful for conceptualizing the semiotic functioning of the Alechinsky-Bonnefoy wall – Arnheim notes that there exist "such intermediate features as onomatopoetic speech sounds, ideographs, allegories and other conventional symbols"[16] which prevent us from placing verbal and pictorial languages in separate categories: "It is not true [...] that verbal language uses constant, standardized shapes whereas a pictorial language such as painting uses shapes of infinite individual variety. Of course, no two pictures of flowers are alike whereas the word *flower* persists unchanged. However, verbal language is not composed simply of words but, first of all, of their meanings."[17]

Now, we know that it is not just the meaning of words that counts for issues of reference as verbal language is neither a simple combination of words nor a combination of the meanings of words. Although the word "flower" remains unchanged in its many usages, the meaning accruing to the word changes according to the contexts in which it is used. Thus it is impossible, in spite of Goethe's belief, and contrary to the case of words, to remain fixed on the singular relationship obtaining between an object and the image purported to convey it. This digression into Arnheim's thinking allows us – just as Frege's idea of *Vorstellung* suggested a little earlier – to follow neither Goethe nor Diderot along the path of distinguishing between the visual and verbal on the basis of a referential relationship that is more precise in one case than it is in the other.

However, if what we have just stated is not too far from the truth, we still must show that a drawing could be universal, that the Alechinsky-tree does not, in its capacity as drawing, correspond to a definite description; that is to say, that it does not refer to any singular object in the same way that the expression "Alechinsky-tree" does.

We previously mentioned that the theme of a tree is frequent in Alechinsky's work. The verbal expression "Alechinsky-tree" can thus refer to a series of drawings. In order for our tree to be attached to a unique referential object, it needs to be supplemented by something else, that is by a context, that which by its very nature gives precision to the meanings accruing to verbal concepts. One thing is clear for our discussion: the drawing is in no way an illustration of the poem because the poem refers to the tree as drawn by Alechinsky. The pictured tree clearly precedes the poem, a fact further suggested by its place on the wall to the left of the poem, in a cultural environment where writing moves from left to right. The drawing cannot be considered first as a drawing: it is seen first in the context of the wall on which it appears.

# A Specific Relationship with Space and Time?

In his text on the *Laocoon* statue,[18] Gotthold Ephraim Lessing stipulates that poetry and painting have their own specific relationships with time, and this is because they both have different relationships with space. As painting deals with forms and colours in space, it works with objects that coexist with one another to the extent that they are placed alongside one another. On the other hand, since poetry functions along the linear chain of written language, it deals with actions, because linearity is entirely appropriate inasmuch as actions unfold in time. However level-headed this view may at first appear, it seems to be invalid for our modernity; that is to say, it seems to hold neither for painting which would juxtapose objects (in Johannes Vermeer's *Woman in Blue Reading a Letter*,[19] I do not first see a woman and then a letter, but rather I see the act of reading a letter as performed by a woman; that is to say that I see an action, a fact that Wollheim will explain in the clearest of terms) nor for poetry which would be appropriate for actions because of its linear functioning (when, between 1942 and 1967, the poet Francis Ponge writes his poems on "things,"[20] it would be irrelevant to understand his poetry in terms of an action unfolding in a sequential manner, while, for Vittore Carpaccio's *Legend of Saint Ursula*,[21] the painter uses a series of pillars to mark off the various episodes that happened in the saint's life).

It is not uncommon today to see Lessing used as a theoretical foil justifying a desire to contrast the tabular nature of an image with the linear nature of a text. Besides the fact that an image can be described in a linear fashion (something seen when we scan an image electronically), we must also take note of the fact that a text (especially in the case of Chinese calligraphy)[22] can be taken "globally." In addition, the idea of a sequential deciphering of texts is the source of a large number of misunderstandings, a fact that becomes clearly visible whenever one attempts to translate word for word from one verbal language to another. For these and other similar reasons, it is difficult to follow Arnheim when he declares the following: "A pictorial image presents itself whole, in simultaneity. A successful literary image grows through what one might call accretion by amendment. Each word, each statement, is amended by the next into something closer to the intended total meaning. This build-up through the stepwise change of the image animates the literary medium. It is an effect beyond the mere selection and sequence of features."[23]

While it is difficult to refuse in their entirety each and every thesis concerning the differences in the ways in which texts and images deal with space, and while common sense dictates that we not dismiss Ferdinand de Saussure's second principle concerning the linear nature of speech as outrageous just as it encourages us to retain the principle according to which a painted canvas works simultaneously with two dimensions, we are nevertheless inclined to believe that the linearity involved in the act of reading also has something to do with a global processing of meaning. It is therefore counter-intuitive to maintain that the global nature of vision has little or nothing to do with a punctuated attention span which concentrates first on one specific aspect and then on another. All this suggests the usefulness of returning to a passage we saw earlier, culled from Diderot's *Notes on Painting* and annotated by Goethe: "Oh, my friend, what an art is painting! I capture in one line what the painter barely manages to rough in over the course of an entire week. It's his misfortune to know, see, and feel just as I do, yet be incapable of rendering things to his satisfaction; despite these feelings prompting him onwards, to misjudge his capacities and so spoil a masterpiece: he was, without his realizing it, at the very limits of art."[24]

These observations suggest a number of questions concerning *what* it is precisely that is compared when one decides to contrast painting and poetry, or for that matter texts and images. What is the object of the comparison Diderot suggests when he refers to a single line of his writing? Is he comparing this line with a painting? It seems natural to understand the word "line" as a metonymy. Diderot alludes to the time involved in producing a picture: taking up to a week only for its first sketch, the picture is contrasted with the almost immediate nature of the writing of literature (it is well known that Diderot was a very quick writer). A comparison of these two types of production necessitates an examination of their respective treatments of time and space. First, in view of the almost lightening-like effect that a text can achieve when describing its objects, Diderot suggests that we think of the relative slowness with which a painter arrives at a similar result. Why is it that those of us who, when attempting to write, have been haunted by the blank-page syndrome are not convinced? Second, we should also do a cross-comparison of the respective treatments of time using, on the one hand, the tabular nature of the image and, on the other, the now-famous linearity of texts. Is it possible to envisage such a comparison on the basis of what we can deduce from our Alechinsky-Bonnefoy example?

First remark: the time of one's visual recognition is obviously not the same as the time of artistic production and we recognize that this time is different for painting and writing: a single glance is enough for the recognition of a tree; a similar glance cast in the direction of the text will only reveal that the nature of the text we see is that of a poem. Recognition of the object occurs immediately in the case of the drawing, the only textual recognition possible during a quick glance is that of knowing what literary genre we are about to read.[25] Moreover, in order to gain a deeper understanding of what it is we are about to read or about to examine visually, significantly more time is needed both for the painting and for the poem. We might further ask whether the problem of self-referentiality presents itself differently in the case of an image in comparison with a written text. For this question, we turn to the philosopher Jacques Morizot: "While [...] the word 'tree' denotes trees whereas the word 'word' denotes words, we also notice that 'word' is also itself a word whereas nothing directly similar is true of the word 'tree'."[26]

The drawing of a tree is no more a real tree than a picture of a pipe is a real pipe. René Magritte taught us this lesson long ago.[27] In contrast, it is true to say that the drawing of a tree is indeed a tree-drawing.

Passers-by who are familiar with Alechinsky's fondness for playing with framing devices are not surprised by what they see on the painted wall. They immediately recognize Alechinsky's signature style on the wall: that tree is an Alechinsky-tree. It has all the distinctive features: with its various smaller images, including those suggesting path-ways,

MARIE-DOMINIQUE POPELARD

the complex frame compresses (or even cuts) the tree not only on the top, but also on the bottom and on the sides. Is it the city which limits the tree, with its streets and its rooftops, its factories too, all visible on the wide frame painted by Alechinsky? A host of other questions now come to mind, even after only a cursory glance at the drawing. And we naturally need words in order to formulate them.

For the pragmatic approach, the image is open to verbal language, but not merely to serve as an illustration, as for example in a text book on anatomy where the pictured parts of the body each receive a verbal designator. The image is open to words in another sense, for example when it invites verbal comments, something one often notices when studying an artist's notebooks. In such instances, we could even say that the image is made possible by the intellectual work accomplished by an artist writing private verbal commands about how to draw or paint an as-of-yet non-existing picture. The image is open to words on the pragmatic plane of a future action, open to words on the epistemological front of learning and knowing: together they indicate how a specific act can be accomplished, they explain how to make a particular gesture, they show how to assemble a piece of furniture from the three hundred and fifty little pieces sitting in the large box you have just bought.

Alechinsky's image is open to Bonnefoy's words in order to become "the" tree about which the poem will speak. In this instance, an artistic image lends itself to new usages, the same thing that happens when, for example, an artwork is taken out of the museum and is placed on the street; that is to say, when it loses its classical frame, its reserved space, exactly what can be observed in the case of the Bonnefoy-Alechinsky wall.

## The Image and the Visual (The Visible and the Visual?)

Might we say in this case that art has lost a part of its specificity? When it becomes part of the everyday landscape, do the visible elements thereby become indistinguishable from merely visual elements? This is an aspect we have not yet commented upon: our wall not only shows a drawing accompanied by a poem, the digital reproduction of the wall we have provided in this essay also shows an advertisement that could very well attract my personal attention as a passer-by if I were more inclined to appreciate commercial messages.... How can we develop an argument concerning the discriminatory powers that allow us to focus on certain objects in our visual field while filtering out others?

The work of Richard Wollheim will be of great assistance in this part of our inquiry, for he has affirmed the irreducible nature of an image with respect to a visual object.[28] This irreducibility is based on five factors:

1) the image is irreducible because of its being an artefact;

2) the image is irreducible because it has specific contours and its own characteristics;

3) the image is irreducible because one perceives an image *as* an image of something, an image of, say, $X$ (in this instance of a tree);

4) the original contribution of Wollheim's thinking consists in his claim that one can see *inside* an image: we see $X$ *in* the image, and as a second step we can replace $X$ not only by a name (which is the case for *seeing as*) but also by a complete proposition (for the example of the Vermeer painting we can say that I do not merely see a woman or a letter but rather I see *the fact that a woman is reading a letter*). For Wollheim, the image does not represent objects but actions;

5) when confronted with an image, we have a unique experience comprising what he calls *twofoldness* ("simultaneous attention to what is represented and to the representation, to the object and to the medium"),[29] a property which, according to Dominic Lopes, can be described as a variable of iconicity.[30]

1B. THE ALECHINSKY-BONNEFOY WALL, 40 RUE DESCARTES, PARIS
(WITH AN ADVERTISEMENT).

Assuming that all these characteristics are relevant both for the painted tree along with its poem and for the advertisement we see on the bottom left, it would seem that there exists a contextual property that allows us to distinguish between the various things we see: the visible wall achieves a certain independence from what is merely visual precisely because it is a wall. Remarkably, the continuity of what we see by virtue of the medium's characteristics ensures that the (painted and/or read) tree on the wall (and here we have a first instance of twofoldness, a double nature without duplicity) is also, thanks to the wall, part of a piece of architecture in the city. Because it is much more than a simple support for a drawing, like the canvas for a painting, the wall provides the very material upon which the tree "grows." Such being the case, one is tempted to speak in this instance of *threefoldness*, to the extent that in a city trees often grow in the intimate proximity of rocks and bricks. It would be useful to flesh out this hypothesis a little further.

Let us suppose for a moment that the image, like the poem as Lessing described it, is itself an action or, according to the vision developed by speech-act theorists for verbal language, let us suppose that the image not only describes (the equivalent of "asserting" in verbal language) but also "does" something else. We could examine the periphery of Alechinsky's tree-image a little more carefully. The series of smaller images in the frame seems to present themselves like sequences in a story in much the same way as a comic strip cuts a narrative into smaller pieces, or like the sketches provided in a scenario, a film's synopsis, or a storyboard. However, it is difficult to find any such succession in the various drawings surrounding our tree; it is just as tricky an enterprise to attempt to read a dialogue into the poem, that is, a dialogue that would, as it were, accompany the scenes presented by the smaller images of the frame. Still, one is tempted to see something that is analogous to the movements and shots of a movie camera: a description of some action seems to be visible. But what action could this be? Perhaps we could agree to see several shots taken from the development and growth of the tree: at one point we see a branch growing, at another we see a path leading to the tree, and then we notice a factory at the edge of the path, a few clouds in the sky, and maybe a few other trees as well.

Could we say, then, that the singularity of the tree lies in the plurality that is sketched out of other possible trees and represented by the large, central tree we see, as if a condensing operation had reduced their multiplicity to oneness? In this instance, the suggestive nature of the image would take on a further meaning, one whose aim would no longer consist in containing an entire temporality within a single representative instant, but rather a meaning that would allow us to see a whole set of possibilities within the image we have before our eyes. This singular tree refers back to itself at the same time as it suggests a universality of treeness which would include all trees, if not the whole of nature itself. One finds oneself on the doorstep of that same universal subjectivity which, for Kant, was a defining characteristic for judgments of taste.[31] This of course brings several other issues into play.

The action effected by an image is not only internal to the same image: something else occurs at the moment when I see it. It happens when I produce an act of vision in the same way that something occurs in language at the moment when I produce a speech act. This visual "something" that occupies us in the case of the Alechinsky-Bonnefoy wall is somewhat complex: the painting is not alone on the wall, the mural painting also contains the poem, and we might even go so far as to say that it also includes an advertisement. The wall is the context which both allows the text-image nexus to function and regulates that functioning. City dwellers are accustomed to a building environment where architectural elements are duplicated in plastic form and where, in particular, walls without windows have become relatively rare. If I as a passer-by remain sensitive to the wall on 40 Rue Descartes in Paris, this is no doubt because in my mind, alongside the contemporary view of the wall that I now have before me, there still remains my memories of how the wall was once when, as a student walking from the Sorbonne to Censier, I passed by it nearly every day, that is, before the time when the wall was painted. Those were the days when the zone in front of the Henri IV High School had not yet been renovated, the days before the then-minister of culture, André Malraux, had not finished his ambitious project of "whitening" all of Paris. But I also remain sensitive to the Alechinsky-Bonnefoy wall for another reason, i.e., because I feel personally implicated by the vocative case used by Yves Bonnefoy at the beginning of his poem, as if the wall were calling out to me, as if I were *the* passer-by named by the text, and perhaps even more so since I have become a professional philosopher. What's more, I remember my visit to the Alechinsky Museum in southern France where I once took my children who (at the age of eight and ten respectively) laughed out loud because of the "funny comic strips" they saw in his work, before they had learned to appreciate his style later on in life. There is all this, of course, and there is also the colour of the tree, a flamboyant blue whose ardour is becoming less and less noticeable with each and every drop of acid rain that washes it down.

- And then there is that blue tree, and everyone knows that there's no such thing as a blue tree!
- Oh yes there is, you only need to walk down Rue Descartes to find one.

No doubt mindful of a famous slogan from May 1968 – "walls can speak" ["les murs ont la parole"] – the poet and the painter work closely together as two muralists in order to make a Parisian wall speak. Together, they give it both an image and a text; they make image and text work and signify together within a conjoint action comprising both words and pictures, the latter working so closely together that it is difficult to separate their tasks or to identify any separate roles:

> The greatest problem of iconography – one haunting all of art history – can often be seen, as we well know, when one attempts to divide within a single work of visual art that which belongs to verbal language and that which belongs to the image. Both the art historian and semiotician get lost when they try to do this. In one of his most brilliant intuitions, Aby Warburg once invited the art historian to look for those regions of art where language and visuality should not be separated out, instances where it is not desirable to decide between the ambiguities their mutual games create – there is already an ambiguity in the word *figure*, belonging as it does both to the vocabulary of rhetoric and to that of the image – instances where there is no desire to resolve them or to suppress them. Warburg insisted on the need to expose these instances as if the project were part of the *work of figures*, however unsteady, however confusing, however unreasonable such a project might prove to be.[32]

Whenever attempting to make separate categories for the semiotic and aesthetic potential of poetry and painting, one soon finds oneself pursuing a dead end. There are so many problems and issues that attest to the desirability of a conjunctive methodology, one combining both word and image, a pragmatic approach no doubt, one capable of taking stock of the aims pursued by acts of meaning, one sensitive not only to spatial and temporal contexts but to social and communicational ones as well. Far from being able to decide once and for all what meanings need to be constructed, words and images are seen as working together in a commonly constructed enterprise. The trivial nature of such an assertion no doubt hides an important facet, the possibility of discerning those functions and activities that are common to both. Amongst the latter we have already placed referential choices and modes, world-making, and imaginative powers.[33] And we realize too that in saying this our work has only just begun.

## BIBLIOGRAPHY

Alpers, Svetlana. *The Art of Describing. Dutch Art in the Seventeenth Century.* Chicago: University of Chicago Press, 1983.

Apollinaire, Guillaume. *Oeuvres poétiques*, ed. Marcel Adéma and Michel Desgaudin, Paris: Gallimard, collection "Pléiade," 1965.

Arnheim, Rudolf. *Visual Thinking.* Berkeley: University of California Press, 1969.

Banfi, Emanuele, and Marie-Dominique Popelard. *Peindre les idées. Sur la calligraphie chinoise.* Paris: Presses Universitaires de France, 2007.

Dagron, Gilbert. *Décrire et peindre. Essai sur le portrait iconique.* Paris: Gallimard, 2007.

Diderot, Denis. *Salons* (4 vols.). Paris: Hermann, 1984–95.

———. *Diderot on Art*, vol. I, trans. John Goodman, New Haven, CT: Yale University Press, 1995.

Didi-Huberman, Georges. *L'Image ouverte.* Paris: Gallimard, collection "Le Temps des images," 2007.

Frege, Gottlob. "On Sense and Reference." In *Translations from the Philosophical Writings of Gottlob Frege*, ed. Peter Geach and Max Black, 56–78. Oxford: Basil Blackwell, 1960.

Goethe, Johann Wolfgang. *Diderots Versuch über die Malerei* [1799]. In *Sämtliche Werke nach Epochen seines Schaffens*, ed. Norbert Miller and John Neubauer (Munich edition). Munich: Carl Hanser, 1991, vol. VII.

Goodman, Nelson. *Ways of Worldmaking*. Indianapolis: Hackett, 1978.

Kant, Immanuel. *The Critique of Judgment* [1790], trans. Werner S. Pluhard. Indianapolis: Hackett, 1987.

Lessing, Gotthold Ephraim. *Laocoon: or the Limits of Poetry and Painting*, trans. William Ross. London: Ridgeway, 1836.

Lopes, Dominic. *Understanding Pictures*. Oxford: Clarendon, 1996.

Magritte, René. *Les Mots et les images*, commentary by Éric Clémens. Bruxelles: Labor, 1994.

Morizot, Jacques. *Interfaces: Texte et image. Pour prendre du recul vis-à-vis de la sémiotique*. Rennes: Presses Universitaires de Rennes, 2004.

———. *Qu'est-ce qu'une image?* Paris: Vrin, collection "Chemins philosophiques," 2005.

Peirce, Charles Sanders. *The Collected Papers of C.S. Peirce*, vol. 2, ed. Charles Hartshorne and Peter Weiss. Cambridge, MA: Harvard University Press, 1931–35.

Peyré, Yves. *Pierre Alechinsky ou la pluralité du geste*. Besançon: Éditions Virgile, 2008.

Ponge, Francis. *The Nature of Things*, trans. Lee Fahnestock. New York: Red Dust, 1995.

Rougé, Bertrand, ed. *L'Index*. Pau: Presses Universitaires de Pau, collection "Rhétorique des arts," 2008.

Stoffregen, Thomas. "On the Nature and Perception of Depictions." The virtual colloquium *Les Images dans la Cognition et dans la Science*, http://www.inter-disciplines.org/artcognition.

Vouilloux, Bernard. "La description du tableau dans les Salons *de Diderot*: la figure et le nom." *Poétique* XIX, 73 (1998): 27–50.

Wittgenstein, Ludwig. *Tractatus logico-philosophicus*. London: Routledge & Kegan Paul, 1922.

Wollheim, Richard. "On Drawing an Object." In *Aesthetics*, ed. Harold Osborne, 121–44. London: Oxford University Press, 1972.

———. *Painting as an Art*. Princeton, NJ: Princeton University Press, 1987.

Zemach, Eddy M. "Description and Depiction." *Mind*, New series 84, 336 (1975): 567–78.

# NOTES

1 An example of this phenomenon can be seen in books of anatomy where one assigns a label to the different parts of the body being illustrated.

2 Teachers regularly sketch drawings or graphs on the blackboard, illustrations whose sole purpose is to regulate the imaginative processes set off in students' minds by the words used by the teacher.

3 Ludwig Wittgenstein, *Tractatus logico-philosophicus* (London: Routledge & Kegan Paul, 1922), § 7.

4 Single-modal depictions can set off multimodal perceptions, a fact demonstrated by Thomas Stoffregen in his paper, "On the Nature and Perception of Depictions," which is part of the virtual colloquium on *Images in Cognition and Science* available at http://www.interdisciplines.org/artcognition (site consulted in May 2008).

5 See "Description and Depiction" (*Mind*, New series, vol. 84, 336, 1975, 567–78), where, after having analyzed arguments taken from Nelson Goodman and Kendall Walton on the same subject, Eddy Zemach argues that understanding a depiction, as well as a description, needs to be aware of conventions. Descriptions and depictions are quite similar to one another.

6 One should note in addition that the *readable* should be included in the *visible* because everything that is readable is indeed visible, whereas the converse is not true.

7 Johann Wolfgang Goethe, *Diderots Versuch über die Malerei* (1799) in *Sämtliche Werke nach Epochen seines Schaffens*, Munich Edition, eds. Norbert Miller and John Neubauer (Munich: Carl Hanser, 1991, vol. VII), 564–65: "Freilich ist die Malerei sehr weit von der Redekunst entfernt und wenn man auch annehmen kö-nnte, der bildende Künstler sehe die Gegenstände wie der Redner, so wird doch bei jenem ein ganz anderer Trieb erweckt als bei diesem. Der Redner eilt von Gegenstand zu Gegenstand, von Kunstwerk zu Kunstwerk, um darüber zu denken, sie zu fassen, sie zu übersehen, sie zu ordnen und ihre Eigenschaften anzusprechen. Der Künstler hingegen ruht auf dem Gegenstande, er vereinigt sich mit ihm in Liebe, er teilt ihm das Beste seines Geistes, seines Herzens mit, er bringt ihn wieder hervor."

8 This is our translation of Bonnefoy's poem on the wall.

9 See on this point Gilbert Dagron, *Décrire et peindre. Essai sur le portrait iconique* (Paris: Gallimard, 2007), 107.

10 See on this point Bernard Vouilloux, "La description du tableau dans les Salons *de Diderot*: la figure et le nom," *Poétique* XIX, 73 (1998): 27–50.

11 Our emphasis.

12 Guillaume Apollinaire, "Le Pont Mirabeau," in *Oeuvres poétiques*, ed. Marcel Adéma and Michel Desgaudin (Paris: Gallimard, collection "Pléiade," 1965), 45.

13 See on this point Bertrand Rougé, ed., *L'Index* (Pau: Presses Universitaires de Pau, collection "Rhétorique des arts," 2008).

14 This examination requires that we pass over the fact that, in his discussion of verbal concepts, Arnheim adopts an outdated theory of verbal language (outdated already in the 1960s), one more or less equivalent to a theory of names in which verbal language would consist of a catalogue of labels corresponding to a second catalogue of things in the world; in addition Arnheim limits the expressive powers of verbal language to those of telling a story – the narrative placement of events in sequential order – while leaving aside the ability

of verbal language to construct arguments; he goes so far as to confuse verbal signs with the signals making up a code in the manner of a highway code.

15  Rudolf Arnheim, *Visual Thinking* (Berkeley: University of California Press, 1969), 251.

16  Arnheim, *Visual Thinking*, 85.

17  Ibid., 85.

18  Hagesandrus, Polydorus and Athenodorus, *Laocoon and his Two Sons*, 1st century A.D., sculptural group in marble, Vatican City, Museo Pio Clementina, 224 cm (height).

19  Johannes Vermeer, *Woman in Blue Reading a Letter*, ca. 1662–64, oil on canvas, Amsterdam, Rijksmuseum, 46.5 x 39 cm.

20  See for example Francis Ponge, *The Nature of Things*, trans. Lee Fahnestock (New York: Red Dust, 1995).

21  Vittore Carpaccio, *The Legend of Saint Ursula*, cycle of nine large canvasses, ca. 1490–1495, Venice, Gallerie dell'Accademia.

22  See Emanuele Banfi and Marie-Dominique Popelard, *Peindre les idées. Sur la calligraphie chinoise* (Paris: Presses Universitaires de France, 2007).

23  Arnheim, *Visual Thinking*, 249–50.

24  This passage is culled from Diderot's *Notes on painting* quoted and glossed by Johann Wolfgang Goethe in *Diderots Versuch über die Malerei* (1799), 564. The English translation comes from "Notes on Painting" in *Diderot on Art*, I, trans. John Goodman (New Haven, CT: Yale University Press, 1995), 201.

25  According to Eddy Zemach ("Description and Depiction"), "reading a description is a one-step process, while seeing a depiction as such involves two steps." And Zemach chooses a tree-depicting picture as an example for explaining why the two steps are not discernible. However, whenever we fail to understand what the picture is supposed to represent, then words may become necessary.

26  Jacques Morizot, *Interfaces: Texte et image. Pour prendre du recul vis-à-vis de la sémiotique* (Rennes: Presses Universitaires de Rennes, 2004), 59.

27  In a series of paintings, the most famous one being René Magritte, *La Trahison des images (Ceci n'est pas une pipe)*, 1929, oil on canvas, Los Angeles, Los Angeles County Museum of Art, 49.5 x 80 cm. See on this account René Magritte, *Les Mots et les images*, commentary by Éric Clémens (Bruxelles: Labor, 1994).

28  Richard Wollheim, "On Drawing an Object," in *Aesthetics*, ed. Harold Osborne (London: Oxford University Press, 1972), 121–44.

29  Richard Wollheim, *Painting as an Art* (Princeton: Princeton University Press, 1987), 46.

30  Dominic Lopes, *Understanding Pictures* (Oxford: Clarendon Press, 1996).

31  Immanuel Kant, *The Critique of Judgment* [1790], trans. Werner S. Pluhard (Indianapolis: Hackett, 1987), § 35.

32  Georges Didi-Huberman, *L'Image ouverte* (Paris: Gallimard, collection "Le temps des images," 2007), 198.

33  While naturalists believe in the descriptive power of an image which nevertheless reconstructs reality in order to enforce its visual objectivity, conventionalists believe that art possesses social and communicational values. Some authors hold the view that both of these beliefs are mixed together. On this point, see once again Eddy Zemach ("Description and Depiction") and Jacques Morizot, *Interfaces*, 19.

# 2

# Mary Magdalene in the Village of Emmaus: Notes on Two Paintings by Laurent de La Hyre

*Bruno-Nassim Aboudrar*

At the mid-point of his *Élévation sur Sainte Madeleine*, the mystical writer Pierre de Bérulle pens a chapter which he entitles "The Angels' Words and Those Addressed by Jesus to Mary Magdalene before the Holy Sepulchre."[1] In this chapter that deals with the encounter between the risen Christ and the woman he loved, Bérulle notes that their meeting occurs at that difficult moment in time when Mary Magdalene was wandering around the empty tomb, that is, just after the Resurrection, but before the risen Christ would disappear again. Bérulle wrote the following words, as if he were speaking directly to his Saviour: "You pronounce the sweet name of Mary and her eyes open up when hearing it, just as the apostles' eyes were opened up at the mysterious moment when He broke bread at Emmaus."[2] Such an attempt to establish a parallel between the episode of the supper at Emmaus, as recounted by Luke, and the story of Christ's encounter with Mary Magdalene, as related by John, is rather rare in Biblical exegesis.

The contrast one normally finds is constructed in a shroud of mystery. It occurs when one compares two consecutive episodes found in the Gospel according to Saint John: in the first one, known by its Latin name as *Noli me tangere*, Jesus asks Mary Magdalene not to touch him; in the second one, he orders Thomas to touch the still-open wounds on his hands and side. For an explanation of this particular contrast, Saint Augustine proposes the opposition of two separate modes of sentient knowledge: on the one hand, we have the sense of sight exhibited by Mary Magdalene; on the other, there is the sense of touch imposed upon Thomas. Augustine continues: this opposition is part of the superficial appearance which shrouds a deeper contrast underlying both narratives. First of all, we must remember that the Gospel literally compares touch with sight and not the other way around: "When, therefore, the Lord said to Thomas, *Come, thrust hither thine hand, and be not faithless but believing*; and when he exclaimed, having touched the places of the wounds, and said, *My Lord and my God!* he is rebuked, and it is said to him, *Because thou hast seen, thou hast believed.*"[3] Further, and more importantly perhaps, the sense of touch is disconnected from the profession of faith *per se* because, as Saint Augustine will insist on several occasions, Thomas will touch a human body while he must begin to believe in God. In other words, he does not really believe in what he is touching: "Thus even he to whom it was said, *Because thou hast seen thou hast believed*, did not *believe* the thing that he saw: it was one thing that he saw, another, that he believed: he saw the Man, believed the God. He perceived namely and touched that flesh living, which he had seen dying; and he believed the God latent in that same flesh."[4] When examined from a different angle, the sense of touch is forbidden in Mary Magdalene's case only in the episode that recounts her exclusive encounter with Christ before the Holy Sepulchre. Concerning this particular point, Augustine observes that, according to the Gospel of Saint Matthew, we are led to understand that in another instance she was indeed allowed to touch her Lord, that is, when she was in the company of the several other holy women who had come along with her to visit the tomb. "For we read it of females also, that after His Resurrection, before he ascended unto the Father, they touched Jesus: among them too, this same Mary Magdalena: as Matthew relates that Jesus met them, saying, *All Hail: and they drew near, and held him by the feet, and worshipped Him*" (Matt. 28, 9).[5] In the final analysis, the test of either touch or sight presents itself as a sort of illusory trap, one that places a person's religious faith in a realm lying beyond that of our bodily senses.

This conviction leads Augustine to stress the second half of Christ's forbiddance; that is to say, he underscores the justification provided immediately after the negative command: "Touch me not; for I am not yet ascended to my Father." Here, Augustine glimpses a mystery. If we wish to unravel this secret truth, we must first recognize certain figures lying hidden underneath those literal words, which have left us no doubt unsatisfied, or even perplexed. He identifies two such instances: on the one hand, Mary Magdalene can be seen as a figure for the Church of the gentiles who "believed in Christ only after He had risen to the Father" and, on the other, "Jesus wanted to show that believing in Him, that is touching Him spiritually, is believing that He and the Father are one."[6] In both readings, this particular episode, when seen figuratively, pointed to a profession of faith that would be regulated posthumously. When the episode of *Noli me tangere* is combined with the story of Thomas's doubts, which occurs later on, they together constitute a relatively homogeneous and coherent whole. The resurrected Christ thus becomes the defining feature of the faith which will be professed by nations of men and women who are able to believe despite His physical absence: these people must believe without ever having seen or touched Him – that is without any tangible proof – and they must further believe in an article of faith that forms the very heart of Augustine's theology: the hypostatic union of the Father and the Son.

In the devotional literature of seventeenth-century France, one finds just such an assimilation of Father and Son as expressed syntagmatically by two successive passages found in the Gospel according to Saint John. One particular reader, the Oratorian (and later Jansenist) Pasquier Quesnel, took it upon himself to explain what may at first appear to be an unjust distribution of divine favours in the cases of Mary Magdalene and Thomas. Despite his Jansenist leanings, Quesnel provides a clearly Oratorian reading of the episode at hand. "You did not allow the loving Mary Magdalene to touch you after your Resurrection even though she had always remained faithful to you, and despite the holy ardour with which she hoped to kiss your sacred feet, just as she had earlier done; and yet you invite Saint Thomas to put his finger into your wounded hand and to place his entire hand into your open side even though you also scold him for his disbelief."[7] The reason for such an apparent injustice lies in the fact that Mary Magdalene's soul was much "more advanced along the paths of spiritual perfection" than was Thomas's: her soul, and not his, could thus bear the weight of even the most trying of spiritual tests. On the other hand, for weak souls such as Thomas's (and for ours as well!), Jesus adopts "a gentler path of conduct, one that is both softer and more sensitive, one that uses great care" in light of these same weaknesses.[8] The level of devotional love that Jesus expects of his faithful is proportionate to the state of each believer's soul. Coming from a holy woman, this love must be pure and untarnished by bodily considerations; coming from a sinner – that is, from a weak soul – devotional love may no doubt need the support of bodily proofs. Nowhere does Quesnel spell out which bodily proofs are allowable for all the sinners who are Thomas's contemporaries and for whom Thomas can now be seen as the tutelary figure. But one can safely assume that the spiritual exercises of the type encouraged by the Oratorian order, beginning with Quesnel's own text, should be counted among any such material proofs, in the same way that it is permissible to include holy images which the Council of Trent had redeemed precisely because it saw in them an ability to elevate the human soul due to their bodily-material nature. Images can lend precious help in the enterprise of elevating the human soul through the exercise of prayer.

For Saint Augustine, on the other hand, the comparison of these two episodes contained in John's Gospel unlocks the figurative expression of certain truths about the hidden nature of faith. According to Nicene symbolism, faith must be free of tangible proofs when belief in the hypostatic union is professed. In the case of the spiritual director living in modern times, that is, for an Oratorian such as Quesnel, the parallelism of these two stories leads back to such articles of faith in yet another fashion. When religious faith is no longer considered in relation

BRUNO-NASSIM ABOUDRAR

to its nature, but rather in terms of the (psychological) relationship it establishes between Christ and the believing Christian, one can thus contemplate faith from the devotional point of view. In their thinking, the role attributed to images by Quesnel or Augustine is assigned almost as an aside. For Saint Augustine, images are basically a non-issue because, for him, faith in Christ's Resurrection remains independent of any tangible proofs, precisely that category of proof that Jesus did not want Mary Magdalene to use while demanding it of Thomas. In Quesnel's framework, images assume an auxiliary role because, while bodily-material forms help a soul to progress along its spiritual itinerary when faced with difficult moments, these same images do not partake of the actual nature of faith which, by definition, has no real need of them on its way to the state of perfection. Both positions, in their respective frameworks, are coherent in relation to the status they accord to images. Indeed, Augustine elaborates a theory of resemblance that makes the use of images indifferent to the exercises of spirituality. While the resemblance between the Son and the Father and that between humans and the Son are not identical to the extent that the first subsists in the same substance and the second is constituted within heterogeneous substances, both resemblances share an essential point to the extent that they are both spiritually constituted, that is, not based in materiality. All this means that, whatever it is that forms the divine nature of Jesus, it does not have any images anchored in his physical nature.[9] As for Quesnel, in his admission that the soul elevates itself spiritually by way of the material nature possessed by images, his position remains consistent with several tenets of Tridentine theology.

Given these details, one asks what happens, on the semantic front, when an author no longer considers the episode of Mary Magdalene's encounter with the risen Christ from the syntagmatic point of view which, as we saw, links this story with the one told later on about doubting Thomas. Instead, it can be studied from a paradigmatic perspective, one that places Mary Magdalene's story alongside that told in the Gospel of Saint Luke about the supper of Emmaus. It is possible to formulate this question in two ways, that is, from the point of view of the text and from that of the image. History tells us Bérulle had first suggested the need to compare the effects created in Mary Magdalene's mind when she heard Jesus pronounce her name with those produced for the apostles when they saw Jesus break a loaf of bread before their eyes. Three decades later, the seventeenth-century French painter Laurent de La Hyre, in response to a commission proposed by the Chartreux convent in Grenoble, delivered what would be amongst his very last works of art (the two works are signed and dated in the year 1656, see below **Illustrations 2 and 3**). This pair of paintings represents the same two evangelical scenes of which we have just spoken, respectively the supper at Emmaus and the encounter occurring before the Holy Sepulchre.

On the one hand, the comparison between the *Noli me tangere* episode and that of Thomas's disbelief had been constructed in linear terms along the syntagmatic axis of meaning – the one story occurs *after* the other in John's Gospel. On the other hand, the parallel established between the *Noli me tangere* encounter and the first meal shared after Christ's death operates on the level of the paradigm, that is to say, inside a semantic configuration where the relevant elements work together in either a relationship of equivalence or in one of opposition. In this latter framework, the relevant elements from both episodes function, significantly for us, within the same semantic space, that is to say, in a context where they constantly stand in for one another. In what follows, I propose to adopt a paradigmatic methodology: in other words, I wish to remain attentive to the structural effects of this substitutive relationship. This I propose to do by examining, first in the texts of the Gospel and then in the images painted by La Hyre, the ways in which the relations of equivalence are constructed as well as the nature of these relationships.

Such an examination requires an answer to the question of what justifies the comparison of these two episodes in the first place. And for this answer, we need to go to the very roots of everything else, that is, to return to the Gospel texts themselves.

If we compare the story of the Resurrection as told in the four Gospels, one immediately notices a contradiction in relation to the rule according to which one should normally contrast the three synoptic

Gospels with John's. Indeed, John and Luke contain a number of congruent elements, which are both thematic and structural in nature (see **Table 1**) and which, taken together, distinguish them from Matthew and Mark. Whereas both John and Luke mention two young men or angels present at Christ's tomb, both Matthew and Mark say that there was only one. In Luke's Gospel, as soon as Peter learns that the tomb is empty, he immediately goes to see for himself. According to John, when he goes, he is accompanied by someone else, namely by John himself. On the other hand, neither Matthew nor Mark evokes any such visit. More significantly (see **Table 2**), we notice that, the first appearance of the risen Christ as witnessed either by Mary Magdalene along with the other Mary who is James' mother (according to Matthew) or by Mary Magdalene alone (according to Mark) is expedited by Matthew and Mark in the space of a single sentence.[10] However, in Luke's version we find a long narrative development concerning Christ's appearance in the midst of a group of pilgrims heading towards the village of Emmaus and, in John's version, in the equivalent passage, we find the episode of Christ's appearance before Mary Magdalene. Once again, in John and Luke, we read complete narrative versions of the events whereas in Matthew and Mark we find only passing mentions.

If, on the one hand, a number of similarities can be adduced that link the story of Mary Magdalene to that of Thomas, on the other, these two narratives are vastly different from one another both in terms of the tone of the language they use and regarding the persons who are included in their respective narratives, which further differ in the events they relate. In one version there is one woman, in the other version we find two men: the woman weeps, whereas the two men are merely saddened – one of these men is called, traditionally at least, Cephas and the other is probably Luke himself. More importantly, the single woman mentioned is *there*, present at the tomb and the journey to Emmaus; the long walk to Emmaus, reminiscent of the military mission mentioned in the first book of Maccabees (3, 40), takes on the air of a hurried retreat. However, it is not exactly a matter of opposing movement to immobility but rather of contrasting the desire to flee with that of establishing continuity, the

**TABLE I: DISCOVERIES AND ANNOUNCEMENTS.**

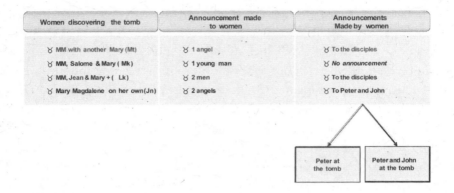

| Women discovering the tomb | Announcement made to women | Announcements Made by women |
|---|---|---|
| ☿ MM with another Mary (Mt) | ☿ 1 angel | ☿ To the disciples |
| ☿ MM, Salome & Mary ( Mk ) | ☿ 1 young man | ☿ No announcement |
| ☿ MM, Jean & Mary + ( Lk ) | ☿ 2 men | ☿ To the disciples |
| ☿ Mary Magdalene on her own (Jn) | ☿ 2 angels | ☿ To Peter and John |

Peter at the tomb    Peter and John at the tomb

**TABLE 2: APPEARANCES OF JESUS.**

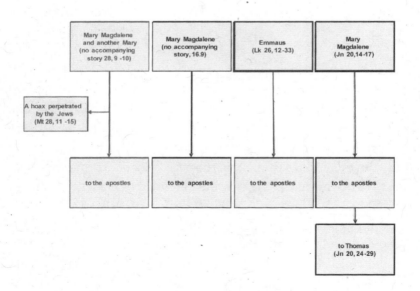

| Mary Magdalene and another Mary (no accompanying story 28, 9 -10) | Mary Magdalene (no accompanying story, 16.9) | Emmaus (Lk 26, 12-33) | Mary Magdalene (Jn 20,14-17) |
|---|---|---|---|
| A hoax perpetrated by the Jews (Mt 28, 11 -15) | | | |
| to the apostles | to the apostles | to the apostles | to the apostles |
| | | | to Thomas (Jn 20, 24-29) |

difference between a centripetal movement and a centrifugal one (one might even speak of a "crucifugal" movement). In seventeenth-century representations of this scene, Mary Magdalene is anything but an immobile figure. Her visible movement consists in getting closer to the cross, getting closer to the Holy Tomb, getting closer to her Master, whereas the apostles are forever getting further and further away from the site where Christ was put to death. For example, in 1628, Charles de Saint-Paul gives an epic, indeed almost sublime, version of the scene in which he depicts Mary Magdalene's deep agitation as compared with John, who merely holds back his tears:

> However, the multiple forms of suffering inflicted on Jesus were not enough to make her want to flee from his side, as had been the case of his Apostles. Even when she was drenched in his blood, she still remained at the foot of the cross. Nor did the weapons carried by nearby soldiers frighten her off, for indeed she had earlier made her way through great numbers of armed soldiers in order to reach the spot were Jesus was crucified. And, in the end, not even death itself would be powerful enough to take her away from him: she went to look for him in his tomb, and not finding him there, she continued her search everywhere, trying to imagine all the possible places where he might be.[11]

A little later, when she discovered an empty tomb, she cried: "Upon my eyes, pour torrents of tears. As for you my feet, be prepared to make endless journeys, without respite or rest, for I must find the one man who makes me burn with impatience."[12] And then, as we read in Luke's Gospel, Jesus was suddenly walking alongside his apostles. During the walk, he began explaining passages of the Old Testament to them. He showed them everything in the Scriptures that pointed to his life and suffering. But does Jesus ever give such a lesson to Mary Magdalene? If ever he does, he does so only implicitly, and such a lesson would not be about the events that had culminated in his suffering and death – a lesson about Christ made flesh – but rather about his future Ascension, about the Son without flesh: "I am not yet ascended to my Father."

When sitting down with his disciples, Christ suddenly became recognizable for them due to a special gesture, that is to say, by the way he broke the bread they were going to eat. This was of course something he had done during his earthly life, at that precise moment when he instituted the sacrifice of the Eucharist during the Last Supper, as described in Luke 22, 19: "And he took bread, and gave thanks, and brake it, and gave unto them, saying, This is my body which is given for you: this do in remembrance of me."

If, on the one hand, the sudden ability of the disciples to recognize their master was founded on a repeated act, on the other hand, in the garden surrounding the Holy Sepulchre, the sign that would allow Mary Magdalene to recognize him would not be gestural in nature, but rather oral. As pointed out in Bérulle's text, it was, to be more precise, the way in which Jesus pronounced Mary's name. In the village of Emmaus he designates himself explicitly while in the garden near Golgotha he calls out, not his own name, but Mary's. This situation presents a clear contrast between gesture and name, between self-designation and calling out for someone else. On this particular point, the difference between the Gospels of Luke and John is grounded on something other than on chance, or even on a literary genre: it is an exceptional difference, one that partakes of contrary modes of language. But what about the motif of repetition, which can be found in both Gospels? Is there not, in Luke, the repetition of a gesture while, in John, we find the repetition of a name? Yes, but there are subtle differences in the modes in which these repeated semiotic acts occur. In Luke's text, the relevant gesture consists in repeating the same act (in two separate instances, Christ breaks the Eucharistic bread, which has just been blessed). But in John's Gospel, the name called out points not to the repetition of the same but rather in itself repeats a difference. The fact that the name used to call Christ's lover is also his mother's did not escape the vigilant attention of a mystical reader such as Bérulle. The latter meditates on this homonymy in two distinct ways, which can themselves be described as logically contradictory. Of course mystical thinking is precisely able to free itself of logical contradiction by presenting itself as a discourse that lies beyond any such principle. On the one hand, Jesus pronounces the name of Mary (Magdalene) just as he would pronounce the name of Mary (his mother). In this instance we have repetition of a name, and Mary is thus the name for a love capable of creating bonds: "That name had a much too strong a connection between Jesus, on the one hand, and the persons of his holy Mother and of that simple disciple, on the other, for it not to be able to link together two such close and well-prepared hearts and minds in a love that was both holy and mutual."[13] On the other hand, Jesus pronounces this same name (the exact one he did not pronounce as a newborn infant, since as a child he did not speak) when he is a resurrected man (and he uses it to call out to a woman who is not his mother).

> When you are born, my Lord, in Bethlehem, in all truthfulness the first glances of your mortal eyes are for your holy Mother, while at the same time you do not speak to her, you do not pronounce her name, which is in fact the same as Mary's, and even though her name was destined, by her innocence and her divine maternity, to be part of her holy person [...] You did not pronounce this name and you remained both silent and prisoner of the holy impotence which is that of an infant. When, at the Holy Sepulchre, you are reborn, my Lord, into your life of glory, the first glances of your immortal eyes, both so glorious and so brilliant, fell upon the Magdalene, and the first name which you pronounce is her name, that same name Mary, a name destined by her love and by her penitence, to be part of her person.[14]

The repetition of a name that occurs here does not belong to an intention inherent in the name – that is, it is not part of the name *per se* – rather it is part of a homonymic relationship that covers a series of antinomies: innocence and maternity versus love and penitence; mortal eyes versus immortal eyes; birth versus resurrection.

At the same time, however, we must understand that use of the name *Mary* underscores an operation of repetition, one constituted in difference, an operation which in Bérulle's thinking grounds the principle of resurrection as a glorious rebirth. As the founder of the Oratorian order, and as a disciple of Saint Francis of Sales, Bérulle inherits a joyous kind of mystical thinking from his spiritual predecessor, one which obliges us to recognize that the Sepulchre is, in and of itself, a matrix of happiness. First sketched out in Bérulle's *Élévation sur Marie Madeleine*, the theme of a joyous sepulchre receives a fuller rendition in his *Discours de l'état et des grandeurs de Jésus*: "For indeed, just as is the case for a birth not of the Virgin Mary, that is, birth into a mortal life, one is born on this earth and our earth is the place which must adopt us with this humble birth, so too is a birth occurring outside of the sepulchre a birth into everlasting life: here you are born into heaven and heaven is the place which must literally take you in with this happy birth in the state of glory."[15] A member of the Dominican order, the mystical writer Louis Chardon meditates on this same idea, but he comes at it from a darker side: the virginal womb is *already* a sepulchre, in the same way that the pregnancy following which Jesus was born was *already* a cross. In Chardon's thinking, incarnation occurs in the realm of mire. As he writes: "I must admit of this mud in the virgin that it is holy and immaculate. And yet it is precisely because he chooses it as the path toward human regeneration, alongside his mother, that it is also prone to pain; he calls it a mud from the deepest of trenches and by this one must understand the sacred womb of divine Mary."[16] In another passage, Mary's womb is assimilated with the cross of suffering: "Whereas Mary will be his first altar, the Cross will be his last. On this second altar he will suffer only for a period of three hours. However, on the first altar he will suffer for nine months. The Cross of Calvary is merely an artificial one whereas Mary is a natural cross, and this is because man was not created according to the model proposed by the cross since, on the contrary, it is she who constitutes the model for mankind."[17]

Nevertheless – and this is the important thing – behind all the apparent differences between these stories visible on the narrative level, we should not forget that at Emmaus Jesus disappears before his disciples' eyes. This scenario stands in contrast with the encounter with Mary Magdalene where he merely announces his later disappearance from earth. Here, for the time being, he formulates what appears to be a strange forbiddance to touch him. Recent exegesis, having at its disposal the linguistic resources found in multiple translations, has harkened back to the exact meaning lying behind the verb "to touch." Getting away from Jerome's Latin translation of *Noli me tangere* – literally meaning "Do not touch me" – Guy Lafon stresses the imperfective sense of the Greek words we can read in the Septuagint Bible. Here the verb of this passage is better understood as something like "stop touching me" for, as Lafon goes on to explain, in this instance the verb "to touch" must be understood as a variant of the verb "to take."[18] However, in addition, Bérulle's meditation clearly stresses the laconic nature of Christ's negative injunction. Seeing in it a model for the type of love that must unite the believer with Christ until the time of the Second Coming, Bérulle understands that the core notion must be one of "a love that separates." I shall later come back to this moment of loving separation that painting is so well able to represent. For the moment, I wish to give a quick overview of the state known as "separating love," which can be found in the language Bérulle uses: "Allow me, oh divine soul, to say this to you: lying at the feet of our glorified Jesus you have just begun to enter the school of separating love, in the same way that, when you lie at the feet of our humiliated Saviour, you have only just entered the school of unifying love. These are two sacred schools in Jesus's grand academy: both are schools which function in the love of Christ, each according to a love which is different."[19] For this reason, it is impossible to say that the differences between the story of Emmaus and that of the encounter before the Holy Sepulchre are only minor in nature. At the same time, however, one notices that these differences can be compared on

TABLE 3: MISRECOGNITION.

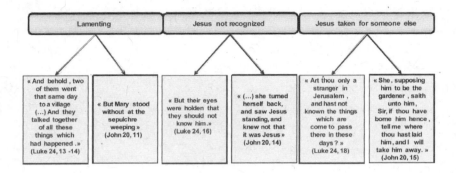

| Lamenting | Jesus not recognized | Jesus taken for someone else |
|---|---|---|

« And behold , two of them went that same day to a village (...) And they talked together of all these things which had happened .» (Luke 24, 13 -14)

« But Mary stood without at the sepulchre weeping » (John 20, 11)

« But their eyes were holden that they should not know him .» (Luke 24, 16)

« (...) she turned herself back, and saw Jesus standing, and knew not that it was Jesus » (John 20, 14)

« Art thou only a stranger in Jerusalem , and hast not known the things which are come to pass there in these days ? » (Luke 24, 18)

« She, supposing him to be the gardener , saith unto him, Sir, if thou have borne him hence , tell me where thou hast laid him, and I will take him away. » (John 20, 15)

TABLE 4: RECOGNITION.

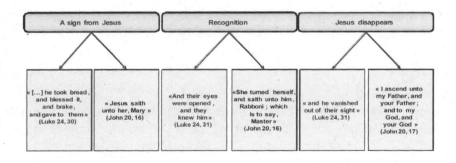

| A sign from Jesus | Recognition | Jesus disappears |
|---|---|---|

« [...] he took bread , and blessed it, and brake , and gave to them » (Luke 24, 30)

« Jesus saith unto her, Mary » (John 20, 16)

«And their eyes were opened , and they knew him » (Luke 24, 31)

«She turned herself, and saith unto him, Rabboni ; which is to say, Master » (John 20, 16)

« and he vanished out of their sight » (Luke 24, 31)

« I ascend unto my Father, and your Father ; and to my God, and your God » (John 20, 17) a point-by-point basis since both narratives are based on an identical narrative structure (**see Tables 3 and 4**).

Both stories can be divided into two episodes, the first of which is premised upon the failure to recognize the risen Christ, the second on his eventual recognition. Further, both episodes contain three actions, and these actions are basically the same in each instance, their differences being mainly ones of intensity or having to do with the relative importance that tradition has attached to each one of them individually. Thus we can focus for a moment on examples which do not concern traditional iconography as it related to the encounter between Christ and Mary Magdalene, serving rather as a prelude of sorts to that same encounter: let us mention the journey on foot undertaken to Emmaus, or the lament at the foot of the cross. As for the latter episode, it is treated rather differently according to the Evangelical exegesis one reads. Concerning the former episode, the apostles' journey on foot is dealt with in a matter-of-fact fashion, and one might even claim that its style is somewhat stuffy. For example, near the end of the seventeenth century, the French preacher Louis Bourdaloue gave the following derogatory comments in one of his sermons:

> When I consider, my fellow Christians, the attitude displayed by his two disciples in the story told to us in the Gospel, I get the impression that the Saviour of our world is dealing with two sicknesses, lying in their very persons, which he now must heal. For this healing he will need to resort to some very powerful remedies, ones enlisting all the strength of his divine grace. First, they did not possess the faith that they should have had in him, and second, they were already beginning to grow distant from him even though they had always considered themselves to be among his closest disciples. They had already begun to disbelieve and already they were becoming cold and listless: they no longer believed what they should have believed. This can be seen in the fact that,

despite his divine nature, they spoke to him as if he were just another man [...][20]

As is well known, it would be easy to fill entire volumes with the words written about the tears Mary Magdalene shed before the Holy Sepulchre. For our purposes, it will suffice to take only those descriptions written during the Baroque era about this scene. A typical example can be found in the following prose passage written by Charles de Saint-Paul: "We see you overwhelmed with pain, overwhelmed under the weight of an unbearable sorrow, a violent sadness that burdens you in such a way that you no longer know what you are doing, you drown in your tears, and one sees on your face all the distinctive marks of extreme affliction."[21] Another can be culled from the poetic verses composed by Desmarets de Saint-Sorlin: "Face to the ground she moans in grief, she weeps and cries/ This pitiful place where she now lies/ She has chosen as her abode, able to leave neither her lover nor her God."[22] Despite the quantitative differences we can observe therein, we notice two clear cases of lamentation. In the first of them, Mary Magdalene's weeping is described while highlighting the appropriate differences, in the scene where the risen Jesus is both misrecognized and mistakenly addressed. And in both instances, the same narrative device is relied upon at the exact same moment: just like Mary Magdalene, the apostles find themselves in the presence of the risen Christ, and they too do not recognize him, speaking to him without ever realizing who he is. And then comes the second episode during which Jesus lets himself be recognized. In this narrative sequence, there are once again three necessary actions: first, Jesus gives a special identifying sign, either orally or in the form of a gesture; second, the apostles or Mary Magdalene recognize this sign and thereby show that they have recognized Jesus; third, Jesus suddenly disappears (he disappears from Magdalene's sight only to reappear a little while later at the supper table with his apostles) or he announces – not as something which is yet to come but in the inchoative mode as something already in motion – that he would soon be disappearing again: "I ascend unto my Father" (John 20, 17).

If we focus on this particular moment, one that the story of the encounter before the Holy Sepulchre shares with the Emmaus episode, the narrative undergoes a significant change in relation to the meaning it once assumed when it was approached in a linear fashion, that is, in relation to an episode that follows it chronologically, to wit, the trial inflicted upon Thomas. The Magdalene-Thomas couple transmitted a message concerning religious faith. It dealt either with the nature of faith itself (seen as independent of material proof, faith concerning the hypostatic relationship, which is to say that faith implies believing without any tangible proof that the Father and the Son share a single divine substance) or with the state of belief proper to a Christian. The Magdalene-Emmaus nexus specifically deals with how it is possible to recognize Jesus in his state of absence. In the second nexus, we see a lesson given posthumously by Christ to those who are closest to him, either to his fellow male disciples or to his "betrothed" (as classical texts of devotion are wont to call her). Assuming the appearance of a testament or will, the relevant episodes thus take on an emotional charge. In this context, language (the linguistic sign) clearly possesses the ability to invoke that which is absent, and this is the case even if it derives its meaning from contradiction as it does in mystical discourse.

What is interesting is that both Mary Magdalene and the Eucharist appearing at Emmaus short-circuit language by standing in its place. Insomuch as Mary Magdalene possesses the name "Mary" and insofar as the Eucharist is present despite Christ's absence, Jesus offers himself to his followers in the form of a substitution, that is, in the form of a linguistic sign that will refer back to him during the great time of his absence, a sign that thus opens itself up to this absence. It is at this level that we can see a profound identity between John's and Luke's version of the story: by calling out to Magdalene (this is what allows her to recognize him), Jesus displays the same form of love which is that of the Eucharist. And this calling out is itself a Eucharistic form because, like the Eucharist, it is unrecognizable on the formal level: Jesus does not look any more like a gardener than he looks like a piece of bread. This is why Louis Chardon mentions the Eucharist in his chapter on Mary Magdalene; it is also why he does this at that very moment where the difference between ignorance and recognition is momentarily suspended:

> With Saint Bernard, we can speak either of a present absence or of an absent presence. There is no better explanation for this relationship than in the example of Christ appearing in the form of the Holy Eucharist, that is to say, where the absence of any perceptible presence – that which the empyrean realm must contain until that moment when Christ returns in his capacity of Universal Judge – does not detract in any way from its present reality; and even though his love does not at this point exercise any movements of life, it does not thereby cease to be both ravishing and effective.[23]

In its claim to be a substitution, the meaning of the Eucharistic sign – at once both a present absence and an absent presence – must nevertheless pass through the operations of language, ideally through the language of mystical devotion. But what will happen to the meaning we assign to the double episode of Mary Magdalene before the tomb and of the meal partaken at Emmaus when these same episodes – whose meaning are given in the Gospels in a shrouded form – are presented not in the guise of words but by the images of painting, as in the case of two works painted by Laurent de La Hyre?

La Hyre insists on the fact that these two episodes occur virtually at the same time, just as he underscores their obvious differences. In fact, in moving from the Tomb to Emmaus, we are faced not just with two settings that are simply different from one another but with two settings that are opposed to one another. In the first instance, the episode involving Mary Magdalene, we have a mountainous backdrop – in fact, this is a high mountainous terrain and not simply the site of Golgotha, which is normally represented as a rather unimpressive hill close to Jerusalem,

2.   LAURENT LA HYRE, *Noli me tangere*, 1656, OIL ON CANVAS, GRENOBLE,
     MUSÉE DE GRENOBLE, 162 X 175 CM. (SEE ALSO P. 240 FOR COLOUR
     REPRODUCTION.)

the city being visible on the horizon. Curiously, mountains as such are
represented very rarely in classical seventeenth-century French art: here
the idea of a mountain lies in stark contrast with that of a garden, an
element of the scenery that is explicitly given in the verbal version of
the episode. In La Hyre's painting, not only does Jesus not appear in
the guise of a gardener, but in addition the depicted scene occurs on
rather hard ground, the only vegetation being of a rustic nature, growing wild, visible on the bottom left corner of the canvas. The mountain
we see might constitute a pictorial reference to the actual location of
the monastery that commissioned La Hyre to do the painting, that is,

3. LAURENT LA HYRE, *The Appearance of Christ at Emmaus*, 1656, OIL ON
CANVAS, GRENOBLE, MUSÉE DE GRENOBLE, 162 X 165 CM. (SEE ALSO P. 240
FOR COLOUR REPRODUCTION.)

the Chartreuse monastery of Grenoble. In this instance, the grandiose
nature of the mountainous terrain expresses the moral qualities of the
monastic institution where the painting will be exhibited: isolation, re-
nunciation, asceticism. But bearing in mind the exact same values, we
might also claim that the mountain points to the French hermitage of
Sainte Baume, "a mountain cave" where there was "neither water nor
herb nor tree,"[24] the site where, according to the mediaeval legends related in *The Golden Legend* by Jacobus de Voragine, Mary Magdalena
lived for thirty years, wishing to remain there, unknown to everyone, in
order to contemplate the things of God, and sustained there by nothing

other than the heavenly food provided by angels. Whatever the truth of the matter may be, the depiction of a mountainous landscape would be perceived, for seventeenth-century viewers, as something rather frightening or hostile. In those rare instances where mountains appear in seventeenth-century French art, they are seen, as in the case of Sébastien Bourdon,[25] as a site rife with bad encounters. In addition, we notice that the mountain that La Hyre has painted was itself the site of a recent and violent storm, as can be deduced by the tree knocked down just above the rocky peak, no doubt constituting an allusion to the exceptional atmospheric conditions, described by both Matthew and Luke, that accompanied Christ's death on the cross.

In direct contrast with the wild site chosen by La Hyre for the Holy Sepulchre, the meal at Emmaus takes place in a marble courtyard next to a villa built beside a thick forest: there two palm trees are shaking in the winds of an impending storm. These trees are the only indication of the fact that the scene is supposed to occur in the Orient; with its fountain and the baker, seen in front of it, who must set the table, the building with its beautiful Doric order is not just part of a Roman décor, but more particularly indicative of a certain level of urbane sophistication. A sense of realism, replete with the appropriate symbols, is established on a first level by the elegant architecture which includes two beautiful vases placed on a stairway, by the lush vegetation of the forest seen in the background, and by the simplicity of the table and of the bench where an apostle is already seated. More significantly, it is created by the visibly worn-out nature both of the stones making up the depicted buildings and of the marble slabs that are part of the courtyard patio: starting at the moment when Christ rises from the dead, the days remaining in the civilization of antiquity are now numbered since the process of a long decay has already begun that will lead to its inevitable demise.

Beyond the obvious opposition between these two sites, several elements of their respective compositions maintain a tight level of cohesion linking the two scenes – and this in turn is reflected in the Evangelical texts to which they refer. The most discreet and the most mysterious element of all has to do with the relationship linking, on the one hand, the tree trunk placed on Christ's left (this trunk functions as a foreground for the mountains that make up the décor needed for the encounter occurring near the tomb) with, on the other hand, the log that is being carried by a shirted character about to enter the courtyard in front of the workshop we see behind the area where the meal at Emmaus will soon be shared. Bearing in mind the need to avoid over-interpretations, one nevertheless notices that the tree trunk is a motif that functions almost like a signature in La Hyre's work. In contrast, a character running in the background constitutes something much less frequent for him. The man seen running is nevertheless reminiscent of the types of figures painted by Poussin, characters whose function lies in giving indications about an impending storm.[26] As Daniel Arasse once remarked, an iconographic motif can only take on meaning within a "figurative network": here the tree trunk and the log-bearing man are placed in similar places within their respective compositions, that is to say, in the background to the left. Clearly visible at this spot on the canvas, they are not any less enigmatic for their visibility. Further, the tree trunk is presented on a slope, which explains in part the running movement undertaken by Mary Magdalene. We notice in addition that the moment at which these scenes take place – to wit, the meal at Emmaus and Mary Magdalene's encounter with Christ – is situated at a time occurring after the suffering on the cross. As is well known, the cross of Golgotha is still visible in the background of several renderings of the *noli me tangere* scene (for example in Holbein's – see below **Illustration 7** – and in Le Sueur's[27] versions of the event); we can say that, in all these cases, instances of "wood" or "trees" stand in a metonymic relationship with Christ's cross.[28] For this reason I propose to read the relationship between the tree trunk in the one painting and the wood-bearing character of the other as a pictorial suggestion concerning how a religious relic is made. As such it becomes an integral part of one of the central themes in both paintings: how is it possible in the future to live with Christ when He is no longer present? Alongside the Eucharist and the holy image, the religious relic – and in particular pieces of the Holy Cross – constitutes one of the solutions proposed by militants of the Counter Reformation, such as Louis Richeome,[29] that is to say, weapons to be used in defence of Catholicism against the criticisms launched by Protestantism.

Obviously, in all this, the strongest and most organic link of all between the two paintings can be found in the figure of Christ himself, in both cases painted rigorously in the same manner. Since we are still dealing with a figurative network, one can ask whether there are any problems in the way Christ is represented. If his physical appearance seems bereft of problematic aspects in the Emmaus painting, it attracts our attention for several reasons in the Magdalene painting. Concerning the way Christ looked when Mary Magdalene saw him, we should once again point out that she at first mistook him for a gardener. There are in fact two iconographic traditions dealing with what Mary Magdalene must have "seen." In the first, he has "the look of a rustic man" ["la sembianza di huomo agreste"], according to the words written by Pietro Aretino;[30] in the second, still draped in his death shroud, Christ offers his almost naked body to the pious desire of his betrothed. Paintings of this scene play a sort of game with the problem of how Christ is recognized, a triangular game involving Mary Magdalene, Jesus, and the painting's viewers, all of whom have different stakes in the outcome of the operation.

When Christ is painted as a gardener, we literally see the same thing that Mary Magdalene sees. We recognize Christ only by means of the appearance under which Mary Magdalene sees him; we also see Christ through the admiration she feels for him at that very moment when she finally recognizes him. The painters Nicolas Poussin and, before him, Lavinia Fontana, make extensive use of this representative device. Normally, the beholder should not be able to recognize Christ under the guise either of a gardener wearing a linen shirt (as is the case for Poussin) or of a totally dishevelled labourer (as is the case for Fontana) whose head is covered by a straw hat. If in the end certain beholders are indeed able to recognize Christ in this disguise, this is only because they recall their readings of the written Gospel, but not because of what they actually see in iconographic language. Indeed, such figures do not partake of any established iconography at all. In this way, both the intimacy and the

4. NICOLAS POUSSIN, *Noli me tangere*, 1653, OIL ON WOOD PANEL, MADRID, MUSEO DEL PRADO, 47 X 39 CM.

BRUNO-NASSIM ABOUDRAR

5. LAVINIA FONTANA, *Noli me tangere*, 1581, OIL ON CANVAS, FLORENCE, GAL-
LERIA DEGLI UFFIZI, 80 x 65.1 CM.

mystery of the scene are preserved as well as another important element that the painter was unable to represent, namely the calling out of Mary Magdalene's name. Mary opens up her arms to the gardener whom she has just recognized as her master through the sound of her name. And let us point out in addition that, for these more prudish types of depiction, the painter is able to find an elegant visual solution to the problem of how to deal with the desire felt by Christ's loving fiancée, that is to say, by showing this desire as something spiritual. Mary Magdalene is not Lady Chatterley and we know perfectly well that it is not because of the vulgarly virile gardener she sees that she decides to open up her arms. Faithful to his reasonable way of interpreting his sources, Poussin wonders what kind of gardener could possibly have been wandering around a gravesite. The Christ he paints has his foot firmly placed on a large hoe or shovel and thus takes on the look of a gravedigger. With a face having such irregular features and a body having such thick wrists, this rustic man must surely have displeased the former high-society courtesan, the seller of expensive perfumes. If in the end she decides to hold on to the man in front of her, this is because of something she senses in Jesus that is no longer part of his body.

The lesson works the other way around in relation to the iconographic tradition that presents Jesus wearing his shroud. The most prominent example of this tradition is of course the *Noli me tangere* painted by Titian in 1512. This painting would in and of itself constitute sufficient justification for the mistrust that members of the Tridentine clergy felt towards those types of images that were capable of igniting the erotic imagination of women. In Titian's painting, not only does Jesus present the arousing charms of his flesh to the viewing public (one cannot see the slightest trace of any suffering on his body), but the gesture of his left hand appears to be pulling the shroud in an upward movement, i.e., toward a very distinctive organ of his humanity, one that is scarcely hidden by the transparent nature of his loincloth. It would almost seem as though he were trying to protect himself from the gesture of Magdalene's hand moving in his direction. As far as I know, no other painter after Titian, not even Correggio,[31] nor the Spaniard Alonso Cano – who

6. TITIAN, *Noli me tangere*, CA. 1512–1514, OIL ON CANVAS, © LONDON, NA-
TIONAL GALLERY, 110.5 X 91.9 CM.

represents a direct reworking of Correggio[32] – exploit the erotic potential
of this scene the way Titian does. And yet, in all these later versions,
the same principle is at work: the viewer has had the chance to recognize Christ well before Mary Magdalene does. The gardening tools
or other like paraphernalia serve merely as an iconographic reminder
about a detail from the scene. Christ's physical beauty and the brilliant
light with which his body is presented are given as obvious figurations of
both the spiritual perfection and the glorious corporeal nature that the

resurrection has bestowed upon him. That Christ would want to interrupt the gesture of touch initiated by Mary Magdalene further reminds us of the ambivalent nature belonging to a human figure whose sacred dignity lies in the fact that she was able to love incarnation more than anyone else, even to the point of loving it in the suffering brought on by separating love. And, like Mary Magdalene, the painting is already itself ambivalent: the beauty present in the pictorial depiction is supposed to be a support mechanism for those wishing to contemplate the nature of celestial beauty. However, this same quality presents the risk of trapping the beholder inside the immediately visible qualities of physical beauty. The *Noli me tangere* painting not only depicts the injunction that Jesus gives to his perfect lover at the same time as it shows the desperate desire she feels in the presence of his glorious body, which has just vanquished death itself by rising up from the tomb, but also, as an image, it transmits a paradoxical piece of advice to all of us who, standing beside the Magdalene, are really just like her. We need to be told not to hang on any longer; we need to let him return to the evanescent visibility from whence he came. We too need to be told not to hold ourselves back any longer.

Between the two options of the gardener or the fantastic ghost, La Hyre chooses to follow a third way, the one first sketched out, more than a century earlier, by Hans Holbein. This being said, La Hyre adopts this path with an entirely different intentionality. Dressed as he is from head to toe with an all-covering blue garment and a coat possessing even a slightly more noble colour, the only "nude" body parts belonging to La Hyre's Christ figure are those that are totally necessary for the devotional narrative being told: the feet towards which Mary Magdalene throws herself, the hands with which he will bless and break the bread, the same hands with which he will signal his refusal to Mary Magdalene, and finally his head. In this painting too, the represented body of Christ shows no physical signs of the suffering he has just undergone; there are also no agricultural tools, and no straw hat of the type traditionally placed on a gardener's head to protect it from the hot sun. If, in this painting, the Christ figure does not radiate the physical beauty of

a pagan god in the way Titian's Christ does, he is nevertheless far from
repeating the same rustic features of the Christ figure represented by
Poussin, and even further from the cold morality of the figure painted by
Holbein who pushes Mary Magdalene away from him "with an expression that is more hostile than it is loving."[33] In La Hyre's *Noli me tangere*,
Jesus is a loving man. He is also handsome: his Venetian blond head of
hair is particularly remarkable as it gracefully falls with its natural curls
onto his shoulders, in a way that reflects the words written by Charles de
Saint-Paul: "the simple presence of this monarch of our hearts is more
than enough to set us burning with his love. At the same time, his hair,
more beautiful than anything you can imagine, embraced the souls of

men with a bond made of an everlasting love."[34] The theme of Christ's physical beauty does not in and of itself represent anything original. But in the example before us, with its stress on hair – normally an attribute belonging to Mary Magdalene – Christ is given a beauty that is almost feminine, thus producing a mirror image of the love relationship being suggested. Exceptionally, in La Hyre's painting, Mary Magdalene's hair is kept in the shadows while Christ's hair, along with his beard, receives the soft light emanating from the left side of the frame. In fact, Christ's hair is painted in the same colour as Mary Magdalene's: the distinguishing feature par excellence of Mary has now been transformed into a visible quality of Christ.

By lifting up his robe, ever so slightly, Jesus allows us to see his bare right foot; this same foot has a sandal strapped on it in the Emmaus painting (in contrast with the apostles who, as pilgrims, should traditionally be shown with footwear but who, in La Hyre's painting, are depicted barefoot). This detail should make us pay careful attention to the way Christ's feet are painted in works depicting the *Noli me tangere* scene. Feet, it would seem, assume a double role that combines both narrative and devotional functions. Just as in the ritual of love and devotion played out in the Pharisee's home by Mary Magdalene while washing Christ's feet with her tears,[35] feet must be brought into a semantic relationship with the head and its hair, both of which, in the abode of Simon the Leper in Bethany, she once covered in expensive perfume.[36] In contrast once again with traditional iconography, La Hyre's Magdalene has no perfume and she sheds no tears. In dressing Jesus in a celestial gown, one that appears rather abstract and not exactly belonging to any identifiable iconographic usage, La Hyre is able to reserve special attention for the head and feet (and also for hands, as we will soon show) and thereby to display in visual terms the extraordinarily fragmented nature of Christ's resurrected body. This is in accordance with Luke, the same Evangelist who recalls the story of Emmaus: "Mine head with oil thou didst not anoint: but this woman hath anointed my feet with ointment" (Luke 7, 46). And it also complies with the poetic ardour with which Bérulle describes this same scene:

Over the entire face of the earth, she is the only person chosen for […] spreading her perfumes on the sacred feet and on that very same head that makes the heavens rejoice and is adored by hosts of angels […]. She alone is often seen at your feet, she alone is allowed to bathe them with her tears, she alone on several occasions showered them with her precious liquors, she alone wiped them with her hair, she alone covered your head with her perfumes […].[37]

All this is because, for Bérulle, Christ's feet are themselves an eminence; that is, they are like a head, the lofty place where a loving exchange can occur, one which takes the form of a mystical exchange of liquids. In La Hyre's work, both Mary Magdalene and Jesus are alike: both are beautiful, desirable, long-haired, and chaste. Furthermore, certain elements of Jesus appear in Mary Magdalene, just as there are elements of Mary Magdalene in Jesus:

In the shadow cast by his sacred feet, a source of grace and purity now flows into that principal soul, one of the most eminent, and then pours into the love shared by Jesus; and also from that humble heart, or rather from that heart so elevated because placed next to divine feet, there springs forth a source of fresh water which washes in purity as it cleanses Jesus' feet. These are two remarkable sources, two remarkable flows: one of these sources is found at Christ's feet and flows into Mary Magdalene; the other of these sources is found in Mary Magdalene's heart and flows onto Jesus' feet. Two lively and heavenly sources, and also heavenly while on the earth, because the earth becomes part of heaven when Jesus is on the earth.[38]

And this is exactly the form that Jesus assumes when dressed in blue: a heavenly source of life-giving water.

From the narrative point of view, however, Jesus' right foot is slightly turned toward the right side of the canvas (that is to say, in the opposite direction from where Mary Magdalene has arrived). Along with his left one, and with the help of Christ's body depicted in *contrapposto*, this foot appears almost like a racer's, already in the starting block. Thus depicted, it indicates that Jesus is already on the verge of leaving. As a consequence, La Hyre's painting does not exactly represent the *Noli me tangere* scene *per se* but rather the Biblical verse closing the narrative: "I ascend unto my Father." It is only through her eyes and through her eyes alone – certainly not because of her hands – that Mary Magdalene is now able to retain an image of her Lord.

In the same way, in the scene of the meal partaken at Emmaus, everything appears as though the scene itself had already come to an end. The bread is already broken, and Jesus is in conversation with his Father; the two disciples present have already recognized who he really is. In this respect, there is nothing exceptional in the way La Hyre has chosen to paint the scene, even if it can be considered rather rare in comparison with the traditional iconography of this same Gospel story. Paintings normally depict the beginning moments of the meal, the moment when Jesus has only just begun to break the bread, that is to say, the point where one of the apostles is *on the verge* of recognizing Christ (whereas the other apostle is of course still in a state of ignorance). At the beginning of the seventeenth century, this is the way painters as diverse as Caravaggio[39] and Velazquez[40] depict the meal. Near the end of the century, however, in one of his last works, Philippe de Champaigne will choose the exact same moment as that selected by La Hyre.[41] Another small difference displayed by La Hyre in relation to traditional iconography can be seen in the details he paints of the table. His table at Emmaus is not *just* a table because it is also an altar and, as such, it can be "set" in a number of ways: sometimes for a meal, replete with fowl and fruit, at other times displaying only the Eucharistic bread. In most cases, however, it will be adorned with a knife, but one that is usually in a precarious position, as if about to fall to the ground. Part of normal table cutlery, the knife is also the sign of a sacrifice about to be renewed. At the very edge of the table, in the place normally occupied by a knife, La Hyre paints several white napkins, folded in a small pile, the third of which is however open, hanging off the edge of the table in our direction, in front of the table cloth itself. The whitish colour of the tablecloth becomes much whiter as well, since in the spot where it appears, it takes on the form of Christ's body, that is, it is draped over his knee. In this sense, the napkin and the tablecloth together remind us of Veronica's veil, even if here they have no image printed on them.

In the encounter with Mary Magdalene as painted by La Hyre, Jesus's gesture toward her does not consist in pushing her away. Rather, he brushes her forehead in a classical manner which, according to mediaeval legend, left a lasting mark in her cranium at the spot where his radiant fingers touched her brow. In touching her forehead, he thereby casts a shadow over her face and is thus hidden from her view in the same manner in which he will remove himself from the sight of the two pilgrims at the very moment when, after having broken bread with them, they have finally begun to recognize him.

Thus, it is safe to say, for both of the La Hyre paintings we have just discussed, that Christ is not really present, that is to say, not *physically* present. That which the apostles and Mary Madeleine see is a remanence, a retinal persistence of vision. Perhaps we could claim that their state of mourning has taken on the form of what the Greeks called *pothos*, in reference to the agitated mind of a nostalgic Achilles while in his sleep, a presence which is none other than that of Protroclus' *psuche*[42]. Or we might wish to show that the resurrection was never anything but the result of the loving desire of the apostles, and that of Mary Magdalene in particular, an ardent desire to see their Lord again after they had seen him die. Both Mary Magdalene and Saint Luke produce the same gesture – in fact it is identical with the one depicted by Caravaggio in his portrait of Narcissus:[43] it consists in trying to embrace a fleeting image. What we viewers see when we look at La Hyre's two paintings is the power of the image, a power that is different both from that of the Eucharist and from that of relics. It is the power to give presence to things which are absent and to give them this presence insofar as they are absent. They give form to this power even to the point of showing the object's dissipation in the effects of desire. Such a lesson about power is not exactly of the type that texts are able to impart.

## BIBLIOGRAPHY

Arasse, Daniel. "L'excès des images." In *L'Apparition à Marie Madeleine*, ed. Guy Lafon, 79–121. Paris: Desclée de Brouwer, 2001.

Aretino, Pietro. *I quattro libri de la humanità di Christo, libro quarto*. Venice: Francesco Marconlini di Forli, 1538.

Augustine (Saint Augustine). *Homilies on the Gospel According to Saint John, and his first Epistle*, vol. I, translated by members of the English Church. Oxford: John Henry Parker, 1848 [first written in the 5th Century A.D].

————. *Homilies on the Gospel According to Saint John and his first Epistle*, vol. II, translated by members of the English Church, Oxford: John Henry Parker, 1849 [first written in the 5th Century A.D].

Bérulle, Pierre de. *Œuvres complètes*, vol. III, 1. Paris: Éditions du Cerf, 1996.

————. *Élévation sur sainte Madeleine*, Grenoble: Éditions Jérôme Millon, 1998 [1st ed. 1627].

Bourdaloue, Louis. *Sermon sur la Résurrection de Jésus Christ (sermon pour le lundi de Pâques)*. In *Œuvres*, Besançon: Outhenin-Chalandre fils, 1882, vol. III.

Chardon, Louis. *La Croix de Jésus*. Paris: Éditions du Cerf, 2004 [1st ed. 1647].

Desmarets de Saint-Sorlin, Jean. *Marie-Madeleine ou le triomphe de la grâce*. Grenoble: Éditions Jérôme Millon, 2001 [1st ed. 1669].

*Holy Bible*. King James Version. Grand Rapids, MI: Zondervan Publishers, 2002.

Lafon, Guy, ed., *L'Apparition à Marie Madeleine*. Paris: Desclée de Brouwer, 2001.

Origen. *An Homilie of Marye Magdalene: newly translated*. London: Reginalde Wolfe, 1565 [first written in the 3rd century A.D.].

Quesnel, Pasquier. *La piété envers Jésus Christ, ou médiation sur les mystères et sur les paroles de JCNS*. Rouen: Pierre Ferrand et Antoine Maury, 1697.

Richeome, Louis. *Trois discours sur la religion catholique*. Paris: Jacques Reze, 1602.

Saint-Paul, Charles de. *Tableau de Magdeleine en l'état de parfaite amante de Jésus.* Grenoble: Éditions Jérôme Millon, 1997 [1st ed. 1628].

Vernant, Jean-Pierre. *Myth and Thought among the Greeks,* trans. Janet Lloyd and Jeff Fort. New York: Zone Books, 2006.

Voragine, Jacobus de. *The Golden Legend,* trans. Granger Ryan and Helmut Ripperger. New York: Arno Press, 1969 [first written in the thirteenth century].

Wirth, Jean. *L'Image à l'époque romane.* Paris: Éditions du Cerf, 1999.

# NOTES

1   In French: *Les paroles des anges et de Jésus à Madeleine au sépulcre.*

2   Pierre de Bérulle, *Elévation sur sainte Madeleine* [1627] (Grenoble: Éditions Jérôme Millon, 1998), 99. ["Vous proférez le doux nom de Marie et ses yeux sont ouverts en la prolation de ce nom, comme ceux des deux disciples en la fraction mystérieuse faite en Emmaüs"].

3   Saint Augustine, *Homilies on the Gospel According to Saint John, and his first Epistle,* vol. I, translated by members of the English Church (Oxford: John Henry Parker, 1848), Homily XVI, 254.

4   Saint Augustine, *Homilies on the Gospel According to Saint John and his first Epistle,* vol. II, translated by members of the English Church (Oxford: John Henry Parker, 1849), 822 [Homily LXXIX].

5   Augustine, *Homilies on the Gospel According to Saint John and his first Epistle,* vol. II, 1055 [Homily CXXI].

6   Augustine, *Homilies on the Gospel According to Saint John and his first Epistle,* vol. II, 358.

7   Pasquier Quesnel, *La piété envers Jésus Christ, ou méditation sur les mystères et sur les paroles de JCNS* (Rouen: Pierre Ferrand et Antoine Maury, 1697), 150.

8   Quesnel, *Homilies on the Gospel,* 151.

9   Jean Wirth, *L'image à l'époque romane* (Paris: Éditions du Cerf, 1999), 32 *et passim.*

10   Matthew recounts an additional detail concerning the priests' attempts to bribe the soldiers who came to tell them about Christ's disappearance. They wanted the soldiers to tell everyone that Christ's apostles had stolen his corpse.

11   Charles de Saint-Paul, *Tableau de Magdeleine en l'état de parfaite amante de Jésus* [1628] (Grenoble: Éditions Jérôme Millon, 1997), 88.

12   Ibid., 89.

13   Bérulle, *Elévation,* 100.

14   Ibid., 102.

15   Bérulle, "Discours de l'état et des grandeurs de Jésus, Discours XII" [1629], *Œuvres complètes,* III, 1 (Paris: Éditions du Cerf, 1996), 464.

16   Louis Chardon, *La Croix de Jésus* [1647] (Paris: Éditions du Cerf, 2004), 428.

17   Ibid., 435.

18   Guy Lafon, *L'Apparition à Marie Madeleine* (Paris: Desclée de Brouwer, 2001), 67.

19   Bérulle, *Elévation,* 107.

20   Louis Bourdaloue, *Sermon sur la Résurrection de Jésus Christ (sermon*

*pour le lundi de Pâques), Œuvres* (Besançon: Outhenin-Chalandre fils, 1882, vol. III), 607.

21 Charles de Saint-Paul, *Tableau de Magdaleine*, 88.

22 À terre elle gémit, et sanglote et pleure.

Elle veut en ce triste lieu,

Pour toujours faire sa demeure; et ne saurait quitter son amant et son Dieu.

(Jean Desmarets de Saint-Sorlin, *Marie-Madeleine ou le triomphe de la grâce* [1669], [Grenoble: Éditions Jérôme Millon, 2001], 192).

23 Chardon, *La Croix*, 867.

24 Jacobus de Voragine, *The Golden Legend*, trans. Granger Ryan and Helmut Ripperger (New York: Arno Press, 1969), 360.

25 Sébastien Bourdon, *The Brigands*, middle of the seventeenth century, oil on canvas, Lyons, Musée des Beaux-Arts, 38 x 59.5 cm.

26 Nicolas Poussin, *Landscape with Pyrame and Thisbe*, 1651, oil on canvas, Frankfurt, Städelsches Kunstinstitut, 192 x 273.5 cm; Nicolas Poussin, *Landscape of a Man Killed by a Snake*, ca. 1648, oil on canvas, London, National Gallery, 118.2 x 197.8 cm.

27 Eustache Le Sueur, *Jesus Christ Appearing to Mary Magdalene*, ca. 1651, oil on canvas, Paris, Louvre, 145 x 129 cm.

28 An example of this metonymic relationship can be seen in the following passage written by Origen (and quoted in French in Chardon, *La Croix*, 878): "She but a little before, with her very eies, to the great dolour of her heart, beheld she her whole hope, to be hanged upon the tree, and saieste thou nowe unto her, why wepest thou? She the third day beheld thy handes wherwith she hath ben often blessed, thy feet which she had kissed, and whiche she had watered with her teares nailed upon the crosse, and thou being her whole sorow, saiest unto her: why wepest though?" (Origen, *An Homilie of Marye Magdalene: newly translated* [London: Reginalde Wolfe, 1565], no page number).

29 Louis Richeome, *Trois discours sur la religion catholique* (Paris: Jacques Reze, 1602).

30 Pietro Aretino, *I quattro libri de la humanità di Christo, libro quarto* (Venice: Francesco Marconlini di Forli, 1538), 221.

31 Correggio, *Noli me tangere*, ca. 1525, oil on canvas, Madrid, Museo del Prado, 130 x 103 cm.

32 Alonso Cano, *Noli me tangere*, ca. 1640, oil on canvas, Budapest, Szépmûvészeti Múzeum, 141.5 x 109.5 cm.

33 Daniel Arasse, "L'excès des images," *L'Apparition à Marie-Madeleine*, ed. Guy Lafon, 121.

34 Charles de Saint-Paul, *Tableau de Magdeleine*, 47.

35 Luke 7, 38.

36 Matthew 21, 7; Mark 14, 3.

37 Bérulle, *Elévation*, 58.

38 Ibid., 51.

39 Caravaggio, *The Supper at Emmaus*, 1606, oil on canvas, Milan, Pinacoteca di Brera, 141 x 175 cm.

40 Velazquez (Diego Rodriguez de Silva y Velázquez), *The Supper at Emmaus*, ca. 1622–1623, oil on canvas, New York, Metropolitan Museum of Art, 123.2 x 132.7 cm.

41 Philippe de Champaigne, *The Supper at Emmaus*, ca. 1656, oil on canvas, Angers, Musée des Beaux-Arts, 137.5 x 179.5 cm.

42 Jean-Pierre Vernant, *Myth and Thought among the Greeks*, trans. Janet Lloyd and Jeff Fort (New York: Zone Books, 2006), 325.

43 Caravaggio, *Narcissus*, ca. 1594–1599, oil on canvas, Rome, Galleria Nazionale d'Arte Antica, 110 x 92 cm.

# 3

# PAINTING THE READERS OF THE EIGHTEENTH CENTURY

*Anthony Wall*

Every period in the history of European art can boast about the quality of its painted readers. Eighteenth-century painters of readers are no different in this respect from their predecessors or from their successors. People are painted in the act of reading, painted as they learn to read, painted as someone else reads to them. They are depicted while reading out loud just as they are shown while reading in silence. Nevertheless, in what follows, I propose to pursue a line of questioning that has a distinctly eighteenth-century quality in its way of representing painted readers: the complicated relationship between reading in public and reading in solitude. Painted images of readers of this century often depict a person attempting to read in solitude, attempting to be alone. As it turns out, when you are a painted character trying to read in peace and quiet during the eighteenth century, it is not exactly easy to be alone. At a crucial moment in the cultural history of the West, at a time when reading practices are slowly changing from the older, intensive forms of textual consumption to newer ones more geared to more extensive forms of reading,[1] at a time when books are becoming smaller and ever more easily held in the hand, at a time when new spaces are being created in the home and in public for the private enjoyment of texts, at such a time questions about if and when a person can truly read alone would certainly seem appropriate.

8. LANCRET, NICOLAS, *La Malice*, FIRST HALF OF THE 18TH CENTURY, OIL ON CANVAS, DUBLIN, NATIONAL GALLERY OF IRELAND, 36 X 29 CM.

The long tradition of painting readers and the particular genres that allow for this depiction show us the extent to which certain periods of time are more propitious than others for producing reading images.[2] Moreover, certain painters are more prone to paint a person caught in the act of reading than others. The object of the following contribution will be to examine the major characteristics of readers as they appear in eighteenth-century France and England.[3]

## READING IN PUBLIC OR IN PRIVATE?

Of course, all European painters of the eighteenth century who are interested in readers, whether they hail from France, the United Kingdom, or elsewhere, have an enormous debt to pay to the great painters of the Netherlands such as Vermeer, Dou, Ter Borch, Metsu, Elinga, de Hooch, van Ostade, and so many others who, like their idol Rembrandt, were masters at the art of depicting the act of reading. Whereas, with many exceptions of course, Dutch painters of the seventeenth century often specialized in the painting of a particular genre scene, that of writing, receiving, or reading a *letter*,[4] in the present discussion I wish to emphasize the visualized reading of *books*, books which, during the Age of the Enlightenment, were more and more often produced in small formats, sometimes almost like modern "pocket books," what the French of the time referred to as "brochures". And if, for example, it is safe to say that, in comparison with the sixteenth century, the seventeenth century frequently depicts the act of reading, is it also true to say that the eighteenth century paints readers even more often than does the seventeenth?

To be in a position to answer this and other related questions, it is of course highly useful to avoid oversimplified hypotheses and broad-stroke generalizations. For example, it is not entirely certain that even if, from an historico-sociological point of view, it is true to say that there are quantitatively more painted readers in the eighteenth century than there are in the seventeenth, we are entitled to conclude that, qualitatively (that is to say, in relation to the huge corpus of paintings that

9. JEAN-BAPTISTE DESHAYS, *Portrait of a Young Woman Holding a Book* (*Presumed Portrait of Madame Deshays*), CA. 1760, OIL ON CANVAS, PRIVATE COLLECTION, 51 X 43 CM. (FOTO MARBURG/ART RESOURCE, NY).

ANTHONY WALL

the eighteenth century has bequeathed to us), there are proportionately more painted readers in the visual arts of the Enlightenment that in those of the Age of Reason. And such a generalization begs the question about whether the later century stresses different types of reading than the earlier one. Another type of over-generalization worth avoiding, at least in the context of French painting, is related to the hypothesis, first promoted by Michael Fried,[5] according to which reading is simply one subtype of a much wider visual phenomenon of the eighteenth century, to wit, paintings which depict activities of absorption. For Fried, mental absorption is construed as a highly individualized phenomena having very little to do, if anything at all, with the obvious linguistic-aesthetic processes that go on in the head of the reader and which the painter may or may not wish to explore visually. And, of course, if we stress here the important link between genre paintings of the Dutch seventeenth century and visual renderings of the act of reading as they were shown during the French and British eighteenth century, it is debatable whether for the Enlightenment it is useful to refer back to sociological and historical facts concerning the changing reading practices of the Protestant Reformation, which encouraged painters such as Dou and Rembrandt to show simple people reading the Bible. Indeed, for painters such as Greuze and Fragonard working in France, it is not entirely clear that such remarks are entirely useful. And such a hypothesis has nothing to say, for example, about the idealized nature of a father reading the Bible to his children in Jean-Baptiste Greuze's famous 1755 painting,[6] just as it has little to say about the particular ways in which Fragonard adopted and adapted the reading subgenre known as the "Education of the Virgin Mary."[7]

If, for eighteenth-century paintings, it is indeed useful to distinguish, as we have already done, between private and public reading, one must nevertheless be prepared to make room for a multitude of reading practices that are *both* private *and* public, or rather *neither* private *nor* public. Such instances can be visualized in the typically British genre of the *Conversation Piece* and in French adaptations of this same way of painting. Here a family is shown as a tight-knit and self-sufficient unit and, in the context of such paintings, we often find someone reading alone, a person tucked away in the corner of the painted space. Is such a person engaging in a solitary act or is he or she manifesting a typical social act of the time? Issues having to do with absorption are not particularly useful for answering such questions. The instances portrayed partake directly of the compositional tradition already launched by the Italian *Sacre Conversazioni* of the Renaissance, a primary example of which is the figure of Saint Jerome reading both in private and in a group setting at the right side of the canvas.[8] This is the same type of contradictory physical positioning taken up by François Boucher's Virgin Mary, both physically present but mentally busy elsewhere, as she reads in the company of her loved ones amongst all the hustle and bustle of angels, her husband and her Child playing with little Saint John during their flight into Egypt. And even in the case of painted scenes other than those of the British Conversation Piece, compositions in which we can often see someone reading more or less in private, it would seem preferable to concentrate not only on the reading act itself, but also on the multitude of visualized accessories that provide us with a broad view of the context in which this particular act of reading is seen to participate. In such instances, discussions of the absorptive nature of the reader's activity cannot capture the richness of the semantic relationship between a group activity and a solitary one. For as these paintings suggest, some readers prefer to read while surrounded by other persons.

If I now concentrate on private scenes of reading, this is not to say that I do not attach any importance to public scenes. On the contrary, the latter must remain in the background of the viewer's mind whenever he or she looks upon a painting of solitary reading from the eighteenth century. This background knowledge according to which reading in private only occurs visually *in contrast with* reading in public is part and parcel of what we described earlier as the difficulty, for a painted character of the Enlightenment, to be truly alone. When one reads, as the paintings show, one does so for visibly social purposes. A great many highly codified activities await the seemingly solitary reader on a number of social fronts: the reader is expected to speak about what he or she has read later

10.  FRANÇOIS BOUCHER, *Rest during the Flight into Egypt*, 1737, OIL ON CANVAS, SAINT PETERSBURG, STATE HERMITAGE MUSEUM, 139.5 X 148.5 CM.

on, either in a salon, or at the dinner table, or perhaps even at the theatre, or in a private tête-à-tête. Readers read in order to prepare their wits for these various social events. Even amorous couples, those who may wish to read love songs together, in private intimacy, will have trouble finding a time and a place to be truly alone. One of the famous paintings of Jean-Honoré Fragonard, known under the title of "Progrès de l'amour,"[9] shows two lovers whose desired privacy is interrupted by the presence of a pesky artist on the right side of the canvas. With behaviour resembling that of modern paparazzi, the artist appears to be drawing their portrait.

11.   SIR JOSHUA REYNOLDS, *Portrait of Giuseppe Baretti*, 1773–1774, OIL ON
CANVAS, PRIVATE COLLECTION, 73.7 X 62.2 CM.

12. PIERRE SUBLEYRAS, *Presumed Portrait of Giuseppe Baretti*, CA. 1745, OIL ON
CANVAS, PARIS, LOUVRE, 74 X 61 CM. (ERICH LESSING/ART RESOURCE, NY).
(SEE ALSO P. 242 FOR COLOUR REPRODUCTION.)

His very presence points to the pragmatic impossibility of a portrait that could show someone truly alone.

This merely pragmatic difficulty – the presence of the painter destroys the fictitious intimacy – is the cover for a second difficulty of an existential order, that of being alone in the eighteenth century in general, especially when one is a painted character, whether this solitary space is intended to create ideal conditions for reading or for another type of activity. In those rare moments one manages to steal from other activities in order to read in quiet, this solitary reading is anything but anti-theatrical. One could even maintain that reading is destined in large part to allow the social human being *to be* theatrical through his or her wit (and the pithy things one gathers in reading), during the intense social life in which one inevitably must participate. Further on, we will look more closely at two (presumed) portraits of an eighteenth-century socialite named Giuseppe Baretti, which will allow us to reinforce our thesis concerning the social nature even of solitary reading: first, a painting by Joshua Reynolds; second, a portrait of a reading gentleman painted by Pierre Subleyras and today housed in the Louvre.[10] We shall return to this pair of portraits at a later point of this essay.

## THE BOOK AS OBJECT

In France, during the eighteenth century – but not only in France – pictorial evidence would suggest that the proportion of reading scenes painted in relation to all other genre scenes is similar, but in reverse, to that established by a comparison between the total number of portraits painted by Nicolas de Largillierre (between 1,200 and 1,500 according to Jean Chatelus)[11] and those which show someone either holding a piece of paper or a book (approximately twenty to thirty canvasses). We are therefore interested here in artists whose proportion of reader canvasses is considerably higher: exactly the case of Sir Joshua Reynolds whose "numbers" are very different from those posted by Largillierre. On the evidence displayed by David Mannings's magnificently produced catalogue of 2000,[12] one finds in the British artist's oeuvre some 2,250 painted works of which roughly two hundred, with the use of paper, books and the like, make visual reference to the act of reading. Despite these "better" numbers on Reynolds's side, one is obliged to admit that, for the greater part of these two hundred works showing paper or books, the latter are mere accessories, that is to say, just simple components among the incredible arsenal available in Reynolds's inventive machinery for varying the compositions of his portraits. In such instances, paper and book are not at all central to the painted subject's soul or spirit. Furthermore, in those examples where a book is displayed, the latter is more often than not closed, a fact which speaks volumes about the non-centrality of "reading" *per se* in the portraits painted by this great British artist. There are of course a few exceptional portraits, but they are few and far between. Beyond the Baretti portrait, to which we shall soon return, one can mention the several portraits he painted of Samuel Johnson (one of which is commonly known as "Blinking Sam"[13]) a portrait of Mrs. Edmund Burke,[14] a painting of Miss Crewe as Saint Genevieve,[15] and a portrait of his favourite niece Theophilia Palmer (in this instance one can even decipher the title of the book she is reading, Richardson's *Clarissa Harlow*).[16] All of these paintings show real persons caught in the act of reading a book or booklet.[17] At least a dozen or more other portraits (those of Anthony Chamier, Mrs. William Johnson, Mrs. Charles Symmons, John Mudge, The Countess of Mount Edgcumbe, The Countess of Lisburne, The Duchess of Rutland, William Baker, Sir William Hamilton in two separate compositions, Miss Sophia Hoare, Miss Popham, Richard Robinson, Thomas Stuart, and Mrs. Yates) allow one to argue that the painted subjects are *almost* reading their books. For example, in the case of the (untraced) portrait of Emily Wynyard, we see a proud woman holding a large scroll filled with Arab letters in her right hand – and if it is true that she is not herself reading these letters, it is obvious that we are supposed to be impressed by the fact that she *could* read them if she wanted to.[18] One can further point to one of his self-portraits which shows him holding a piece of paper, which he is presumably supposed to be reading (even if he destroyed this painting later on) and to several other subject paintings (two showing old men reading – one perhaps a study for King Lear, the other a possible depiction of Joab). Finally, there are three paintings depicting reading boys (all from private collections, an earlier version of one of these being part of the permanent collection in the Museo de Bellas Artes of Buenos Aires).[19] But all of these works represent barely twenty-five canvasses in a corpus of well over two thousand paintings.

While it can be said that the great portraitists of the eighteenth century sometimes turn to the act of reading as a distinctive sign for the portrayal of the human subjects they are being paid to paint, one should note that, for such a purpose, the use of open books – books that the painted subject could thus read theoretically – is relatively rare in the art of portraiture. Pragmatically speaking, this rareness no doubt stems from the fact that it is difficult for a subject to look the painter in the eye and to read a book at the same time. As we saw with Reynolds, such a pragmatic problem can be resolved when the act of reading is depicted in a work that does not purport to be a portrait: here it can form the central theme of work, as was the case of Reynolds's three reading boys, just mentioned. In its continuation of Dutch genre painting from the seventeenth century where reading had been explored in the context of everyday life, French painting from Diderot's century further specializes its depictions of reading scene by turning less and less toward the exchange of letters and ever more toward the reading of books. Elements of everyday life often enter into the works of eighteenth-century portrait artists, both major and minor, including for example Louis Aubert, Fragonard, Greuze, Baudouin, Chardin, Charpentier, De Troy, Lancret, Nonotte, Voille, Loir, Mercier, Nattier, Trinquesse, Van Gorp, and many others. These painters often give us images less of a *particular person* than they represent a particular human act. For example, when a painter wants to depict "a" scholar or "an" alchemist, these generic persons will often be shown with a book since the latter can be seen as the primary accessory for showing the social nature of such a character. The painting is not particularly concerned with the question of *who* this person might actually be. Such "nameless portraits," whose purpose is to show someone in the act of reading, avoid the age-old conundrum of the viewer who has trouble deciding what precisely he or she is supposed to contemplate when presented with a "reading portrait": should the viewer pay attention to the book or to the person? Such problems have always plagued theological theories of the icon since the writings of the early Church fathers, and subsequently the Western art of portraiture, especially when the latter purports to use distinctive signs such as a book to confirm the identity of the painted subject.[20] The point of the most powerful paintings of reading lies less in the fame or anonymity of the person being painted than it does in the reading action depicted by such a painting.

## SHOWING WHO IS READING OR SHOWING THE ACT OF READING?

And this is why it is not only possible, but especially important, to recognize that certain artists of the eighteenth century, in France as elsewhere, are better able than others to render the nuances of the reading act. Many artists, particularly portraitists, concentrate on the "model"; but others are extremely inventive in their efforts to analyze the "act." This act can of course be studied from a multiplicity of perspectives; that is to say, for example, in its inchoative stages, *in medias res*, or in its effects. At one moment, the reading subject is busy reading before our eyes; at another, he or she is engaged in a moment of pause, dreaming about the words that have just been read, or meditating on their possibilities. Reading is sometimes portrayed as a single-staged act, at other times it is seen in a multiplicity of stages. When this portrayed act does not fit into a larger story line, reading itself is the "story" being depicted on the canvas. The book is physically attached to the reading persons or separated from them in space (for example, because it is on the ground or perched on a lectern, not physically touched by the person reading). The act of reading is itself part of a larger series of actions, or it can, in and of itself, constitute the principal subject of the canvas. It occurs in the middle of a much larger landscape, a large interior, or it fills up the entire painted space in which it occurs, interior or exterior.

While certain artists paint scenes of reading much more frequently than others, it is wise to avoid easy generalizations regarding the relative frequency or rareness of such scenes in a given painter's oeuvre, hypothesizing for example that depictions of reading constitute signals of this painter's more or less high level of culture. One is also well-advised to refrain from suggesting that painters (especially portraitists) are more or less *grands artistes* to the extent that, ever since the dignified image of Madame de Maintenon as painted by Pierre Mignard in 1694, they were cultured enough to show the human subject as the recipient of France's great literary culture.[21] Here, the "honour" of the accessory is transferred to the model at the same time as the prestige of the "model" also spreads to the "act." In this line of thinking, certain painters of the European Enlightenment – for example Fragonard, Liotard, Quentin de la Tour, Roslin, Grimou, Colson, Raoux – would suddenly become masters to the extent that they themselves have mastered the art of painting readers; they would be far above those painters who paint readers on an irregular basis.

The personal penchants belonging to a particular artist, whether portraitist or not, along with his or her choices concerning the painted subject matter are not of course the only factors determining whether or not the act of reading appears on a given canvas, wood panel, or copper plate. An equally important set of considerations concerns genre. Several religious and non-religious sub-genres call out for images of readers as if by necessity. In the case of religious paintings of eighteenth-century France, compositions treating subjects such as the Young Christ's Debates with the Temple Scholars, the Holy Virgin's Education, or Mary Magdalene's penitence will contain almost per force at least one character who is reading. Questions of physical rapprochement between reader and book are of prime importance for the penitent Mary Magdalene; questions of the size of the book come into play in eighteenth-century paintings of the Education of the Virgin, issues of the isolation of the reader from the rest of the crowd come in the Young Christ in the

13. MICHEL-BARTHÉLEMY OLLIVIER, *Thé à l'anglaise chez le Prince de Conti dans le Salon des Quatre-Glaces*, 1766, OIL ON CANVAS, VERSAILLES, MUSÉE NATIONAL DU CHÂTEAU ET DE TRIANON, 53 X 68 CM. (RÉUNION DES MUSÉES NATIONAUX/ART RESOURCE, NY).

Temple with Biblical Scholars. Of course, lay versions of these same genres develop during the Enlightenment period when, in France at least, there are significant numbers of portraits of well-to-do women being cast as Magdalene. The subgenre of the school master teaching his pupils to read is a laicized version of the Virgin's education. Paintings of scholars and alchemists are related to the motif of the Pharisee scholar checking passages in the Bible to ascertain whether or not the adolescent Christ is quoting Scriptures accurately. In addition, we find in the eighteenth century multiple variants of the Conversation Piece on each side of the Channel, and increasing variants of the Musical Soirée, works in which we find either the Musicians intently engaged in reading a score, or scenes of concerts where one or more persons in the "listening" public are seen reading (and not always a score). The painting known as *Thé à l'anglaise chez le Prince de Conti dans le Salon des Quatre-Glaces*, by Michel-Barthélemy Ollivier, provides an interesting example of a reader (the young Mozart's father) absorbed in his reading, despite the music played by his son. This paradoxical character is once again reminiscent of Boucher's Virgin Mary and prefigures Gustave Courbet's magnificent portrait of Baudelaire sitting in a corner of the artist's workshop, while reading all on his own.[22]

On the visual front, such concerted efforts to set the act of reading off against other more or less comparable activities – something to be achieved by placing the act of reading in the midst of these other activities – naturally leads to questions about the specificity, if any, of reading as a social act of language, and about the specificity of linguistic and cultural comprehension (when derived from reading) as compared with the modes of understanding that are related to other means of communication. Reading is portrayed as a special type of understanding and, as such, is an integral part of the general movement of the French eighteenth century intent on promoting painting as a legitimate means of intellectual exchange. Such suggestions about the relative worth of images in relation to reading become both paradoxical and convincing when they themselves are expressed within images that comment upon reading. And this relative stress on reading as a linguistic act casts painting itself as a special form of reading in society. However, we still need to explain why eighteenth-century painters rarely paint the actual words on the page being read (in stark contrasts with artists of earlier centuries). And rarely do they give us the title of the book being read either. In a relatively unknown portrait of a young girl reading, painted by Jean-François Gilles Colson, we see a book shown as a physical object as it is held in the girl's hands. While we are given a definite glimpse of one page, *verso folio*, of the book, on this particular page we can read no words at all since all that the painter gives us are squiggles rather that any properly formed words. Indeed, examples where we can see what precisely a painted character is reading are few and far between. In a painting by Bernard d'Agesci (formerly attributed to Greuze), we see

14. JEAN-FRANÇOIS GILLES COLSON, *Portrait of a Young Girl Reading*,
SECOND HALF OF THE EIGHTEENTH CENTURY, OIL ON CANVAS,
MORLANNE (PYRÉNÉES-ATLANTIQUES, FRANCE), MUSÉE DU CHÂTEAU,
58 X 48 CM (PHOTOGRAPH BY JEAN-MARC DECOMPTE, CONSEIL GÉNÉRAL
DES PYRÉNÉES-ATLANTIQUES). (SEE ALSO P. 243 FOR COLOUR REPRODUCTION.)

a woman in ecstasy as she reads Heloise and Abelard.[23] A lost painting from before 1766 painted by Greuze provides another example. It
shows a young girl reading a religious-meditative text on the Holy Cross,
no doubt Louis Chardon's famous text from the seventeenth century.
However, this piece of information only comes to us from the traditional
title of the painting and not from the visual information displayed by
the work itself.[24] In the same way, when we see Don Quixote reading,
as illustrated by Fragonard, we only know that he is reading books on
chivalry if we abstract this information pragmatically.[25]

In the eighteenth century, when an actual painting (and not the title
or the pragmatic context) gives us information of the precise contents
of what is being read, these bits of information are highlighted by other
means than by painting the words being read. One of these means, perhaps the most important, is the use of the painted person's finger, which
either points to a page (even if the words on the page are not themselves
painted) or marks the spot in a book, only partially open, where the
reader is going to return, once he or she has finished looking at the
painter. The finger is an invitation addressed not so much to the painter
than to the viewer; it is a physically depicted encouragement to give due
consideration to the reading act as such, rather than to the specifically
semantic content of that act. It thus creates a physical bond between
the reader's body and the contents of what is being read; it points to
the physical nature of the book being visualized, thereby stressing the
necessarily physical nature of reading, which can unfortunately be lost
if interpreted as a purely mental phenomenon. As Alexandre Wenger
has shown with convincing clarity, we should not today underestimate
the importance of the links that the eighteenth century saw between the
book and the reader, links that could be studied in the physical effects
that reading exerted on the reader's body.[26]

All these issues and lines of questioning are relevant for a closer
analysis of two (presumed) portraits, already mentioned, of a certain
Giuseppe Baretti (see above; Illustrations 11 and 12).

15.  LOUIS TOCQUÉ, *Portrait of Arnoldus van Rijneveld*, CA. 1730–1739,
OIL ON CANVAS, AMSTERDAM, RIJKSMUSEUM, 91.5 X 72 CM.

# Distance for Reading: On Two (Presumed) Portraits of Giuseppe Baretti

Both Joshua Reynolds and Pierre Subleyras suggest the need to distinguish between reading from a distance (one that is no doubt accompanied by pauses for reflection) and reading from close up (sometimes so closely that one loses one's critical distance from the object and its contents). This distinction is not bereft of important links with another highly important difference, ingeniously construed by Daniel Arasse, between the viewing of a painted image from a distance, as an indivisible whole, and viewing the same image from close-up (that is, viewing it in its bits and pieces, or in its details).[27] The Reynolds portrait suggests, in particular, a sort of physical, if not mental, madness that can result from a reading that lets nothing come in between the close physical contact between a reader and his or her book: "a form of madness is indeed also part of the (classical) horizon of someone who gets too close to a painting, thereby abandoning all reasonable distancing and drowning oneself in details."[28] On the one hand, attention to detail connotes care, precision, concentration; on the other, it suggests loss of control, obsession, ecstasy, even purposelessness. Baretti as painted by Reynolds makes us wonder when reading closely is not to be condemned as something ridiculous. Such pleasure of indulging in useless details is of course that of the monkey painted by Chardin. In all this, it is important to remember that, in the case of Baretti, the details in question are first and foremost those given by painted words, and not by anything else.

But who was this Giuseppe Baretti? Above all, he was the flamboyant author of several theoretical texts, written in Italian, which dealt with the history of Italian literature; he was also a controversial critic and poet, as well as an advocate of the Italian language in England. Especially remembered for the polemical tone of his writings on literature, he was outraged by the constant flow of terrible books being published in his native Italy. Beginning in 1763, Baretti is the editor of a literary journal entitled "*Frusta letteraria*" – "The Literary Whip" – which he published under a fictitious name. Largely due to the controversies created by his

16. JEAN-BAPTISTE-SIMÉON CHARDIN, *Le Singe antiquaire*, 1740, OIL ON
CANVAS, CHARTRES, MUSÉE DES BEAUX-ARTS, 28.5 X 23.5 CM. (CLICHÉ
MUSÉE DES BEAUX-ARTS DE CHARTRES).

work, he decides in 1760 to move permanently to the United Kingdom, where he had already published a commercially successful *Dictionary of the English and Italian Language*.[29] In 1769, at the time when the Royal Academy is being established by George III, Baretti is appointed as the Academy's First Secretary responsible for foreign correspondence: it is there that he befriends Reynolds, the first President of the Academy, as well as Samuel Johnson, who will later introduce him to the famously rich Henry Thrale and family in whose home he will become both the preceptor of Thrale's children and part of his prestigious literary Salon. In 1773, after more than a year of difficult legal problems for Baretti (the latter is charged with the murder of a pimp in a sordid episode of prostitution), Thrale asks Reynolds to paint Baretti's portrait in celebration of his acquittal (for self-defence). This portrait will become part of the "Streatham Worthies," a series of thirteen portraits commissioned by Thrale, all painted by Reynolds, which includes the most notable members of his literary circle: Samuel Johnson, Edmund Burke, David Garrick, Reynolds, and, of course, Thrale himself along with his wife Hester Lynch Thrale. It is important, when viewing Reynolds's portrait of Baretti, to understand the passionate nature of the man who is reading with such intensity; it is also important to understand the friendly winks of the eye included in the portrait executed by Reynolds, a man who gently makes fun of Baretti's failing eyesight. In the self-portrait destined to become part of the same Streatham Worthies series, we also note the way in which Reynolds also gently mocks his own failing sense of hearing.[30]

Another good angle for appreciating the flamboyancy of the reading character as painted by Reynolds lies in a comparison with the sombre man depicted by Pierre Subleyras. Here, one notices a man pausing in his reading, almost self-consciously beating his chest in a *mea culpa* gesture. The painting hanging in the Louvre is the original of a replica belonging to Turin's *Museo Civico*. Whether or not the sitter for Subleyras was actually the painter's friend Jacques-Antoine de Lironcourt, or Baretti, does not detract from the usefulness of comparing these two reading men:[31] in the case of Subleyras's work, one immediately senses a certain religious solemnity that is foreign to Reynolds's painted character. And if the reader's shirt in Subleyras's work is of high quality, even ornate, it is certainly not overly luxurious, like the coat he is wearing. All this gives us a picture of a French gentleman, a well-dressed *honnête homme* whose general appearance seems subtly different from the dandy painted by Reynolds. Such a contrast can be supported by a comparison of the wigs worn by the two men.

As already mentioned, Subleyras's reader is in the middle of a break during his reading activity while Reynolds's reader is intensely engaged with what he is reading. Subleyras's subject is therefore more pensive than Reynolds's, looking almost as if he were daydreaming. His left hand delicately holds onto the page he is reading while his book is placed between two other closed books. Could it be that the pausing reader is busy looking for a particular passage? Is this passage difficult to find? Is the same passage the source of his meditative pause, even that of his *mea culpa*? The general impression of dignity generated by Subleyras's reader, the calm aura of his facial features, the unitary tone of his entire person present a stark contrast with the much more exuberant and urbane man painted by Reynolds in 1773–1774. Are these changes merely due to the fact that the sitter himself is a much more worldly man in 1773–1774 than he was in the late 1750s, or should we say that Reynolds was a much more active participant in the high society life of London that was Subleyras in the social life of Rome? We know, for example, that Subleyras complains often about how much he is asked to paint by the cardinals and dignitaries of Rome: Reynolds (who is also an ardent painter) at least controls his own destiny and does not suffer from pecuniary shortfall. Reynolds's Baretti places his face virtually against the page he is reading, almost as if there were a physical unity between the intensely reading man and the physical object he is digesting with his eyes. Reynolds's reader is also much more luxuriously dressed than Subleyras's character. The exaggeration of his attire suggests that the reasons for which he is reading with such intensity are not those of the book itself. They might rather be related to the nature of his overly rich costume, extremely elegant clothing. The latter includes a richly brown frock coat made from what appears to be expensive Suede leather and a shirt made of a delicately worked silk, white in colour. Bits of the latter are revealed by those parts of the cuff that exceed the length of the coat's sleeves and by the zone of the shirt that protrudes over the top of the collar. We get additional glimpses from those parts of it that have become exposed between the two open sides of the coat, just under the neck and the chin. The open coat also reveals a dark-grey leather vest, replete with stylish buttons. The gentleman's hands are white, his left hand bearing a large ruby. The author of the prestigious Reynolds catalogue, David Mannings, convinces us even further: one sees here a man who is not only very well aware of high fashion in London, but also full of personal vanity. For whom exactly is Baretti so very well dressed? His own hair is visible: one sees the care with which a small tail is placed at the back of his neck, a dark-coloured bow holding it in place. This style, complete with the "catogan" ribbon, is characteristic of what Londoners of the time refer to as the Macaronic style, that is to say, the clothing of the ultra-fashionable London men of the 1770s. Since this man was already fifty-four years of age in 1773, one needs to ask whether Reynolds is giving us a further wink of the eye in reference to that amorous adventure that led to Baretti's lengthy trial. This is the type of man to whom Denis Diderot's wife would refer, in 1767, as "a smiling, affected, effeminate, old flirt."[32]

Although it appears completely normal for such an urbane man to want to be well-dressed for a portrait, it nevertheless remains possible, even plausible, to see further levels of meaning in Baretti's excessive dress, almost as if the sitter senses that the world is looking at him at all times, even in those moments when he is reading alone. This stylish air functions in direct contrast with the "intellectual aura" that the act of reading is supposed to impart to a sitter. Rather than being completely engrossed in his reading, something the thesis of absorption would suggest, such a fashionable man points to the ulterior motives one possesses for reading. For we have difficulty resisting the temptation to say that Baretti's act of reading has a very peculiar theatrical sense: the theatrical costume he is wearing for public consumption includes reading. Read-

ANTHONY WALL

17.  PIERRE-LOUIS DUMESNIL THE YOUNGER, *The Attending Physician* (*Presumed Portrait of Nicolas Beauton*), 18TH CENTURY, OIL ON CANVAS, BORDEAUX, MUSÉE DES BEAUX-ARTS, 32.3 X 44.1 CM. (ERICH LESSING/ART RESOURCE, NY).

ing, even solitary reading, is utterly social in nature (in Rousseauistic terms, there is no such thing as a pre-social type of reading). As the locus to which one turns for exploring the ins and outs of the current debates of the day, the book represents the place where one finds the details of contemporary scientific debates. Many of the best paintings that depict a person reading thereby display the difference between those difficult forms of reading that put the subject to sleep and other types that are part of stimulating learning experiences. For indeed human learning comprises a sensual dimension that all conceptions of human cognition need to respect, especially if they wish to remain exempt from useless idealism.[33] As depicted by Reynolds in the Baretti portrait, reading can be construed as an operation of decipherment that directly involves the social dimension of a human being: it implicates the body in all its accoutrements and in all its theatricality.

* * *

These examples of painted readers allow us to insert scenes of reading, even solitary reading, into the broader historical narrative of which they are an integral part. They encourage us to see these works as part of the story of how men and women learn to understand their own processes of learning and understanding. In this sense, scenes of reading can be shown to be highly dialogical in nature. This explains why authors such as Diderot build an entire dialogue around the painting of a portrait (we need only to think of the way he discusses his own portrait in the *Salon of 1767*, that is, as the result of a conversation gone astray between the painter and his wife); this also explains why such a prominent portraitist as Maurice Quentin de La Tour was always eager to make his clients speak while he painted their portrait. As Édouard Pommier shows, La Tour believed it necessary to combine the pleasures of verbal exchange with the art of painting.[34]

It now becomes easier to understand why, at the beginning of this essay, we stressed the difficulty, for a painted character of the eighteenth century, of finding a way to be truly alone. A social activity in the same way as having one's portrait painted, reading is also a distinctively social act. The ways in which the reading character is dressed are no less gratuitous than the things one chooses to be shown reading are. Concerned with careful planning for future conversations, reading in the eighteenth century is intimately involved in making a good social impression insofar as it enables a person to contribute to current social debates. Reading enriches one's repertoire of witty replies, gives new ways for thinking through what was earlier said. In this sense it can never be seen as just one of many other absorptive activities. A person wishing to be shown reading is never really alone.

# BIBLIOGRAPHY

Arasse, Daniel. *Le Détail: Pour une histoire rapprochée de la peinture.* Paris: Flammarion, collection "Champs," 1996.

Baretti, Giuseppe. *Easy Phraseology, for the Use of Young Ladies, who intend to learn the Colloquial Part of the Italian Language.* London: G. Robinson in Paternoster Row, 1775.

Basil of Caesarea (Saint Basil). *On the Holy Spirit.* Crestwood, NY: Saint Vladimir's Seminary Press, 1980.

Chartier, Pierre. *Inscrire et effacer. Culture écrite et littérature (XV$^e$-XVIII$^e$ siècles).* Paris: Gallimard / Seuil, collection "Hautes études," 2005.

Chatelus, Jean. *Peindre à Paris au XVIII$^e$ siècle.* Nîmes: Éditions Jacqueline Chambon, 1991.

Diderot, Denis. *Rameau's Newphew.* In *Rameau's Nephew / D'Alembert's Dream,* trans. Leonard Tancock. Harmondsworth: Penguin, 1966.

———. *Diderot's Early Philosophical Works,* trans. Margaret Johnson. New York: Burt Franklin, 1972.

———. *Diderot on Art,* vol. II, trans. John Goodman. New Haven, CT: Yale University Press, 1995.

Duncan, Robinson. "Giuseppe Baretti as a Man of Great Humanity." In *British Art, 1740–1820: Essays in Honor of Robert R. Wark,* ed. Giulland Sutherland, 81–94. San Marino CA: Huntington Library, 1992.

Dunne, Tom, ed. *James Barry. 1741–1806. The Great Historical Painter.* Cork (Ireland): Crawford Art Gallery and Grandon Editions, 2005.

Ferrand, Nathalie. *Livre et lecture dans les romans français du XVIII$^e$ siècle.* Paris: Presses Universitaires de France, 2002.

Fried, Michael. *Painting and the Beholder in the Age of Diderot.* Berkeley: University of California Press, 1980.

Mannings, David. *Sir Joshua Reynolds: A Complete Catalogue of his Paintings,* 2 vols. New Haven, CT: Yale University Press, 2000.

Michel, Olivier, and Pierre Rosenberg. *Subleyras 1699–1749.* Paris: Éditions de la Réunion des musées nationaux, 1987.

Milly, Jullien. "Le silence de l'hôte: *Persona.*" In *Les Images parlantes,* ed. Murielle Gagnebin, 149–67. Seyssel: Éditions Champ Vallon, 2006.

Neyrat, Frédéric. *L'Image hors-l'image.* Paris: Éditions Léo Scheer, 2003.

Pommier, Édouard. *Théories du portrait.* Paris: Gallimard, 1998.

Postle, Martin. *Sir Joshua Reynolds: The Subject Pictures*. Cambridge: Cambridge University Press, 1995.

————, ed. *Joshua Reynolds: The Creation of Celebrity*. London: Tate Publishing, 2005.

Rusnak, Matthew Francis. *The Trial of Giuseppe Baretti, October 26th 1769*. PhD Thesis. Rutgers University, May 2008.

Stewart, Garrett. *The Look of Reading: Book, Painting, Text.* Chicago: University of Chicago Press, 2006.

Sutton, Peter C., Lisa Vergera, and Ann Jensen Adams. *Love Letters: Dutch Genre Paintings in the Age of Vermeer*. London: Frances Lincoln, 2003.

Warner, William Beatty. "Staging Readers Reading." *Eighteenth-Century Fiction* 12, no. 2–3 (2000): 391–416.

Wenger, Alexandre. *La Fibre littéraire. Le discours médical sur la lecture au XVIIIe siècle*. Geneva: Droz, 2007.

# NOTES

1 See on this essential point Pierre Chartier, *Inscrire et effacer. Culture écrite et littérature (XVe–XVIIIe siècles)* (Paris: Gallimard / Seuil, collection "Hautes études," 2005), 162–63.

2 For example, in the fifteenth century, Carlo Crivelli can for all intents and purposes be cited as the virtual champion of reading saints, having few competitors in this subfield of art. In the sixteenth century, we admire the multiple portraits painted by Agnolo Bronzino and Hans Holbein who depict a person sometimes holding a book in his or her hand, at other times holding a piece of paper, but rarely are these characters shown to be actually reading what they have in their hands, as if the paper and the book were merely objects with which to occupy their hands (see, for example, Hans Holbein the Younger, *Portrait of a Young Merchant*, 1541, oil on wood panel, Vienna, Kunsthistorisches Museum, 46.5 x 34.5 cm). We could say, in the case of Agnolo Bronzino's *Portrait of Ugolino Martelli* (ca. 1535, oil on wood panel, Berlin, Gemälde-galerie, 102 x 85 cm) that this particular painted character gets about as close as you can to the actual act of reading, *while still not reading*: he is after all busy keeping his finger in a particular spot within the book that he will no doubt continue to read after his posing session has finished. But, here as elsewhere, it is impossible to determine from what we see in the image what precisely the painted character is trying to read. When, in 1548, Titian paints the Portuguese Empress Isabelle *almost* in the act of reading (Titian, *The Empress Isabel of Portugal*, 1548, oil on canvas, Madrid, Museo del Prado, 117 x 98 cm), in her case too it is impossible to say what it is that she is actually reading. Ambrosius Benson gives us several persons who are busy reading (i.e., *Young Woman Reading a Prayer Book*, ca.

1520–1530, oil on wood panel, Paris, Louvre, 75 x 55 cm), as do artists such as Albrecht Dürer who depict Erasmus (see the latter's *Erasmus of Rotterdam*, 1526, engraving, Amsterdam, Rijksmuseum, 24.9 x 19.3 cm).

3    Although not quoting explicitly from the book, the following essay is obviously influenced by the recent work published by Garrett Stewart, *The Look of Reading* (Chicago: University of Chicago Press, 2006). While providing an excellent overview, both historically and theoretically, of the major issues concerning the painting of readers, Stewart's essay has little to say about the eighteenth century. To this extent, two other recently published works are of direct relevance for the current inquiry, neither of which are cited by Stewart: (1) William Beatty Warner, "Staging Readers Reading," *Eighteenth Century Fiction* 12, 2–3 (2000): 391–416 and (2) Nathalie Ferrand, *Livre et lecture dans les romans français du XVIIIᵉ siècle* (Paris: Presses Universitaires de France, 2002), even if the latter concentrates on literary representations of reading.

4    See on this account Peter C. Sutton, Lisa Vergara and Ann Jensen Adams, *Love Letters: Dutch Genre Paintings in the Age of Vermeer* (London: Frances Lincoln, 2003).

5    Michael Fried, *Painting and the Beholder in the Age of Diderot* (Berkeley: University of California Press, 1980).

6    Jean-Baptiste Greuze, *Père qui lit la Bible à ses enfants* (*La Lecture de la Bible*), ca. 1753, painting exhibited during the Salon of 1755, oil on canvas, Paris, private collection, 80 x 64 cm.

7    For instance: Jean-Honoré Fragonard, *Education of the Virgin Mary*, ca. 1772–1773, oil on canvas, Fine Arts Museum of San Francisco, 84 x 115 cm; Jean-Honoré Fragonard, *Education of the Virgin Mary*, ca. 1772–1778,

oil on wood panel, Los Angeles, Armand Hammer Foundation, 28.8 x 23.2 cm; Jean-Honoré Fragonard, *Education of the Virgin Mary*, ca. 1775, oil on canvas, Amiens, Musée de Picardie, 92.1 x 73.1 cm; Jean-Honoré Fragonard, *Education of the Virgin Mary* [Bérard canvas], ca. 1772–1778, oil on canvas, Paris, private collection, 90 x 72 cm.

8    Giovanni Bellini, *Sacra Conversazione*, 1505, oil on canvas transferred from a wood panel, Venice, Church of San Zaccaria, 402 x 273 cm.

9    Jean-Honoré Fragonard, *Les progrès de l'amour* or *Les Quatre âges de l'amour* (*L'Amour couronné*), ca. 1771–1772, New York, Frick Collection, 317.8 x 243.2 cm.

10   In addition to Subleyras's painting in the Louvre and the 1773–1774 painting by Reynolds (copies of the latter are housed in the National Portrait Gallery in London [75 x 63 cm.] and in the Indianapolis Museum of Art [75 x 63 cm.]), Olivier Michel and Pierre Rosenberg point with relevance to the portrait of Baretti painted in 1773 by James Barry, currently in a private collection (see their *Subleyras 1699–1745*, Paris, Réunion des Musées nationaux, 1987, p.305). In view of Baretti's appearance in the portrait painted by Barry – described by Matthew Francis Ruspak as "a working-class lout" (*The Trial of Giuseppe Baretti*, 165) – it has been suggested by Duncan Robinson that Reynold's 1773–1774 portrait should be seen as an attempt to correct certain negative impressions about Reynolds's Italian friend. This would explain why Reynolds gave the latter a much more elegant demeanour while retaining the same ultra-close reading pose visible in the Barry portrait. For a colour illustration of the latter work, see Tom Dunne (ed.), *James Barry 1741–1806. The Great Historical Painter* (Cork: Crawford Art Gallery and

Grandon Editions, 2005), 82. One must of course deal with the possibility, still debated by specialists, that the sitter for the Louvre portrait was not Baretti but rather a certain Jacques-Antoine de Lironcourt, a close friend of Subleyras. Such a hypothesis does not entirely exclude the possibility that Subleyras could have used his friend as a model to help him finish a portrait already begun of Baretti. On all accounts, this portrait of a reading man gives us a person belonging to a social class similar to that of the Baretti painted by Reynolds, that which allows us to suggest a comparison between competing ways of portraying an elegant man who is busy reading in private. Be that as it may, the fact that the Insel Verlag of Frankfurt uses this same portrait as the cover illustration of its recent (1996) soft-cover edition of the translation Goethe wrote of *Rameau's Nephew* by Diderot, is not without incidence upon the reading we sketch here of this portrait, i.e., as a suggestion that this elegant reader is engaged in reading in order to take into society the information and ideas he needs in order to shine in public. At one point in Diderot's text, the Nephew answers a question about what he looks for when he reads works of literature: "Well, what I find in them is everything I ought to do, and everything I ought not to say. For instance, when I read *L'Avare* I say to myself: 'Be a hypocrite, by all means, but don't talk like a hypocrite. Keep the vices that come in useful to you, but don't have the tone or the appearance, which would expose you to ridicule.' Now in order to avoid this tone and appearance you must know what they are, and these authors have done excellent portraits of them. I am myself, and I remain myself, but I act and speak as occasion requires" (Denis Diderot, *Rameau's Nephew*, in *Rameau's Nephew / D'Alembert's Dream*, trans. Leonard Tancock

[Harmondsworth: Penguin Classics, 1966], 82).

11  Jean Chatelus, *Peindre à Paris au XVIII<sup>e</sup> siècle* (Nîmes: Éditions Jacqueline Chambon, 1991), 170.

12  David Mannings, *Sir Joshua Reynolds: A Complete Catalogue of his Paintings*, 2 volumes (New Haven, CT: Yale University Press, 2000).

13  Sir Joshua Reynolds, *Portrait of Samuel Johnson* (also known as *Blinking Sam*), ca. 1775, oil on canvas, San Marino (California), Huntington Galleries (on loan from Frances and Laurent Rothschild), 75.3 x 62.4 cm.

14  Sir Joshua Reynolds, *Portrait of Mrs. Edmund Burke*, ca. 1767–1773, oil on wood panel, private collection (sold by Sotheby's, New York, May 27, 2004), 76.2 x 61.6 cm.

15  Sir Joshua Reynolds, *Mrs. Crewe as Saint Geneviève*, 1772, oil on canvas, private collection of the Marquess of Crewe (as of 1942), 166 x 175. This painting is part of the same sub-genre practiced in the middle of the century by such French artists as Étienne Jeaurat (*Sainte Geneviève lisant en gardant ses moutons*, oil on canvass, Paris, Church of Saint-Nicolas-des-Champs, 235 x 140 cm) and Carle van Loo (the lost painting *Sainte Geneviève en bergère*, ca. 1740, copies of which can be seen in the church of Saints Pierre and Genevieve in Sommervieu, Calvados [184 x 88.5 cm], in the church of Saint Martin in Valpuiseaux, Essonne, engraving by Jean-Joseph Baléchou, ca. 1758–59 [London, British Museum, 53.6 x 37.8 cm.]) or, latter on in the century, by Élisabeth Vigée-Le Brun, *Sainte Geneviève*, oil on canvas, Louvenciennes, Musée de Marly-le-Roy). As such, Reynolds's painting displays the artist's deep familiarity with the French painting of his time.

16  Sir Joshua Reynolds, *Portrait of Theophilia Palmer reading Clarissa Harlow*,

ca. 1771, Switzerland, private collection, 76 x 63.5 cm (Mannings Catalogue # 1389).

17 There is also a *Presumed Portrait of James Boydell*, attributed to Reynolds, but not catalogued by Mannings, a canvas sold by Christie's of London on the 21st of December, 1921 (59.7 x 48.3 cm).

18 Sir Joshua Reynolds, *Portrait of Miss Emily Wynyard*, 1766, present location unknown, engraving by Samuel William Reynolds in London, National Portrait Gallery, 20.1 x 12.8 cm.

19 Sir Joshua Reynolds, *Boy Holding a Pen (The Studious Boy)*, ca. 1747–1748, oil on canvas, South Africa, private collection, 76.2 x 63.5 cm; Sir Joshua Reynolds, *Portrait of a Young Boy*, oil on canvas, private collection (sold by Sotheby's, London, November 10, 1993), 83 x 69 cm; Sir Joshua Reynolds, *Boy Reading*, 1747, oil on canvas, private collection, 78.7 x 63.5 cm; Sir Joshua Reynolds, *Boy reading*, 1777, oil on wood panel, private collection (sold by Sotheby's, London, November 29, 2001), 76 x 63 cm; Sir Joshua Reynolds, *Boy reading*, oil on canvas, Buenos Aires, Museo Nacional de Bellas Artes, 77 x 64.5 cm (this is an earlier version of the painting sold by Sotheby's in 2001).

20 Whereas, in the foundational writings of Saint Basil (fourth century A.D.), for example in his *De Spiritu sancto* ("On the Holy Spirit"), the problem of the power of icons, and therefore of idolatry, is avoided through an explanation of the image's "honour" passing from the icon itself to its "prototype" or immaterial model (this is why we adore God and not the image of God), or in our context (one of unnamed persons reading), the power of the image passes from the prototype to the accessory, or rather to the immaterial action denoted by this accessory. In *De Spiritu sancto*, Chapter 18, 45, Saint Basil writes:

"For the Son is in the Father and the Father in the Son; since such as is the latter, such is the former, and such as is the former, such is the latter; and herein is the Unity. So that, according to the distinction of Persons, both are one and one and, according to the community of Nature, one. How, then, if one and one, are there not two Gods? Because we speak of a king, and of the king's image, and not of two kings. The majesty is not cloven in two, nor the glory divided. The sovereignty and authority over us is one, and so the doxology ascribed by us is not plural but one; *because the honour paid to the image passes on to the prototype*. Now what in the one case the image is by reason of imitation, that in the other case the Son is by nature; and as in works of art the likeness is dependent on the form, so in the case of the divine and uncompounded nature the union consists in the communion of the Godhead" (Saint Basil of Caesarea, *On the Holy Spirit* [Crestwood, New York: Saint Vladimir's Seminary Press, 1980]; my emphasis). For a psychoanalytical perspective on this point, see Frédéric Neyrat, *L'Image hors-l'image* (Paris: Éditions Léo Scheer, 2003), 82.

21 Pierre Mignard, *Madame de Maintenon (Françoise d'Aubigné) en Sainte Françoise Romaine*, 1694, oil on canvas, Versailles, Musée national du Château et de Trianon, 128 x 97 cm.

22 Gustave Courbet, *L'Atelier de l'artiste*, 1855, oil on canvas, Paris, Musée d'Orsay, 361 x 598 cm.

23 Auguste Bernard, called Bernard d'Agesci, *Lady Reading the Letters of Heloise and Abelard*, ca.1780, oil on canvas, The Art Institute of Chicago, 81.3 x 64.8 cm.

24 Judging at least from the surviving engraving housed in the Musée Greuze in Tournus, Burgundy (executed by Marie-Louise Adélaïde Boizot, 1780, 23.5 x 19.2 cm) or by either the less-

than-perfect anonymous copy that is part of the permanent collection of the Musée Cognacq-Jay in Paris (46.5 x 36 cm) or the anonymous pastel on view in the Fine Arts Museum of San Francisco (38.8 x 35 cm).

25  Jean-Honoré Fragonard, *Don Quixote Reading*, ca. 1780–81, black chalk and bistre on paper, Winterthur (Switzerland), Oskar Reinhart Museum, *Am Römerholz*, 41 x 27.5 cm.

26  See Alexandre Wenger, *La Fibre littéraire. Le discours médical sur la lecture au XVIII siècle* (Geneva: Droz, 2007).

27  Daniel Arasse, *Le Détail: Pour une histoire rapprochée de la peinture* (Paris: Flammarion, collection "Champs," 1996).

28  Ibid., 264. See on this point Jullien Milly, "Le silence de l'hôte: *Persona*," *Les Images parlantes*, ed. Murielle Gagnebin (Seyssel: Éditions Champ Vallon, 2006), 158.

29  Even Baretti's works on the Italian language, destined for Britons, are not without controversy. See, for example, his *Easy Phraseology, for the use of Young Ladies, who intend to learn the colloquial part of the Italian Language* (London: G. Robinson in Paternoster Row, 1775).

30  Joshua Reynolds, *Self-Portrait as a Deaf Man*, ca. 1775, oil on wood panel, London, Tate Britain, 79.9 x 62.2 cm.

31  Before his death in 1748, the French painter Pierre Subleyras was a favourite of the pope and the Roman curie. The painting of the reading man dates from approximately 1745, six years before Baretti's first move to the United Kingdom. It has been objected, even to deny Subleyras's authorship of this painting, that it does not appear in Subleyras's famous *Artist's Studio* (ca. 1747–1749, Vienna, Akademie der bildenden Künste, 130.5 x 101 cm) in which, near the end of his busy life, Subleyras painted miniatures of

many of the most famous works of his entire career. But, then again, there are many of his paintings that were not included in the Vienna painting, especially the large number of licentious paintings, which were intended to illustrate many of La Fontaine's fables and tales.

32  Denis Diderot, *Salon of 1767*, *Diderot on Art*, vol. II, trans. John Goodman (New Haven, CT: Yale University Press, 1995), 20.

33  For Diderot, the sensual dimension of both knowledge and learning is perhaps its most fundamental one. Such ideas are expounded in his *Letter on the Blind*: "Those philosophers, madam, are termed idealists who, conscious of their own existence and of a succession of external sensations, do not admit anything else [...]." (in *Diderot's Early Philosophical Works*, trans. Margaret Johnson [New York: Burt Franklin, 1972], 105).

34  Édouard Pommier, *Théories du portrait* (Paris: Gallimard, 1998), 278.

# 4

---

# THE DECISIVE MOMENT

---

*Stéphane Lojkine*

In 1952, Henri Cartier-Bresson published a book of photographs bearing the title *Images à la sauvette* – "images on the run" – a collection whose introduction provided his personal conception of the photographic "shot."[1] With my own title, "the decisive moment," I wish to recall a phrase first coined by the famous French Cardinal de Retz and appearing in a passage chosen by Cartier-Bresson for the epigraph of his book: "*There is nothing in this world that does not possess its decisive moment* and the highest form of good behaviour consists, first, in recognizing this moment and, then, in seizing it. If in the turn of the events of a State one misses this moment, one thereby risks never finding it again or, worse yet, not ever noticing it."[2]

There can be no better way than this for underscoring the competing forces that underlie the notion of the decisive moment. On the one hand, we have the image caught "on the run," as it were, the fleeting expression on someone's face, the indistinguishable gesture of everyday life appearing as if out of nowhere, the objective randomness – belonging either to a situation or to a pose – which points to a simple photographic moment lying outside of the picture's frame. On the other hand, we have the nobility residing in classical language and the philosophical reflections contained in historical memoirs written at a distance, both of which are destined to circumscribe a scene in history and, within that scene as described by the historian's critical eye, to reveal the central element that allows the grand narrative to function. That which, in history, can be described as a memorable picture is precisely the *decisive moment* in which the fate of men and the turns of events of states are determined.

There can be no doubt that, in an essay dealing with photography – a new art form in search of legitimacy – the grand seventeenth century can provide a noble formula for presenting a simple peasant, a way, that is, to establish from the very start its own distinctive character. The encounter rehearsed here of history and painting meeting up with competing notions of the *decisive moment* (or, if you will, with the idea of the "crucial instant" that speakers of German describe as being *pregnant*) is of course a moment that preceded the invention of photography. Cartier-Bresson intends to place *this moment* at the service of a modern definition of the snapshot or the instant photo, that quick image taken of something lying between the randomness of flowing time and a certain configuration of things which, within that same flow, suddenly becomes essential, necessary, and meaningful, if only for a fleeting moment.

In his essay, Cartier-Bresson not only borrows an idea from the Cardinal de Retz,[3] he also adds a final page to the long history of how the Horatian principle known as *ut pictura poesis* has come to be used in visual thinking. This is the history in the West of how painters and writers dealt with the connection between the visual and discursive aspects of representation. Very early, the solutions proposed for this complex problem had begun to concentrate on the choice made by artists and writers of the particular moment they wished to represent. Not only for painters, but also for historians and playwrights, the decisive moment brings together elements from both visual and discursive languages because, in history, the crucial moment creates a picture, just as, in the image, the moment gives a concentrated formula to an entire story and thereby underscores what is essential in it.

It is important not to reduce this notion to the intricacies of a technical debate, that is to say, to the problem of how best to reconcile two heterogeneous substances of representation: on the one hand, the slow discursive succession of events in history; on the other, the global nature of an image not only in its corporeal immediacy but also in its now-ness containing neither a yesterday nor a tomorrow. The technical problem of how to combine the various media and substances of representation has always been accompanied by a second one having to do with hierarchies. As it is both fragile and guarded by boundaries, the decisive moment harks back to the humble craftsmanship underlying each and every image. As for its decisiveness, and the underlying notion of an artistic choice, these are elements which, both for the artist and for the event chosen, bear the glorious mark of genius. The high profile given by pictorial compositions to that special moment necessarily reveals something of a symbolic protest: while on the technical side an image only gives life to a single instant, on the artistic side the inventiveness of the artist vis-à-vis the story being told is able to bestow an unexpected value upon an intrinsically uninteresting moment in time, a value that is, simply put, *decisive*.

The decisive moment does not merely allow the image to wreak revenge on history. The stakes are the very contents of that history. Within the space of representation, the decisive moment points to the brutal nature of reality, the brutal nature of all things which, since structurally coming from nowhere, are by definition unexpected, meaningless, or even absurd. They appear out of the blue and function as a symptom whose validity lies outside the normal frames of reference, thereby introducing the possibility of hitherto unseen fits within new operative devices and, through their arrival, giving legitimacy to the illogical meanings that are created in the juxtaposition of imagistic elements, the same elements which, historically, have always been of totally different natures.

## I. Poussin's *Manna* Remaining Faithful to Scripture

The question of the decisive moment rose to prominence within the theoretical framework sketched out by Charles Le Brun who, on November 5, 1667, delivered one his most famous lectures to the French Royal Academy of Painting. The passage that concerns us is found near the end of a text entitled *"Les Israélites recueillant la manne dans le désert*

18. NICOLAS POUSSIN, *Israelites Gathering Manna*, 1639, OIL ON CANVAS, PARIS, LOUVRE, 149 X 200 CM.

by Nicolas Poussin": it is presented in the form of a homage paid to Poussin, considered at the time to be the master of the new and emerging French school of painting. Just before Le Brun had finished his lecture, an objection arose from within the audience ("Il y eut quelqu'un qui dit que ..." ["There was someone who said that ..."]), someone who wished to voice two major concerns.

He risked the following: it seemed to him that Poussin was so very precise in his work so as not to omit the slightest detail from the many circumstances that were necessary for the composition of a story. And despite this exactness, he was nevertheless unable to give an overall image in his painting that was close enough to what had really happened in

STÉPHANE LOJKINE

the desert, at that moment when God made it rain manna from the sky. This failure is due to the fact that the scene is represented as if it must have occurred in broad daylight and had been clearly visible for all the Israelites to see, something that is contrary to Scripture which explains that the Israelites had found the manna in the morning, all around their camp, as if it had been a dew that they now were going to harvest. In addition, the objector considered the extreme need and poverty that Poussin chose to represent by means of a woman forced to drink the milk of her own daughter's breast: this too was not appropriate for the time at which the depicted action must have taken place. And this is because at the time when manna began to fall from the heavens the chosen people had already been saved by quails which had previously arrived in sufficient quantities to satisfy even the greatest of hungers. That is to say that this event alone would have saved them from the dire need depicted by the painter.[4]

Let us quickly recall the subject painted by Poussin: after their flight from Egypt where they had been held as slaves, the Hebrew people wandered for forty years across the desert before arriving in the Promised Land. If during this time they did not die of starvation, this is thanks to a series of miracles, amongst which we find the episode of the manna, a miraculous substance that God made fall from heaven in order to feed his chosen ones. The two objections just enumerated concern, first and foremost, Poussin's relative unfaithfulness in relation to the Biblical text he purported to illustrate. Poussin paints the manna as having fallen from the sky at daybreak, whereas it can be deduced from the narrative recounted in Exodus that it had fallen during the night. Furthermore, in choosing to paint a mother drinking milk from her own daughter's breast (see bottom left corner of **Illustration 18**), Poussin would have us believe that the Hebrew people were then suffering from extreme hunger, something that strays significantly from what was told in the episode immediately preceding the text concerning the heavenly manna: the Israelites had already been saved previously when quails had fallen from the sky. In neither of these two examples had the painter respected the spirit of the Biblical text nor did he follow the sequence of narrative events this text presupposes. Let us admit, however, that there is a high level of ambiguity in the notion of *circumstances* as used by the public objector to Le Brun's lecture: he speaks of the necessity to omit none of "the circumstances that were necessary for the composition of a story." But do these circumstances refer to the moment, to the event itself, or rather, quite literally, to everything surrounding that same event? Related as they are to the painted event as something having happened in real history, that is to say, a circumstantial event, the circumstances in question prevent the represented story from achieving any real degree of structural closure: they are given as if they constituted indispensable data; they are further presented according to the vulgarly stubborn and stubbornly contradictory principle according to which "that's the way things were."

## The Layout of Figures

While Le Brun's lecture is really a discourse on figures, this same reference to the *circumstances* contradicts his own text in another important way. Forming a veritable obsession in his lecture, the word *figure* appears no less than forty-five times during the brief exposé presented by the Academician. And Le Brun's discourse on figures turns the event shown into something unreal; it transforms the event into an abstract set of oppositions and configurations. The figures smother the singularity of the event to be recalled within the well-known play of signs, as well as within the formal logic of their possible concatenations.

The figure introduces something new into the realm of representation, namely a market economy for which it will soon become the only legal currency. As an exchange value, the figure is that which, in the midst of representation, can be exported, translated, manipulated, and commercialized. Every act of representation can therefore be understood in terms of a careful laying out of one's figures; it is a configuration of signs, values, occurring within a scenic space, that of the marketplace. Le Brun states that he will speak of "the *layout* in general" and of "each figure in particular": "the general *layout* contains three elements which are just as general in and of themselves, namely the way space is composed, the *layout* of figures, and the colour of the air" (p. 100); "the *layout* of the figures [...] must be made up of parts, groups and contrasts" (p. 101); Moses and Aaron "are accompanied by the elders of the nation who are *laid out* according to several different attitudes"; "even though the landscape is *laid out* in a very learned manner and filled with admirable figures"; "groups are formed by *putting* several figures *together*" (p. 102); "this well-chosen contrast [...] which comes from the various ways in which figures are *laid out*"; "*layout* of the entire work" (p. 103); "this great painter did not *lay* his figures *out* merely to fill in the space of his composition" (p. 106); it is a matter of giving "more freedom and a greater variety in the ways in which all the human characters composing the work are generally *laid out*" (p. 109). In this way, representation acquires the glorious multiplicity present in rich displays: colours and objects are organized in such a way that they take the best advantage possible of potential contrasts and thus ensure the best returns from what can be seen. The human spectator derives the highest level of enjoyment from such a saturated space, one that has been put to the most profitable use possible, and thus it is that the ways in which figures are laid out represent what is productive for making-meaning.

The idea according to which figures have a layout brings the realm of representation back into the territory of rhetoric; that is to say that the layout provides the means for commercializing pictorial representation; it transforms representation into a business endeavour, a verbal exchange. By focussing his comments on the *circumstances* surrounding the rain of manna, Le Brun's anonymous objector replaces a structural mechanism for making things seem unreal with a once-occurrent singularity of content, a unique kind of machine for making history: the unfolding of time is thus able to resist most radically the capitalistic assimilation of the real which had been attempted by the figurative structures of representation.

Time is something that cannot be exchanged. What "has been" may on occasion be recovered, traded in, even disguised, but the order in which things *just plain happen*, the unique succession of unique events, this is something that the structural economy is unable to assimilate. In fact, their uniqueness makes it possible to denounce this very economy. Through *circumstances*, each and every attempt to turn reality into a set of figures is put on trial; circumstances denounce the artificial nature of every figurative *layout*. Deriving both from "a grand necessity" and from "extreme poverty," theatrical effects are incommensurable with the historical scene that Poussin wishes to paint. They are "inappropriate for the time of the events he puts into figures."

What had first appeared as a debate about aesthetics, one that was both technical and scholarly, now begins to reveal some of its ideological stakes: Le Brun is constructing the official doctrine of the Academy on the basis of a conception of figures which would be valid for all artistic genres, a system of freely circulating meanings functioning within a protected zone of representation. This is the same Academy that would decide to found the artistic Salons, itself a protected zone established for the exhibition and marketing of art works. Thus it can be said that the attempt to conceptualize painting in terms of a system of figures is inseparable from the economic enterprise of establishing a marketplace for art.

## The Moment as Compromise

In other words, this discussion, both technical and scholarly in nature, can be said to have hidden its own ideological interests. One should not forget that, when Le Brun defends Poussin from the charge of not having respected the circumstances of his painted episode, he does so by referring to the differences inherent in the expressive means used by the painter in comparison with those employed by the historian.

> To this objection Monsieur Le Brun replied that painting does not function in the way history does. First, an historian

expresses himself with a particular arrangement of words; he relies on a sequence of utterances which will create a picture of the events he wishes to evoke, presenting the chosen action as part of a succession. A painter on the other hand has but one moment at his disposal, a single instant, embedded within the entire event, which he must choose in order to represent what had happened at that particular moment. It is sometimes necessary to combine many incidents that had in reality preceded the actual event he wishes to paint in order to make the subject he is showing more comprehensible. For indeed, without such devices, those who look upon the work would be no better informed about the event than they would be by an historian who, instead of recounting all the matters relating to the story he is telling, decided merely to tell the end of the story. (p. 111)

If, therefore, Poussin has decided not to respect the exact circumstances of the episode he is painting, this is because a painting can represent just one split second of the action. If the painter needs to make the story intelligible by focussing on its ending, he finds himself somewhat obliged to bend the rules insofar as he will represent certain incidents as having happened at the same time when, in reality, they must have happened one after the other. In our case, the falling of manna from the sky will be shown at the same time as the Israelites who are gathering it; the anguish on their faces when faced with hunger, something that was visible before the rain of quails, will now be shown as if it had occurred later on, that is, when the manna had begun to fall. This need to bring together successive elements by showing them as simultaneous events, all occurring within a single moment, finds its motivation in the technical constraints imposed upon the artist by the medium of the painted image.

Le Brun's defence of Poussin, based on the apparent opposition between the rich means available to the historian on the one hand, and the meagre pickings placed on the painter's platter on the other, hides – and rather poorly I might add – his stated ambition to find a single theory and a single framework capable of integrating all the *media* of artistic representation. Whereas, for the artist, he speaks of the "layout of figures," in the case of the historian he speaks of the latter's "organizing words." These are matters of global representation rather than of succession in time, the one corresponding to the other in Le Brun's thinking. For example, when Le Brun evokes a "sequences of utterances," this expression is immediately described as something that "creates a picture"; in other words, the historian's words do the same work as the configurations used by the painter. Later on, Le Brun adds a further qualification: "these groups of figures, accomplishing varying actions, appear as if they were themselves episodes which prepare the arrival of what we call unexpected turns of events" (p. 112).

This opposition between historian and painter, a screen for the difference between poetry and painting, might at first glance look like a simple rhetorical trick devised for allowing the theoretician to present an a-historical conception of representation. For indeed representation functions here according to the formal interplay of neutral and abstract signs. And whatever the concrete means may be within which representation is effected, in each case it is a matter of reducing the importance of the event's temporal circumstances and making their unique succession appear in the guise of a material assembly, a layout of mobile and interchangeable figures. The notion of the decisive moment, as raised in Le Brun's impromptu answer of 1667, might have been nothing more than a pretext for preserving abstraction from the singularity of history pointed out in the objection he had heard.

If the very real differences between the textual and iconic means of representation are in the end an alibi for the manoeuvre needed to generalize a figural conception of representation, it must also be seen that something else is needed. Painting is presented as lacking something discourse already has, painting is the expression of this loss which inhabits its very being, a deficiency which it must constantly try to overcome by displaying it out in the open. This we see in the very conception of pictorial creativity, based on a logic of the supplement, a way of thinking that will provide the enunciatory framework needed for articulating several of the central elements present in Diderot's *Salons*.

> [...] for this reason, when Monsieur Poussin decided to show how manna had been sent to the Israelites, he thought it was insufficient merely to paint it strewn on the ground, ready to be harvested by the men and women present in the scene. It seemed to him that further things were necessary in order to underscore the miraculous nature of the event that had occurred, namely the state in which the Jews found themselves at that particular point in time. He decided to represent the desert surroundings of the Jews, some of whom he painted in a state of languor, others as in a hurry to gather as much of the food as they could, still others thanking God for the favour he had once again bestowed upon them. These various states and the diverse actions accompanying them function in the painting in the way utterances and words would do for transmitting his thought. (p. 111)

The "various states" and "different actions" that Poussin decides to show on his Manna canvas take the place of the missing "utterances" and "words" that would have otherwise allowed him to "transmit his thought." Since the painter has no other means than pictorial figures, the languor of some along with the hurriedness and thankfulness of others assume the role normally played by figures of speech. Painting is here conceived in terms of a language of substitution: it merely places in the space of the painted scene that which speech naturally places along the temporal chain composing the story that must be told.

## Theatre as a Model for Temporal Reduction

And this substitution also allows something else to happen: the uniqueness of the moment is no longer perceived as a technical constraint but rather is fully integrated into the system of poetic constraints belonging to pictorial representation in general. Not only for painting but also for the theatre, it is a question of respecting the Aristotelian rule of the three cardinal unities:

> And someone in the audience added a further point to what Monsieur Le Brun had just stated, namely that if, according to the laws of the theatre, a poet is allowed to bring together several events that had in reality happened at different times with the aim of creating a single unified action – with the proviso that he not thereby create internal contradictions, and that he rigorously respect the conventions of verisimilitude – then it is even fairer to grant this same liberty to painters. (pp. 111–12)

It is clear that the scene depicted on the canvas now takes the place of the theatrical stage: the painted scene is obliged to respect the same laws that a theatrical play does; it is granted the same poetic licence as that afforded to a stage production. The necessity of concentrating representation in a single moment, even if this moment is artificially constructed, is in fact a complex requirement, one which entails reducing the importance of particular circumstances and subjecting them to the needs of internal coherence, that is, to the self-referential play of figures. The heart of the matter lies in the dictum that there be no "internal contradictions" and that conventions of verisimilitude be "rigorously respected"; that is to say that figures must be laid out in relation to one another and that the actions they represent must themselves be part of the Great Code that comprises all the reasonable possibilities that are available, all this according to rules of propriety. This respect of convention is, in the final analysis, much more important than, say, whether or not the decisive moment really happened in history in such and such a manner and whether or not the painter needed to fudge things a little in order to achieve a coherent representation of how the event actually unfolded. The supreme necessity concerns the syntactic correctness of the message, and this requirement remains valid not only for texts but for images as well. It is on this note that the meeting of the Academy reached its conclusion: "This is the reason why these groups of figures, accomplishing varying actions, appear as if they were themselves episodes which prepare the arrival of what we call unexpected turns of events, as if they were the means by which to make known the changes which had occurred in the lives of the Israelites when they move from extreme poverty into a much happier state" (p. 112). A close correspondence is thus established between the action painted on the canvas and theatrical turns of events, between groups of depicted figures and the episodes or scenes composing a theatrical play. This correspondence allows us to say that a painting is not just, strictly speaking, constituted by a single scene, but by several scenes, exactly as things are for a play on the stage. Not only then is the moment depicted by a painting a composite one, but this moment also refers to an overarching reality: it has a vague or general meaning, not a circumstantial one, a meaning that, with relative ease, can be exported, transposed or otherwise made available for several domains. In this light the painting refers less to a particular chapter in the book of Exodus than it addresses the issue of "what changed in the lives of the Israelites," a change that is not so much a single, identifiable event than it is a transformation occurring in the soul, one necessitating a shift toward a non-temporal scene of the soul's passions – one that is universal in its depiction while using all the appropriate tropes. The transformations began, as we have seen, in the passage "from extreme poverty" to a "much happier state." Both poverty and happiness lie at the limits of human time, outside of normal human space, and they do not apply to any single people. The decisive moment works in painting by un-realizing reality within a universalized version of the relevant circumstances.

Diderot knew the lectures pronounced in the Academy very well via their published versions.[5] And although he does not mention Le Brun's text explicitly, he nevertheless refers to Poussin's Manna painting on two separate occasions. In the *Salon of 1767*, his discussion of Joseph-Marie Vien's *Saint Denis Preaching the Faith in France*[6] becomes the springboard for a discussion of groups and masses, which gives rise to another vocabulary for the layout of figures. Diderot begins with an example taken from Poussin of what he calls a group: "But the young woman sitting on the ground nursing her elderly mother at her breast and consoling [with her hand] her standing, crying child for being deprived of the nourishment nature intended for it, a deprivation rooted in a filial tenderness stronger than maternal tenderness" (*Diderot on Art II*, p. 37). This idea of the group and the example of Poussin's *Israelites Gathering Manna* both come from Le Brun's text. And later on, in 1769, in his *Regrets for My Old Dressing Gown*, Diderot provides a description of the personal office he has set up in his home, a description that includes allusions to an engraving he owns of Poussin's *Manna* painting:

> I saw the Bergamo tapestry give up its spot on the wall (where it had been hanging for such a long time) to the Damascene tapestry. And then, two prints not without merit: *The Israelites Gathering Manna in the Desert* by Poussin and *Esther before Ahasuerus*[7] by the same painter; the first one shamefully chased away by an old man painted by Rubens, and the second one, poor *Esther*, blown away by a *Storm*[8] painted by Vernet. (Diderot, *Œuvres, Tome IV*, pp. 821–22)

In 1769, Diderot admits that he is finally becoming a "bourgeois" as he has now decided to redecorate his home. From the passage just read, we learn, as if in an aside, that this same Poussin engraving had adorned his wall for a very long time before finally being displaced by a real painting, one that is much more modern, namely a *Storm* by Joseph Vernet.

STÉPHANE LOJKINE

## II. Choosing the Decisive Moment: On the *Encyclopaedia* Article Entitled "Composition" (1753)

Almost a century after Le Brun's lecture had been delivered in the Academy, the way in which people understood the problem of the decisive moment had of course changed. For Diderot, the question of "the unity of time in painting" had become the central issue expounded in the article he wrote on "composition." He reminds his readers, first, of the fact that a painter has only one moment at his disposal, "an almost indivisible instant" (*Œuvres, Tome IV,* p. 120), and, second, that the poet does not labour under the same restraints imposed by the single moment as does the painter (p. 123). Of course, in Diderot's case, these reminders do not exactly constitute a reply to an objection, voiced in a room, in order to contradict Le Brun's claim that composition in painting is really the same thing as the layout of figures. Nevertheless, for Diderot, the decisive moment becomes a central notion allowing him to reconceptualize the idea of a painter's composition.

### From the Layout of Figures to the Combination of Movements

For this important shift to occur within aesthetic theory, the idea of the figure would have to command much less prominence than it earlier had. Indeed, his article on "Composition" begins with a reminder of the Aristotelian metaphor of the body and its parts:

> A well-composed painting is a single whole [...] whose parts, through their mutual correspondence, form an ensemble that is just as real as that formed by the limbs on the body of an animal; as a result a painted work of art, being made from a large number of characters strewn across the canvas as if at random – without any proportionality, without intelligence and without unity – has not earned the title of being

a *true composition* any more than various studies of legs, noses, eyes that have been placed on a single piece of cardboard have earned the title of *portrait*, or even that of a *human figure*. (Diderot, *Œuvres, Tome IV*, p. 120)

The metaphor of bodily parts should be able to function as the celebration of how the syntagmatic structure of figures coalesces within the painting's general composition. This structure would work in the same way that the various parts of an animal's body contribute to its overall healthy functioning. One notices however that Diderot turns this metaphor on its head, presenting the image of a generalized dismemberment in which the combination of various figures now produces the nightmare vision of *membra disiecta*. Paradoxically, the accumulation of figures leads to a situation of disfigurement to the extent that, by the end of the same paragraph, there is not even so much as the "portrait" of a real "human face." When left to function on its own, according to its own individualized logic, and in its own seemingly untranslatable world, a figure *disfigures*, that is to say that, in a kind of suicidal gesture, a figure will end up destroying itself.

What serves as the organizational principle for painting is therefore not the figure, not even a group of figures, but rather the all-important moment. For the decisive moment is that which coordinates and coalesces. It does this work not so much in relation to figures than in relation to movement: "However, a painter has at his disposal but a single instant, one that is almost indivisible; and this instant must be the point to which all the movements of the composition refer; if, amongst these movements, I notice ones that either precede or follow the central one, then the rule of temporal unity has been violated" (*Œuvres, Tome IV*, p. 120). Le Brun's earlier concessions in relation to temporality are no longer a concern for Diderot. Similarly, what is at issue is no longer the need to accommodate the succession of events in such a way as to make it appear as if non-coincidental events could appear as concomitant. This is because historical circumstances no longer function for Diderot as figures of circumstance capable of placing everything on the canvas that the historian has arranged within the chronology of his story. Since it is indivisible, Diderot's decisive moment has also become instantaneous, no longer catching *figures* on the fly but rather movements, no longer interested in capturing syntagms and symbols but rather actions or transformations.

## The Sacrifice of Iphigenia

Diderot will look somewhere else than to Le Brun for his understanding of what it is that makes time move: the painter no longer injects time between the figures of his painting, those figures which, in Le Brun's thinking, all involved slightly different temporalities. Rather he injects time into the figure itself, which by this very movement becomes disfigured:

> At the moment when Calchas raises his knife above Iphigenia's breast, it must be possible to see all the horror, the compassion, and the pain expressed in the clearest of terms on the spectators' faces; in her fury, Clytemnestra will lunge toward the altar and will attempt, despite the soldiers' arms holding her back, to grab Calchas' hand and to place herself between him and her daughter; Agamemnon will have his head covered by his coat, etc. (Diderot, *Œuvres, Tome IV,* pp. 120–21)

It is therefore not entirely an accident if, in this article on "Composition," the first example Diderot gives of a painting deals with the sacrifice of Iphigenia as composed by the Greek artist Timanthes of Cythnos. For antiquity, this painting served as a canonical example in their aesthetic discussions.[9] It is significant that Timanthes' *Iphigenia* counters both the logic of the figure and the expression of those passions that flow from it. This is because for this painting, whose subject is the greatest and

19. TIMANTHES, *The Sacrifice of Iphigenia*, ACCORDING TO A FRESCO FOUND IN POMPEI, IST CENTURY A.D., NAPLES, NATIONAL MUSEUM OF ARCHAEOLOGY, 138 X 140 CM.

most painful sorrow imaginable, that of a father voluntarily sacrificing his own beloved daughter, the artist is unable to find any expression whatsoever for representing the relevant pain and sorrow. Thus he places a veil over Agamemnon's face. In this sense, *Iphigenia* is a composition that is figuratively incomplete; in its very core the composition bears a glaring hole.

Diderot further develops his idea of disfigurement as occurring in the moment. For him, the moment brings together movements, not figures. The horror felt at the sight of a sacrifice creates mixed emotions amongst the spectators, feelings that are both undifferentiated and confused: "it must be possible to see all the horror, the compassion, and the pain expressed in the clearest of terms on the spectators' faces." It is not merely a question of juxtaposing a face of horror with one of compassion, followed by another of pain; at issue here is an attempt to describe something that is un-figurable, and to describe it both by means of movement and within movement: "in her fury, Clytemnestra lunges toward the altar and will attempt, despite the soldiers' arms holding her back, to grab Calchas' hand and to place herself between him and her daughter." Clytemnestra lunges forward, tries to intercede at the very same time as the soldiers restrain her; Calchas is impeded for a split second, the very second chosen by the artist for his painting. Each character is thus defined by a particular type of movement; the differences in movement now replace the old ways of differentiating between various figures. Diderot concludes as follows:

> Within every action it is possible to discern a host of different instants amongst which a person would have to be rather clumsy not to choose the most interesting one; according to the subject matter, this moment is the most emotional one, or the happiest or funniest; unless the rules specific to painting dictate otherwise; unless it is possible, through effective colouring, shadows and light, or the general layout of figures, to gain back what was lost due to the choice made of a particular moment and to the circumstances belonging to the action shown. (*Œuvres, Tome IV*, p. 121)

This is in essence a neatly formulated way for contrasting the "general layout of figures" as theorized by Le Brun with the particular "choice of the moment and the circumstances." As such, it constitutes the new model of organization we wish to discuss.

## The Decisive Moment is Undecided

Diderot imparts a special orientation to this new model, one that was not part of the original debates engaged in by the Royal Academy of Painting: it is no longer merely a matter of remaining faithful to the special circumstances of a given moment, but more importantly of examining several possible moments and of choosing to paint the one that is most appropriate. Will it be the moment of climax, the one whose intensity gives the greatest theatrical effect possible? Or will it be the aesthetic moment, the one that guarantees the best pictorial effects of "colour, shade and light"? In a first move, Diderot opts for theatricality as opposed to aestheticism and mannerism. It is this idea of choice that is the innovative element in his thinking: Le Brun took it for granted that the moment painted should be that of an action's ending. For him, painting showed the sum of all the constitutive elements making up a particular narrative, the sum of events of which it was purported to be the iconic equivalent. As such, a summing up can only appear at the end of a narrative, only at the last moment. Moreover, Le Brun authorized a certain poetic licence in this regard: he was ready to accept the introduction of new turns of events, certain incidents or figures belonging more properly to earlier moments, which is to say that he was prepared to allow for the condensation of the relevant events in order to obtain a single representation of successive events. Such licence was called for when motivated by the need to make the scene understandable, since in certain instances figures would remain incomprehensible without the assistance of particular circumstances more properly belonging to the immediate past. Still, it is the present event as a sum of earlier events that counts above all else: ancillary circumstances are admissible only in relation to it. In other words, the painted scene is a *terminus post quem*.

Diderot's entire demonstration hinges on a desire to show that the ending, which is the final moment, is never the best one for a painter to choose. The decisive moment is to be found *before* the outcome has been decided, during the moment of hesitation or in the movement preceding the decision. This we already saw in the way Iphigenia's sacrifice was represented: "Calchas raises his knife"; in other words, we are dealing with the moment when nothing has yet been done, when the image thrusts the viewer toward the completion of an action which, for the moment, appears as if it were in suspended animation. The ideal moment is not one of completion, but rather one of dramatic suspense.

## Hercules' Choice

This necessity of suspension, of an undecided moment in the depiction of a scene, can be more clearly seen in yet another example. We are thinking here of the choice made by Hercules, in a painting composed by Annibale Carracci, a composition which, both in its painted and its engraved versions, was very popular in the first half of the seventeenth century.[10]

> Prodicus assumes that, in his youth, Hercules [...] had been welcomed by the goddesses of Glory and of Pleasure into a quiet spot in the forest. Both of the goddesses were in an argument as to who would be best able to entice him: just imagine the number of separate instants that this moral fable could offer a painter who had chosen it as his subject matter. It would easily fill up an entire gallery. There is the moment when the hero is welcomed by both goddesses; the moment when the voice of pleasure lets itself be heard; the instant when he listens to the language of honour, the instant when he weighs in his mind the reasons of honour against those of pleasure; the moment when glory begins to gain the upper hand; the moment when he is altogether set on establishing his glory. (Diderot, *Œuvres, Tome IV*, p. 121)

On this canvas painted by Carracci, considered at the time to be the model for the many paintings and engravings treating the subject, Hercules is shown sitting in the centre of the composition, facing the spec-

20. ANNIBALE CARRACCI, *Hercules at the Crossroads*, CA. 1595–1596, OIL
ON CANVAS, NAPLES, MUSEO E GALLERIA NAZIONALI DI CAPODIMONTE,
237 X 167 CM. (SEE ALSO P. 244 FOR COLOUR REPRODUCTION.)

tator, and leaning on the large bludgeon with which he has just fought
against Erymanthe's wild boar. On his right, Minerva points to the steep
and barren path leading to virtue. And on his left, we see Venus, dressed
in a simple white veil, who shows him a table, easily within his reach, on
which can be seen several theatrical masks. At the foot of this same table
we notice a few violins, which remind us of the pleasures of music, the
same pleasures that will be combined with those of the stage and of the
pending meal. At the same time, this table is placed directly in front of
the inextricable forest of vice.

STÉPHANE LOJKINE

## Narrative as a Gallery Filled with Paintings: An Illusion

The breakdown of Prodicus's story into a sequence of individual moments, that is to say, into a series of possible paintings, gives us a caricature of the actual practices engaged in by painters who relied on narrative cycles. Diderot will allude in passing to a famous narrative cycle when he mentions the gallery, painted by Rubens, and housed in the Palais du Luxembourg by Marie de Medici (*Œuvres, Tome IV*, p. 122). In the *Salon of 1765*, when he tells the story of Coresus and Callirhoe in the form of a dream projected on the walls of Plato's cave – the same story that had given rise to Fragonard's monumental painting[11] – his fictive listener, Melchior Grimm, makes the following observation: "But my friend, at this rate don't you realize that only one of your dreams would suffice to fill an entire gallery?" (*Diderot on Art, I*, p. 143).

We find a further development of the same idea in his *Isolated Thoughts on Painting*: "Moments follow one another in a poet's description which could provide a long gallery of paintings" (Diderot, *Œuvres, Tome IV*, p. 1024). However, by Diderot's time, the narrative cycle as a pictorial form was already rather old-fashioned, and the successive paintings Diderot derives from his dream are not all of equal merit. The gallery of paintings derivable from a single narrative is always evoked along with an ironic undercurrent, as if these paintings constituted an illusion, that of a technical equivalence between poetry and painting functioning on both the syntagmatic and the systematic fronts. This is exactly what the expressive details of the paintings derived from the story of Prodicus reveal:

> Upon seeing the goddesses, [Hercules] must be overcome with admiration and surprise: he must feel great emotion when hearing the voice of pleasure and be filled with fiery passion when he hears that of honour: in that moment when he weighs their respective advantages, he slips into a dreamy state, he is uncertain, in a suspended state; at the same time as the intensity of his internal struggle increases and as the

moment of sacrifice draws ever nearer, he is seized by regret, agitation, torment, anguish: *et premitur ratione animus, vincique laborat. (Œuvres, Tome IV, p. 121)*[12]

For every moment of the narrative, there needs to be a new Herculean figure corresponding to the new passion in his soul that needed to be painted: first we have Hercules' surprise (in seventeenth-century France this was also called "admiration"), second we have emotional pity, and third we have the flames of passionate desire. But when the moment arrives when Hercules must make his choice, the typology of the available figures suddenly goes for a skid, it misses a beat, and new adjectives such as "dreamy, uncertain, and suspended" appear followed by similar nouns ("regret, agitation, torment, anguish"), all of which culminate in a verse by Persius that describes the triumph of reason within the soul: the soul is solicited by reason (*premitur ratione*) and its possible corruption seeks to be conquered (*vincique laborat*).[13]

## The Un-Figurable and the Inexpressive

Is it really a gallery of paintings that is at issue here? Or would it be better to say that there is just a single moment of hesitation coming before the choice, that moment when Hercules' teetering soul, haunted by contradictory movements, cannot possibly be depicted by any single unequivocal figure – precisely because it is, quite literally, un-figurable?[14] Carracci's painting, one which fascinated the viewers of his century to the point that a rather minor and insignificant subject such as "Hercules' Choice" was turned into a veritable fashion, was based on the expressionless nature of the hero's face. Today, we would say he looked almost bored, his eyes seemingly staring into space, his curled eyebrows indicating indecision, all of which, along with the meaningless pouting of his lips, unsettles the painting's viewers. Hercules appears to have no soul, he seems bereft of any feelings whatsoever, and his body is motionless. He remains silent because he has strictly nothing to say.

According to the table of the soul's passions and the typology of their expressions, as established by Le Brun – a series that included movements of the eyebrows, shapes of the lips, and looks of the eyes – Hercules does not correspond to any case at all; that is, he corresponds to no known expressive type. Like Agamemnon whom Timanthes paints with a veil, Hercules is an anti-figure, a blank, a hole in the network of signifiers, a moment of silence in the text, or one of suspension: "he is dreamy, uncertain, suspended."

Hercules in suspension reiterates Agamemnon in a veil. Diderot unwittingly reveals something important when he says that Hercules has been captured by the painter at the very moment when "the sacrifice is approaching." What sacrifice is this? A sacrifice of all the pleasures offered by Venus or that of Iphigenia offered up by Calchas' knife only a few lines later? "When Calchas has stabbed Iphigenia in the breast with his sacred knife, her mother will have to faint."

## The Moment of Decision and the Moment of Sacrifice: The Double Scene of Thought

"The moment of sacrifice" is of course a slip of the tongue (a slip of the pen) for "the moment of decision"; the choice made by Hercules *implies* the sacrifice of Iphigenia: on the one hand, Timanthes paints the horrifying picture of death that, for Diderot, means the mother's death (his heroin is Clytemnestra, not Iphigenia, i.e., Clytemnestra thrusting herself in Calchas' direction, Clytemnestra lying unconscious); on the other, Prodicus writes the scenario of a philosophical choice. Diderot brings together two images within a single device just as, in *The Letter on the Deaf and Dumb*, the episodes of Virgil's Dido on the verge of death and of the plague in Athens, as described by Lucretius, provides him with his final hieroglyph: a primal scene is played out where both the mother's death and philosophical meditation, engaged in the very process of thought, unceasingly repeat the same combination. This is just what we find in the *Salon of 1765* in a passage where Coresus' death is embedded within the myth of the cave, or later on in the *Salon of 1767* where several verses taken from Virgil's *Georgics* provide the backdrop for the philosophical dialogue in the *Promenade Vernet*.

Although the choice of a particular moment determines a painting's composition – it is the obvious goal of the Encyclopaedia article "Composition" to show this –, the choice of the moment can also be seen in relation to the choice that Hercules must make, an instance where the very process of thought unfolds, that split second of pensive indecision that precedes creativity, the final formula, or representation itself.

## III. The Return of the Real: Towards Objective Chance

Following his *Encyclopaedia* article on "Composition," Diderot repeatedly insists on the fundamentally anti-figural nature of the decisive moment. Once the painter feels compelled to choose the moment in a story that will produce the greatest dramatic effect possible, this same painter finds himself, paradoxically, forced to prefer a weak moment, one that, strictly speaking, precedes the action at hand and suspends his characters in a state of indecision, one showing them with their arms in the air in the face of a crime they dare not commit. This weak time of dramatic suspense puts expressionless heroes on stage: their feelings are mixed and their uncertain eyes open up a depressing zone within the space depicted. This was exactly what Agamemnon's veiled face showed us in the scene of Iphigenia's sacrifice. The same holds, in a more discreet fashion, for the vague boredom showing on Hercules's face as he hesitates between two goddesses.

### One Face Hides Another: Marie de Medici and Madame Greuze

Such a depressive zone calls for a viewer whose eye is capable of filling it in. The missing expression on the canvas whets the viewer's imagination: the zone asks to be completed and begs for someone to reconstitute those circumstances that the chosen moment needed to forego. The viewer is

21. PIETER PAU-
WEL RUBENS,
*The Birth of
Louis XIII*, CA.
1621–1625,
OIL ON CANVAS,
PARIS, LOUVRE,
394 X 295 CM.

thus asked to reconstruct the story, or to fill in the missing part. For indeed, the story's missing figure belies a necessary omission as displayed on the canvas. This is why Diderot chooses to replace the fixed figures of passion by his idea of movement. He praises the *Birth of Louis XIII* by Rubens for the facial expression that the painter was able to impart to Marie de Medici, the triumphant queen who had just given birth: "Rubens painted her in such a way that the joy of having given birth to a son did not erase the impressions left by the pains of labour. Of these two contrary passions, one is present and the other is absent" (Diderot, *Œuvres, Tome IV*, p. 122).[15] Impassible and regal, Marie de Medici is seated on the throne where she has just given birth: Mercury puts her new-born child in her hands. The glorious celebration of this royal birth is organized around the empty expression painted on her face, an expression which shows nothing.

Diderot pinpoints something sublime in the moment chosen by Rubens: it plunges the viewer, by dint of the latter's imagination, into the feelings of joy that mingle with those of recent pain, so recent that is still not entirely absent. And yet, this same pain is not depicted by any of the iconic signs belonging to the painting; rather, it is "expressed" by Marie de Medici's inexpressive face. Due to the hole it performs within the network of signifiers, all of which are part of the pictorial representation, her face is thus an anti-figure: it compels the viewer to effect an imaginary figuration, one filled with movement. Part of a State portrait, the royal face is disfigured by the expressions of pain shown on the face of a woman in labour, the same expressions that the viewer's imagination chooses in order to fill in the expressive vacuum shown on the painting. Diderot returns to Rubens' painting in the *Salon of 1765* in a passage where he discusses one of the portraits Greuze painted of his wife: "Look closely at this fine, fat fishwife, with her head twisted backwards, and whose pale colouring, showy kerchief, all mussed, and expression of pain mixed with pleasure depict a paroxysm that's sweeter to experience than it is decorous to paint; it's a study, a sketch for *The Well-Loved Mother.* How is it that in one place a given expression is decent, while in another it's not?" (*Diderot on Art I*, p. 102).

While the official Salon booklet announced a *Portrait of Madame Greuze* in rather neutral terms, Diderot on the other hand attributes a moral meaning to the pastel and characterizes it as a figure. It's *The Well-Loved Mother*, as he tells us: to be more precise, it is a preparatory study for the mother's head in a painting where it will figure amongst many other elements (see the mother on the right side of Illustration 23). The feelings of joy we read on the mother's face, embraced as she is – also pressed – by so many children, are entirely ambiguous: might they not be described as depicting the sexual pleasure showing on a face "twisted backward"? "You've never seen two opposed expressions so clearly evoked together. This *tour de force*, Rubens didn't succeed any better with it in the painting in the Luxembourg gallery, in which the painter showed on the queen's face both her pleasure at having brought a son into the world and the traces of her preceding pain" (*Diderot on Art I*, p. 102). The

22. JEAN-BAPTISTE GREUZE, *Portrait of Madame Greuze* (*The Well-Loved Mother*), 1765, PASTEL WITH RED, BLACK, AND WHITE CHALKS AND STUMPING ON LAID PAPER, WASHINGTON, NATIONAL GALLERY OF ART, 44 X 32.2 CM (IMAGE COURTESY OF THE BOARD OF TRUSTEES, NATIONAL GALLERY OF ART).

23. JEAN-BAPTISTE GREUZE, *The Well-Loved Mother*, 1769, OIL ON CANVAS,
MADRID, COLLECTION OF THE MARQUEE LABORDE, 99 X 131 CM.

mother subjugated by her children's embraces has just left behind some
very different embraces, those received in the company of her husband:
the libertine expression, still visible on her face, will slowly give way
to motherly bliss. Depicted here as if she were a queen amongst her
children, we cannot help but remember that, in the previous moment,
she was enthralled by the convulsions of her sexual pleasure, themselves
resembling pain. The parallel Diderot draws between Madame Greuze
and Marie de Medici is not merely one based on disfigurement or re-
figuration: in both cases we observe a woman who, majestically painted
in all her glory, functions as a screen for another more indecent one, the
body of a woman in labour. An absent signifier becomes the dominant
one; it is the anti-figure for the decisive moment. As such, it refers back

to a female body in orgasm, which is not plainly present in the scene she offers to the viewer's eyes. The effects of something un-figurable work against the theatricality of what we can indeed see. These feminine Majesties display knowledge of another sort, they lead us to an intimate experience (that of sex, life, even death). Here, knowledge and experience have taken on the deceptive figure of pain in order to act out the entire primal scene.

The anti-figure we have just discussed refers to this un-figurable scene. Its depressed zones, brought on by the decisive moment, propel the viewer's eyes toward the un-representable brutality of the female body caught in the middle of its labour, and in all its glory. It is not just a matter of representing movement instead of a figure because, here, the entire composition comes into play. The decisive moment brings together two moments in time, it articulates two scenes and, by means of these, it projects a visibly theatrical set of characters into an invisible brutality, whether steeped in the climax of pleasure or doomed to total oblivion.

## Seizing the Figure as It Vanishes: On Cleopatra's Smile

The interplay of these two scenes is particularly noticeable in the commentary Diderot provided in 1761 concerning Charles-Michel-Ange Challe's painting of Cleopatra:

> Cleopatra lies dying and the snake is still on her breast. What is the snake still doing there? But if it were already far from her body, as the logic of the chosen moment dictated, who would have been able to recognize Cleopatra? The truth of the matter is that this moment is not well-chosen: it would have been better to choose the moment when this proud woman, determined to foil the hubristic designs of Rome to have her adorn its victory, uncovers her own breast, smiles at the snake – with that same smile, filled with disdain, which

she keeps for the conqueror from whose grasp she is about
to escape – and she has it bite her breast. (*Œuvres, Tome IV,*
p. 218)

In accordance with the rules dictated by the Academy, Challe chose to
paint the final moment of the story he wanted to portray:[16] Cleopatra
has already been bitten by the snake and the die is already cast. Logically, she should have thrown the snake's body far away from her but the
principles of poetic licence, as spelled out by Le Brun, allow Challe to go
against the order of the events as they would have occurred in time and
to show the lingering presence of the snake without whose presence the
scene could not be understood. In characterizing Cleopatra, the snake
also brings her to the congealed state of a figure. There is no movement
in the painted scene: the decisive moment has just occurred in the one
immediately preceding the depicted scene.

Diderot will re-imagine this painting using as its core Cleopatra's
sublime smile. The long sentence he writes to describe this suspended
moment accumulates several verbal constructions: "uncovers," "smiles,"
and "has it bite." Indeed, we have a temporal succession of events but the
latter is represented in terms of space: "uncovers" involves her left hand
exposing her breast; "smiles" refers to her face; "has it bite" indicates her
right hand dropping the dangerous animal on her breast.[17] The smile
"filled with disdain" contained in Diderot's prose[18] is an oxymoronic
expression; it combines the seductions of the body with the sovereignly
cold expression she assumes in the face of death.

To bolster his demonstration, Diderot moves ever so slightly from
the moment he has chosen to that represented by Challe in his painting:

Perhaps this expression would have been more frightening,
more powerful, if Cleopatra had smiled at the snake as it bit
her breast. Here, the expression of pain seems pitiful, that
of despair seems rather common. The choice [by Challe] of
the moment when Cleopatra breathes her last breath does not

LA MORT DE CLÉOPATRE

Dedié a Monseigneur Emmanuel Félicité de Durfort de Duras Duc de Duras
Pair de France, Prince de Bournonville, Chevalier des Ordres du Roi et de la Toison d'Or, Lieutenant
Général de ses Armées, Premier Gentilhomme de la Chambre de Sa Majesté, Gouverneur et Lieutenant
Général du Comté de Bourgogne, Gouverneur Particulier des Ville et Citadelle de Besançon.

Par son très humble Serviteur Michel Ange Challe Ecuyer Peintre ord.re du Roi Dessinateur de sa Chambre et de son Cabinet.

A Paris chez Chereau rue S.t Jacque aux deux Piliers d'Or, et chez Buret, mueur de sa Maj.té Dauine.

24. CHARLES MICHEL-ANGE CHALLE, *The Death of Cleopatra*, 1761, ACCORDING
TO THE ENGRAVING BY JEAN-BAPTISTE MICHEL (CA. 1770–1778), LISBON,
BIBLIOTECA NACIONAL DE PORTUGAL, 40.6 X 28.7 CM.

give us an imperial Cleopatra; it only gives us a woman who is dying after having been bitten by a snake. This is no longer the story of the queen of Alexandria but a simple accident of life. (Diderot, *Œuvres, Tome IV*, p. 218)

At that very moment when the snake is biting Cleopatra's breast, the queen's smile reaches both its maximal tension and its highest expressive power. But after the bite is complete, the expression of pain becomes pitiful and the smile falls from its initial moment of grandeur. With the arrival of death, Cleopatra will simply be overcome with despair. That unique expression, the distinctive mark of the previous split second, is now lost and replaced by the banal and vulgar moment of a dying woman. Thus Diderot has underscored the figure as it is being shaped, he shows how it congeals, how it takes on an extraordinary splendour, only to disappear once again as quickly as a drawing in the sand. When cut from those circumstances that make it a special event in history, a momentous scene of tragedy, Cleopatra's death becomes a mere "accident of life," an unfortunate – even fortuitous – encounter of a woman with a snake.[19]

It would seem, then, that the decisive moment flirts with chance. Indeed, Cartier-Bresson refers to "objective chance" when speaking of the way a movement lays itself out so fortuitously in reality; he suggests that we must seize the photographic instant before it disappears, that is, before the space we see falls back into meaninglessness. By setting the scenes he describes in the *Salons* into anamorphic movement, Diderot sets the stage for a new type of artistic relationship, one that is creative. This relationship involves the real and the instantaneous as evoked by Cartier-Besson and later theorized by Roland Barthes in his *Camera Lucida*.

## The Moment of Intimate Federation: The Paralytic (Filial Piety)

While studying Challe's *Cleopatra*, Diderot claims to be able to dominate this element of chance. He also believes he can protect an historical scene from the triviality of life's accidents. However, with the arrival of several new genres within bourgeois painting, the decisive moment tends to fuse with the same element of chance it was supposed to control. Thus, he writes the following words concerning Greuze's painting of 1763, *Filial Piety*: "They also say that the undivided focus of all the characters in the painting is not natural, that it would have been better if just a few of them had taken care of the old man while all the others would have thus been free to attend to their own tasks. They say that in this way the painted scene would have been simpler and truer, because they are certain that this is the way things are" (*Œuvres, Tome IV*, p. 277). Greuze had painted a sick old man surrounded by everyone in his family, all of whom, as if in one large circle, were caring for him simultaneously. It is not true-to-life that everyone from such a large family, however much they loved and respected their father, would all be taking care of a single sick person at the exact same time. For such a scene, the classical rules of composition call for different actions for different characters. As assumed by certain characters, the loving care for the old man would become meaningful, that is visible, only when opposed to a second, less worried-looking group of characters. Filial piety can only be shown by contrast, if not in relation to impiety, or even indifference, then at least with respect to persons busy doing something else. The care given to the old man can only be seen against the backdrop of other domestic chores, all the other necessary tasks of everyday life, many of which the painter should portray in order to create a system of differences, a way of laying out the various figures of the painting. Diderot will argue against this conception of pictorial composition:

> The moment that they are asking for is a common and un-
> interesting one, while the moment chosen by the painter is

25.  JEAN-BAPTISTE GREUZE, *Filial Piety* (*The Paralytic*), 1761, OIL ON CANVAS,
SAINT PETERSBURG, THE STATE HERMITAGE MUSEUM, 115 X 146 CM.

special. By coincidence, on that particular day, it so happened
that the son-in-law was feeding the sick old man and that the
latter, moved by the young man's care, expressed his gratitude
so strongly, and so penetratingly, that it caught the attention
of everyone in the house who dropped whatever it was that
they were doing. (*Œuvres, Tome IV*, p. 277)

And so it is that the decisive moment goes against the grain of verisimilitude. It lies at the antipodes of the vague and universal qualities
advocated by Le Brun who saw the moment of the painted scene as a
way of opening things up to meaningful transactions, to both verbal and
commercial exchanges. But the moment chosen by Greuze is "special,"

says Diderot, and as such it exposes an encounter that can only have meaning if it is anchored in its own particular time and place. Both unique and priceless, the encounter captures everyone's attention. Its act of suspension ("everyone in the house ... dropped whatever it was that they were doing") is not that of a tragedy, the moment familiar to all and anxiously awaited, the moment that theatrical plays will repeat each and every time that they are staged, but rather suspension occurs here in an instant because this is a snapshot that will be engraved in the family's memory as a most important event, a snapshot that will thus set this time off for humble people against the course of history. The decisive moment inscribes itself in reality as something of an exceptional occurrence; it is not an historical event but rather the symptom of a federating intimacy: not a simple observation such as *that was the way things were* but a more collective one, i.e., *we were all there when it happened*, that is to say, that the whole family circle was present.

No pre-existing system of differences is sufficient for staging such a federating intimacy. Painting ceases to function as a system of signs because now it calls for a sense of touch:[20] "the old man was *moved*," "so penetratingly," "it caught the attention of everyone." The decisive moment also becomes contagious: it passes from one person to the next; it spreads its dramatic suspense.

## From the Single Instant to the Instantaneous: Vernet's Occupations of the Riverbank[21]

The famous *Promenade Vernet* provides the moment when objective chance will reveal itself with stark brilliance. Pretending never to have seen the paintings Vernet exposed during the Salon of 1767, Diderot goes for a long hike during which he describes the landscapes he sees, dividing them into seven sites which, as it turns out, are really Vernet canvasses after all. He sees the fourth site during the morning hours while sitting in the armchair he had found on the terrace of the country manor where he was staying. Suddenly, before his eyes, the landscape he is looking at becomes a painting. This is the decisive moment:

Vernet, my friend, take up your charcoal, and make haste to enrich your portfolio with this group of women. One, bending over the surface of the water, wets her laundry; another, crouching, wrings it out; a third, standing, has placed a basket filled with some of it on her head. Don't forget the young man near them, seen from the back, bending over, engaged in the same task. Make haste, for in an instant these figures will assume other positions which will, perhaps, be less attractive. (*Diderot on Art II*, p. 98)

Within reality, at a given moment in time, Diderot's eye catches a special combination that may very well dissipate "in an instant." The three washerwomen accomplish successive stages of their common task: wetting the laundry, wringing it, and then placing it in a basket, ready to be carried away. Coincidence splits this time into several micro-narratives unfolding within the depicted space, thus making time visible. A young man seen from behind, on the far side of the woman carrying her basket, frames the scene, marking it as a background figure. Beyond him stretches the greater decor, the pure landscape in all its splendour.[22]

Is this not merely a rhetorical device, one whose aim is to sneak the classical layout of figures back into the picture via a walk through nature? Let us admit that this trick is also the symptom of a paradigmatic change. As soon as the layout of figures is no longer conceived of in terms of a formal arrangement found in a space without time, but rather as the conjunction of several movements inscribed into a single and singular temporality, then the painting ceases to be a semiotic structure and becomes rather an operative device; that is to say, it articulates a structure onto a conjuncture[23] and maps a real-life space occupied by chance coincidence onto a symbolic space, ideally reconfigured.

* * *

I have attempted to show how the notion of the decisive moment was born in the seventeenth century at the crossroads between painting and history. It was important to explain the extent to which this notion can be seen as an attempt to articulate the modes of representation valid for both.

The first lectures of the *Académie royale de peinture* were marked by a conflict between a theory of figures and the resistance offered by circumstances. The decisive moment was thus a compromise: since painting represented only a single instant, it needed to lay out its figures in a logical manner within a fixed and immobile space; and yet the decisive moment will artificially incorporate the circumstances that historically preceded it in order to make the story intelligible, which it has as its mission to represent.

From the very beginning, in the "Composition" article written for his *Encyclopaedia*, Diderot reverses the compromise position put together by the Academy's founding members: the decisive moment becomes the core principle for pictorial organization and composition; it deconstructs the figure which now splits into many expressive movements or, quite literally, turns it into an anti-figure, referring back to an earlier, unfigurable scene of representation. The decisive moment now changes: it both ceases to be identified automatically with the end of the story and it begins to weaken, all this in order to allow viewers to complete the scene's movement within their own minds.

The decisive moment thus becomes the indecisive moment of dramatic suspense. But above all, since it is not automatically given, it must always be chosen: this choice provides the opportunity for Diderot to browse through the stories that painters refer to and to move the temporal cursor of the painted scenes he has chosen to examine. From this moment forward, an anamorphic game is put into place, one that progressively dethrones the classical frame of the painted scene in favour of the instantaneity of the snapshot, which is yet to come.

# Bibliography

Barthes, Roland. *Camera Lucida*, trans. Richard Howard. New York: Hill and Wang, 1981.

Cartier-Bresson, Henri. *The Decisive Moment*. New York: Simon & Schuster, 1952.

———. *The Decisive Moment*: *Images of Man*. New York: Scholastic Magazines, 1973.

Chouillet, Jacques. *La Formation des idées esthétiques de Diderot*. Paris: Armand Colin, 1973.

Cicero. *De oratore*, trans. James M. May and Jakob Wisse with the title *Cicero on the Ideal Orator*. New York: Oxford University Press, 2001.

Diderot, Denis. *Œuvres. Tome IV* (*Esthétique-Théâtre*), ed. Laurent Versini. Paris: Robert Laffont, collection "Bouquins," 1996.

———. *Diderot's Early Philosophical Works*, trans. Marguerite Jourdain. New York: Burt Franklin, 1972.

———. *Diderot on Art*, vol. 1, trans. John Goodman. New Haven, CT: Yale University Press, 1995.

———. *Diderot on Art*, vol. 2, trans. John Goodman. New Haven, CT: Yale University Press, 1995.

———. *Selected Writings on Art and Literature*, trans. Geoffrey Bremner. London: Penguin, 1994.

Eustathius of Thessalonica. *Commentarii ad Homeri Iliadem pertinentes ad fidem codicis Laurentiani* [Commentaries on the Iliad and the Oddeyssey], ed. Marchinus van der Valk. Leiden (Netherlands): Brill, 1971.

Laclos, Choderlos de. *Dangerous Liaisons*, trans. Helen Constantine. London: Penguin, 2007.

Le Brun, Charles. *Les Conférences de l'Académie royale de peinture et de sculpture au XVII<sup>e</sup> siècle*, ed. Alain Mérot. Paris: Éditions de l'École Nationale des Beaux-Arts, 1996; re-edited by Jacqueline Lichtenstein and Charles Michel, Paris: Éditions de l'École Nationale Supérieure des Beaux-Arts, 2007.

Lichtenstein, Jacqueline. *La Tache aveugle. Essai sur les relations de la peinture et de la sculpture à l'âge moderne*. Paris: Gallimard, 2003.

Ortel, Philippe. *La Littérature à l'ère de la photographie*. Nîmes: Éditions Jacqueline Chambon, 2002.

————. "Valences dans la scène: pour une critique des dispositifs." In *La Scène. Littérature et arts visuels*, ed. M. Th. Mathet, 303–22. Paris: L'Harmattan, 2001.

Panofsky, Erwin. *Herkules am Scheidewege*. Leipzig: Studien der Bibliothek Warburg, 1930.

Persius. *The Satires of Persius*, trans. Guy Lee. Liverpool: Francis Cairns, 1987.

Pliny the Elder. *Natural History*, 10 vols., trans. Harris Rackham. Cambridge, MA: Harvard University Press, collection "Loeb Classical Library," 1938–1963.

Quintilian. *The Institutione oratoria of Quintilian*, 4 vols., trans. H. E. Butler. Cambridge, MA: Harvard University Press, collection "Loeb Classical Library," 1920–1922.

Retz (Cardinal de Retz). *Mémoires*. In *Œuvres*, ed. Marie-Thérèse Hipp and M. Pernot, Paris: Gallimard, collection "Pléiade," 1984. English translation: *Memoirs of the Cardinal de Retz, containing all the great events during the minority of Lewis XIV and administration of Cardinal Mazarin*, Dublin: R. Reilly for Stearn Brock, 1736.

————. *Mémoires*, vol. II, ed. Simone Bertière. Paris: Garnier.

Richardson, Jonathan. *Essay on the Theory of Painting*, ed. John Churchill. London: W. Bowyer, 1715; 2nd ed. 1725.

Richardson, Samuel, *Clarissa*, ed. Angus Ross. London: Penguin, 2004.

Testelin, Henry. *Sentiments des plus habiles peintres*. Paris, 1680 and 1696.

Ritschald, Claude, Allison Morehead, Mieke Bal, and Bettina Baumgärtel. *Cléopâtre au miroir de l'art occidental*. Paris: Les Cinq Continents, 2004.

Shaftesbury, Anthony. *An Essay on Painting: Being a Notion of the Historical Draught or Tablature of the Judgment of Hercules, according to Prodicus*, vol. I. London: printed by John Darby, and sold by J. Roberts, 1714.

Starobinski, Jean. *Diderot dans l'espace des peintres* suivi de *Le Sacrifice en rêve*, Paris: Réunion des Musées Nationaux, 1991.

# NOTES

1   The American edition of *Images à la sauvette* was entitled *The Decisive Moment* (New York: Simon & Schuster, 1952). See also Henri Cartier-Bresson, "*The Decisive Moment*: Images of Man" (New York: Scholastic Magazines, 1973).

2   Cardinal de Retz, *Mémoires*, II, 5, ed. M.-Th. Hipp and M. Pernot (Paris: Gallimard, "Pléiade"), 252. The Cardinal reuses this formula several times in his writing (which I have highlighted in italics): "Il n'y a point de qualité qui dépare tant celles d'un grand homme, que de n'être pas juste à prendre le *moment décisif* de sa réputation. L'on ne le manque presque jamais que pour prendre mieux celui de sa fortune" (II, 8, 359). "Voici, à mon sens, le *moment fatal et décisif* de la révolution. Il y a très peu de gens qui en aient connu la véritable importance. Chacun s'en est voulu former une imaginaire" (II, 22, 735; I have corrected an error in the printed text, which reads *final* instead of *fatal*. See the edition prepared by Simone Bertière [Paris: Garnier, vol. II], 253).

3   It would be useful to quote, in addition, several occurrences where this notion appears in novelistic form. For example, in Letter CCXXIV of *Clarissa*, Lovelace writes the following words to Belford: "Or is it that I am taken in a cowardly minute? For heroes have their fits of fear; cowards their *brave* moments: and virtuous ladies, all but my Clarissa, their *moment critical*" (Samuel Richardson, *Clarissa*, ed. Angus Ross [London: Penguin, 2004], 722, Richardson's emphases). Likewise, in Choderlos de Laclos' *Dangerous Liaisons*, Madame de Merteuil gives the following description to Valmont when writing about the young Dancenis: "Tomorrow afternoon is to be the *fateful occasion*" ["c'est demain après-midi que

sera cet *instant decisif*"] (Letter 51) and later at the end of Letter 70, she writes: "Send me your excellent instructions and give me the benefit of your sage counsel at *this critical time*" ["Faites-moi passer vos sublimes instructions et aidez-moi de vos sages conseils, dans ce *moment décisif*."] See *Dangerous Liaisons*, trans. Helen Constantine [London: Penguin Books, 2007], 113 and 148 (my emphases).

4   *Les Conférences de l'Académie royale de peinture et de sculpture au XVII$^e$ siècle*, ed. Alain Mérot (Paris: Éditions de l'École nationale supérieure des Beaux-Arts, 1996), 110; re-edited by Jacqueline Lichtenstein and Charles Michel (Paris: Éditions de l'Ecole Nationale Supérieure des Beaux-Arts, 2007, I, 1), 171. It has been postulated that the objector in question may very well have been Philippe de Champaigne.

5   The *Conférences de l'Académie Royale de Peinture & de Sculpture pendant l'année 1667*, published under the editorship of Félibien, appeared in 1668. For further information see Henry Testelin, *Sentiments des plus habiles peintres*, 1680 and 1696.

6   Joseph-Marie Vien, *Saint Denis Preaching the Faith in France*, 1767, oil on canvas, Paris, Church of Saint Roch, 665 x 393 cm.

7   Nicolas Poussin, *Esther before Ahasuerus*, ca. 1654, oil on canvas, Saint Petersburg, State Hermitage Museum, 119 x 155 cm.

8   Joseph Vernet, *A Storm*, 1769, oil on canvas, private collection (once the personal property of Denis Diderot).

9   Pliny the Elder, *Naturalis historia* XXXV, 39 ; Quintilian, *De institutione oratoria* II, 13 ; Cicero, *De oratore* XXII; Eustathius of Thessalonica,

Commentaries on the Iliad and the Odyssey (12th century), §1343, 1.60.

10 Erwin Panofsky, *Herkules am Scheidewege* [*Hercules at the Crossroads*] (Leipzig: Studien der Bibliothek Warburg, 1930).

11 Jean-Honoré Fragonard, *Coresus Sacrificing Himself for Callirhoé*, 1765, oil on canvas, Paris, Louvre, 309 x 400 cm.

12 Here Diderot gives a loose translation for a passage culled from Shaftesbury's *Judgment of Hercules*, a text which he likely read while translating the latter's *Inquiry Concerning Virtue, or Merit*: "This Fable or History may be variously represented according to the Order of Time. Either in the instant when the two Goddesses (Virtue and Pleasure) accost Hercules. Or when they are entered on their Disputes. Or when their Dispute is already far advanced, and Virtue seems to gain her Cause. According to the *first* Notion, Hercules must of necessity seem surprised on the first appearance of such miraculous Forms; he admires, he contemplates, but is not yet ingaged or interested. According to the *second* Notion, he is interested, divided, and in doubt. According to the *third*, he is wrought, agitated, and torn by contrary Passions. 'Tis the last Effort of the vicious one, striving for possession over him. He agonizes, and with all his strength of Reason endeavours to overcome himself. *Et premitur ratione animus, vincique laborat*." (Shaftesbury, *An Essay on Painting: Being a Notion of the Historical Draught or Tablature of the Judgment of Hercules, according to Prodicus* [London : printed by John Darby, and sold by J. Roberts, 1714, I, 1–2], 6–7). When Jacques Chouillet linked Diderot's "Composition" article to Jonathan Richardson's *Essay on the Theory of Painting* (London: W. Bowyer, ed. John Churchill, 1715; 2nd ed.1725), he did not point to this

further intertext. See J. Chouillet, *La Formation des idées esthétiques de Diderot* (Paris: Armand Colin, 1973), 381.

13 The original, as with everything else concerning Persius, is difficult to understand: "*Teneros tu suscipis annos / Socratico Cornute sinu. Tum fallere sollers / Adposita intortos extendit regula mores, / Et premitur ratione animus vincique laborat / Artificemque tuo ducit sub pollice vultum*." ["You raise my tender years, / Cornutus, on Socratic breast. Then unawares / The skilful rule, applied, straightens my crooked ways, / My spirit, under reason's pressure, strives to lose / And by your thumb is moulded into artistic shape." (Persius, *Satires* V, vv.36–40, *The Satires of Persius*, trans. Guy Lee [Liverpool: Francis Cairns, 1987]).

14 In this passage Diderot distorts his source. Shaftesbury has indeed chosen his decisive moment and he has chosen it according the logic of his time, that is to say, the last one: "Of these different periods of Time, the latter has been chosen, as being the only one of the three, which can well serve to express the *Grand Event*, or consequent Resolution of Hercules, and the *Choice* he actually made of a Life full of Toil and Hardship, under the Conduct of *Virtue*, for the deliverance of Mankind from Tyranny and Oppression. And 'tis to such a Piece of Balance in our pondering Hero, that we may justly give the title of the *Decision* or *Judgment* of Hercules." (Shaftesbury, *An Essay on Painting*, I, 3, p. 7)

15 This is also an idea that Diderot borrows from Shaftesbury: "How is it therefore possible, says one, to express a Change of Passion in any Subject, since this Change is made by Succession; and that in this case the Passion which is understood as present, will require a Disposition of Body and Feature wholly different from the

Passion which is over and past? To this we answer, that notwithstanding the Ascendancy or Reign of the principal and immediate Passion, the Artist has power to leave still in his Subject the Tracks or Footsteps of its Predecessor; so as to let us behold not only a rising Passion together with a declining one, but, what is more, a strong and determinate Passion, with its contrary already discharged and banished. As for instance, when the plain tracks of Tears new[ly] fallen, with other fresh tokens of Mourning and Dejection, remain still in a Person newly transported with Joy at this sight of a Relation or Friend, who the moment before had been lamented as one deceased or lost." (Shaftesbury, *An Essay on Painting*, I, 10, pp. 10–11).

16    For a discussion of the Western iconography of Cleopatra, see Claude Ritschald, Allison Morehead, Mieke Bal, and Bettina Baumgärtel, *Cléopâtre au miroir de l'art occidental* (Paris: Les Cinq Continents, 2004). Among the numerous stage productions portraying Cleopatra during the seventeenth and eighteenth centuries, we point to Jean de La Chapelle's tragedy of 1681, *La Mort de Cléopâtre* (Théâtre de Guénégaud), which was restaged in 1723. In 1750, Jean-François Marmontel also staged a play written in verse about Cleopatra at the Théâtre de la rue des Fossés Saint-Germain. In 1784, it was restaged, in a totally revised version, by the Comédie française.

17    The roles played by Cleopatra's two hands vary according to the composition one studies: in two separate compositions Guido Reni (1630–1640) places the snake in Cleopatra's right hand (see appendix "Other Cited (but unillustrated) Works of Art"), while Alessandro Turchi (*The Death of Cleopatra*, ca. 1631, oil on canvas, Paris, Louvre, 267 x 255 cm) puts it in her left hand, just as do Claude Vignon (*Cleopatra's Suicide*, ca. 1640–1650, oil on canvas, Rennes, Musée des Beaux-Arts, 95 x 81 cm), Louis-Jean-François Lagrenée (*The Death of Cleopatra*, 1755, oil on canvas, Paris, École Nationale Supérieure des Beaux-Arts), and the engraver Jean-Baptiste Michel (1775) – but no doubt in reverse form in relation to Jean Michel-Ange Challe's original painting of 1761, which he was reproducing.

18    This expression was probably invented by Diderot in contrast with those depictions of Cleopatra that normally show her in a state of pain with her eyes looking upward, something he forcefully criticizes. The Cleopatra painted by Andrea Solario (*Cleopatra*, ca. 1514, oil on canvas, private collection) is rare in its depiction of a queen who looks at the snake – but she does not smile. Elisabetta Sirani's painting *Cleopatra* (ca. 1650, oil on canvas, Flint [Michigan], Flint Institute of Arts, 99.7 x 75.6 cm) indeed shows her smiling, but this work shows her holding a pearl, not a snake.

19    This encounter is full of resonances for Diderot who, fascinated by Poussin's *Landscape of a Man Killed by a Snake* (1648), saw in this painting (and he alone saw this) a woman being devoured by a snake. See, on this subject, his *Letter on the Deaf and Dumb* ("*serpentem fuge*," *Diderot's Early Philosophical Works* [New York: Burt Franklin, 1972], 181), the *Salon of 1765* (where he compares Chardin's still life to a snake, *Diderot on Art* I, 62), the *Salon of 1767* (both when speaking of Juliard's landscapes, *Diderot on Art* II, 140–41 and when describing a landscape by Loutherbourg, p. 243) and his *Paradox of the Actor* (in *Selected Writings on Art and Literature*, trans. Geoffrey Bremner [London, Penguin Books, 1994], 102), where he refers to Racine.

20  For a discussion of the ways in which eighteenth-century painting reversed the traditional hierarchy of the bodily senses, see Jean Starobinski, "Diderot dans l'espace des peintres" (Paris: Réunion des Musées Nationaux, 1991, 23–26), and Jacqueline Lichtenstein, *La Tache aveugle. Essai sur les relations de la peinture et de la sculpture à l'âge moderne* (Paris: Gallimard, 2003).

21  Joseph Vernet, *Occupations of the Riverbank*, 1766, oil on canvas, Paris, private collection, 49 x 39 cm. This is the first of two known versions of this composition, the second one being housed in the Hermitage Museum of Saint Petersburg (*Occupations of the Riverbank*, ca. 1767, oil on canvas, 47.5 x 37.5 cm).

22  Diderot does not mention the fisherman visible in the foreground, seated beside a dog on the left in front of the washerwomen. This fisherman assumes the function of a visual shifter in this scene as can be seen in the surviving oval versions of this composition (the version exhibited in the Hermitage Museum is either a variant or a copy of the Paris version, no doubt the painting exhibited during the 1767 Salon). The reason for Diderot's omission is this: the Philosopher assumes the fisherman's position in this fourth site of the Promenade Vernet. As such he can both introduce the scene and place himself between the painted scene and the viewer/reader.

23  "While, from the beginning, a structure puts meaning into the zone that it organizes by polarizing its components (the near and the far, the good and the bad, etc.), the device for action – best represented as a three-dimensional object – appears each and every time that a *structure* opens up to a *conjuncture*, that is to say, to an element which is heterogeneous in relation to the structure in its entirety" (Philippe Ortel, *La Littérature à l'ère de la photographie* [Nîmes: Éditions Jacqueline Chambon, 2002], 345). See also Ortel, "Valences dans la scène: pour une critique des dispositifs," ed. M. Th. Mathet, *La Scène. Littérature et arts visuels* (Paris: L'Harmattan, 2001, 303–22).

# 5

# On the Strategies of Portraiture in the Images and Texts of Seventeenth-Century Spain

*Pierre Civil*

The eminent art historian André Chastel once remarked, with good reason, that "the Renaissance is full of faces."[1] In saying this, he sought to underscore the fact that the Renaissance can indeed be seen as the "Golden Age" for the artistic genre of the portrait. Today, the flourishing of portraiture that occurred during this period is recognized as a fundamental feature of what has come to be known as Early Modern European culture, if not of modern culture in the wider sense. As their principle characteristics, portraits proclaim the excellence of the person painted while, at the same time, proposing this same person as an edifying example. They thereby claim to perpetuate the memory of that person, even after death. The aesthetic theories that accompanied the evolution of painting during Italy's *Quattrocento* were keen to renew the representational tools that its painters had inherited from classical antiquity: portraits were seen as arousing the desire to acquire an idealized image of the human subject, an image filled not only with all his or her social, political, moral and spiritual values, but also endowed with aesthetic and symbolic qualities as well.[2] Thanks both to recent criticism and several contemporary theories of portraiture, all of which are informed by semiotic approaches to painting and by philosophical thinking on the impact images have on us, it is now possible to imagine a well-rounded way of understanding the ways in which a person is represented along with all the relevant socio-historical trappings that we must take into account when studying this artistic genre.[3] In this context, the portrait can truly be raised to the status of a privileged object among all those examined by cultural studies.

In its time, the artistic model provided by Italian artists to the rest of Europe entailed several possible variants and various pictorial types, all of which led to the establishment of various representational systems according to the geographic and historical contexts in which they were developed.[4] At the outset of the early modern period, as the seat of the leading political power in Europe, the Iberian Peninsula was quite naturally a zone where various cultural influences mixed together. It became, moreover, an important incubator for new and creative forms of artistic expression. Given that the Iberian Peninsula possessed its own special conception of the human individual, its art of the portrait would therefore evolve in an original manner. As just one historical trace, amongst many others, of the tremendous interest there was at the time in Spain and Portugal for portraiture, let us for the moment cite but one example, that of an essentially technical treatise written in 1548 by the Portuguese artist Francisco de Holanda, *Do tirar pelo natural* ("On the art of life-like portraiture").[5] In this treatise, the artist-technician transmits his rich personal experience as a portrait artist, specifically that gained during his long stay in Italy, which allowed him to learn his trade.

Even if, in principle, the artistic portrait did not have, as its principle objective, the project of illustrating any particular written text, one is nevertheless struck by the permanent relationship that was established between portraits *per se* and verbal discourses. A first proof of this assertion lies in the rich literature that surrounded the painting of portraits. Beyond the many commentaries and generic definitions we are able to find, we will turn our attention here to those texts that point to a direct link either with the creation of a specific art work or with more formal possibilities that inject various forms of written language into the very representational space of art. An implicit encounter arises between, on the one hand, the artistic figure of the model (organized on the canvas or wood panel by the presence of visible lines and coloured nuances) and, on the other, practices of the rhetorical portrait, a rigorously codified motif belonging to literary narratives or poetry. There are of course many possible variants for how such an encounter – a constant parameter of the portrait genre – will evolve.

As far as this parameter is concerned in the context of the Spanish Golden Age, a number of case studies can shed meaningful light both on actual artistic practice and on the reigning conceptual configurations. If one starts with the basic premise that a portrait is itself an image, one can pinpoint the special effects that written words, when presented within a painting, bring to the overall assessment of the work. As a second step, one needs to consider the omnipresence of a particular theme, that of the "fraternity" between painting and poetry. It is important to observe the extent to which this theme is part and parcel of the ways in which the effigy of a given person circulates in society, more particularly in the case of an image said to be that of the poet himself. As a further step in this process, we shall turn to an analysis of the ways in which portraiture unfolds when part of an identifiable group of paintings, as is observable in seventeenth-century Spain. We shall thus examine four concrete examples of portraits that partake in an elaborate interplay between word and image. By concentrating on such a grouping of portraits, we are of course obliged to neglect other sub-groups of the genre, all of which present their own special problems, most notably those represented by portraits of the Prince and of prestigious persons of the court.[6] Be this as it may, we shall not thereby neglect engraved portraits, especially when they involve authors, those portraits that are printed in the opening pages of a book, the lofty place from which such images appear to overlook the lively world of writing.[7]

# Words Appearing in the Portrait[8]

In a book published in France in the year 1522 under the title *L'Imagination poétique*, the French poet and humanist Barthélemy Aneau tells a story about what he found one day in a printer's workshop in the city of Lyons: "Several little figures, both drawn and etched, prompted the question as to what their purpose was, and I was soon answered. No purpose at all except that of providing an inscription appropriate for them [...] and so, thinking that these figures had been made for no apparent reason from silent and still characters, I promised that I would make them lively and give them speech, using living poetry to breath a soul into them."[9] This cute little anecdote aptly underscores the idealized ability of verbal language to breathe life into dead images, a variation on the well-known *topos* consisting of speaking either of eloquent painting or of silent poetry. At the same time, however, it highlights the material reality of the book itself and reminds us of all those editions that often contained a haphazard collection of engraved effigies designed to recall the act of writing. In such an editorial world, images of authors, patrons and other personalities are multiply present all over the title pages of a book; as such they strongly suggest an intricate relationship with its contents. Such is the role attributable to the engraved portrait of Pedro Mexía, a famous writer of the time from Seville: his portrait adorns the opening pages of the 1570 edition of Mexía's book, *Silva de varia lección*. His portrait was accompanied by two lines of poetry written in Latin:

> *Ingenio quantus fuerit Mesias videbis*
> *Intus, at effigies corporis ista fuerit.*[10]

The portraitists of this period were wont to place written indications directly on the painted surface of the canvas, or directly in the engraved portrait. Such indications could include the name of the painted subject, his or her age (more often than not the person's age is given by means of the standard Latin formula *aetatis suae* ...) or even his or her social status. While these written comments sometimes constituted a more or less well-developed hymn of praise, they could also serve to certify that the portrait being viewed indeed resembled the person being painted. Without delving any further into these verbal commentaries – they were already considered somewhat archaic during the first half of the sixteenth century and thus would soon be abandoned – we should nevertheless insist on the fact that written words provided an indispensable answer to a number of fundamental questions concerning the subject's identity and social status. Moreover, they incarnated certain types of deictic meaning that naturally accrue to any such forms of representation. In the end, one of their purposes consisted in giving rise to the semiotic work that a portrait must accomplish, and this they did by pointing to the very act of painting a portrait, thereby underscoring in an explicit fashion the illusory character of the represented figure while treating the materiality of the image as contributing to a truthful enterprise. Concurrently, they bestowed full artistic merit upon the image of likeness of which they were a part.[11] Such words written in the space of the portrait made it possible (a fundamental part of portraiture as art) to distinguish between referential identity and pictorial identity, the two poles between which the represented human figure oscillated as if by definition.

## LOPE DE VEGA

The Spanish engraver Juan de Courbes left us with a portrait of Lope de Vega, a towering cultural figure in Spain who was without a doubt considered to be the most famous poet and playwright of his time. This portrait serves as the frontispiece of an early edition of Vega's *Laurel de Apolo*, a poetic text first published in 1630.[12] Such representations of the man whom Madrid called "the phoenix of spirits" were systematically present in the opening pages of virtually every one of his publications: they provide a case where an author engages in a unique kind of self-affirmation that can be compared with other literary practices of the day. Furthermore, the portrait clearly underlined the dignified social rank of

Nacio Don
Luis de Gongo
ra Iueues XI de
Iulio de M.DL.
XI.en Cordoua

Murio Don
Luis de Gongo
ra Lunesta XX
III. de Mayo de
M.DC.XXVII
en Cordoua.

Vixit Don Luis de Gongora LXV. Años. X. Meses. y XIII. Dias.

De amiga Idea de valiente mano
Molestado el metal, viuio en mi vulto
Emulo tibio; y el intento vano
Si vida se vsurpo, me indio culto

*A.     A.M.*

Bien asi o Huesped doctamente humano
Copias perdona demi Genio culto
(Quando aun la Fama del pincel presuma)
Que no ai de mi mas copia que mi pluma.

*L.    L.*
P. I. de Courbes F.

26. JUAN DE COURBES,
*Lope de Vega,*
ENGRAVING, 1630.
IN *Laurel de Apolo
con otras rimas,* BY
LOPE DE VEGA,
MADRID: JUAN
GANZÁLEZ, 1630.

the model, since it represented him wearing the dress of the Order of Saint James. Clearly, this was a man at the height of his fame. Through the portrait, he was inscribed into the realm of classical heroes, as if his effigy had been struck on an elaborate medallion. Along the circumference of the image, a Latin inscription quotes the poet's name and proposes, hyperbolically, to sing the praises of a man who would not be content to be a simple disciple of the poetic Muses, but rather their rival. These written comments quite literally surround the part of the image that shows Vega's physical appearance; their place within the engraving constitutes, as it were, a sort of physical boundary that serves to set the identity of the represented poet off against everything else. Several other quotations insist upon the eternal glory achieved by his grand poetry. In Spanish we read: *La sagrada poesía de Lope nació de las musas, aquella puede desaparecer, éste no puede desaparecer.*[13] Respectful of the rhetorical traditions of the time, this dithyrambic discourse serves to organize the meanings attributable to an image whose main mission is to underscore the glory of this great man of letters. In many ways, such commentaries are the equivalent of a modern-day publicity campaign.[14]

## Góngora

During that same year of 1630, our engraver executed another portrait, this time of one of Lope de Vega's greatest rivals, Luis de Góngora who, at the time of this engraving, had already been dead for three years. This second portrait was included in the opening pages of José Pellicer's *Lecciones solemnes*,[15] or to be more precise, it constituted its frontispiece. This pictorial representation is therefore seen to be a commemorative monument, conceived as it was in terms of a stele overladen with a multitude of symbolic layers. Appearing on a medallion, this image of the man known as the "Prince of Spain's lyrical poets" once again takes up (at the same time as it reproduces the picture in reverse) a famous portrait of Góngora painted by Velazquez in 1622.[16] In contrast with the austere restraint visible in the painted work, the engraver preferred to give a bombastically enthusiastic image of Góngora, one representing the model wearing the crown of Fame. Numerous written discourses can be seen everywhere on the portrait, all alluding to the birth and death of this great poet and proclaiming his eternal glory. In the lower portion of the engraving, serving as it were as the foundation for everything else, we find a poem consisting of two quatrains, which alludes not only to the literary activities of this illustrious poet from Cordoba, but also to the traditional rivalry between the author's pen and the painter's brush. In this way, the poem engages in a metalinguistic game of the type practised by the represented poet himself. This is therefore a "portrait that can talk" and, as such, partakes of an academic exercise frequently utilized

27. JUAN DE COURBES, *Luis de Góngora*, ENGRAVING, 1630. IN *Lecciones solemnes a las obras de Don Luis de Góngora*, BY JOSÉ PELLICER DE SALAS Y TOVAR, MADRID: IMPRENTA DEL REINO, 1630.

at the time. The words "No hay de mí más copia que mi pluma"[17] are proudly proclaimed in the poem's last verse. In all its redundancies, such visualized praise is part and parcel of the codified ways in which words and images are normally used, and in this instance they are set to work within a portrait whose aim is to celebrate the aesthetic achievements of Góngora himself, the same achievements that have been recognized as lying at the pinnacle of poetic creativity.

# THE COMMONPLACE OF THE *UT PICTURA POESIS*
# ADAGE: PORTRAITURE AND POETRY

This bringing together of art and literature was justified by the traditional *topos* linked to the Horatian expression *ut pictura poesis*, a veritable commonplace of thinking about art and culture. For people of the time, Horace's expression advocated the ideal of fraternity among the various arts just as it encouraged complementarity between painting and poetry. Such comparisons between text and image are all the more justified, it was claimed, given that both artistic forms are used to make actually absent things appear to be present. On this same subject, there was no dearth of reflections and theoretical manoeuvrings within the very first treatises written on the art of painting and on the imitation of the models provided by Italian aesthetics.[18] The principle of apparent equivalency between art and poetry was the result of a rhetorical scheme destined to fuel a number of fascinating academic debates. At the same time, it constituted an efficient instrument for pleading in favour of painting's overall excellence and nobility. In Spanish, the common use of the verb *pintar* ("to paint") instead of the verb *describir* ("to describe") as well as reliance on traditional metaphors for referring either to the one art or to the other turned the written page into a sort of canvas (and vice versa) thereby testifying to the widespread generalization of these very comparisons.

Imbued with exalting qualities, the visual art of portraiture was particularly well placed for illustrating the Horatian formula to which we have already alluded. As we have already seen, the most productive comparisons between the pen and the paintbrush occur in a context of praise. For its part, the literary portrait claimed to represent a lucid examination of a single individual through its enumeration of this same person's physical features. All this was done according to the canons at the core of rhetorical practice.

Well before the onset of the new fashions of the seventeenth century, which greatly favoured collections of portraits, the temptation to associate the written poem with a visual effigy was expressed in terms of a game of mirrors put into place in order to reflect either the painted portrait or the literary one. In Spain, the book entitled the *Libro de descripción de verdaderos retratos*, written by the Sevillian author Francisco Pacheco, that is to say, by a man who was both a painter and an aesthetician, both a poet and a quiet observer of the Inquisition, offers an original example of artistic thinking, one that includes some fifty-six pen drawings representing famous men either from the second half of the sixteenth century or from the beginning of the seventeenth. Here one finds portraits of ecclesiastical figures, artists, writers, aristocrats, all of whom came from the city on the Guadalquivir. Each of the figures shown as a bust obeys a systematic pattern of representation; each portrait is followed by a text, written either in prose or in verse, extolling the merits and virtues of the represented person, and presented in beautiful calligraphic style. Here the writing we see appears to be the object of an epiphany of the human face. Each chapter of the book closes with a few poems written with the intention of glorifying the portrait's human model. Moreover, many of these poems refer to a sketched portrait and can themselves be seen as a hybrid between literary homage and academic exercises; they are written by well-known poets and fit in well with the literary tastes of the time.

Let us look for a moment at a particularly meaningful example, that of the image portraying the poet Fray Luis de León. The sketched portrait is accompanied by a rhetorical one directly relating to it:

> *Fue pequeño de cuerpo en devida proporción; la cabeza grande,*
> *bien formada, poblada de cabello algo crespo; la frente espaciosa,*
> *el rostro más redondo que aguileño (como lo muestra el retrato),*
> *trigueño el color, los ojos verdes y vivos.*[19]

This portrait gallery, filled with both comments and exemplary figures, had been inspired by the aesthetic models provided by Flemish and Italian artists; it constituted a very personalized case of the *livre d'artiste* appearing, so to speak, ahead of its time, a work that takes on special meanings in the

Implevit
eum Dominus spiritu
sapientiæ et intellectus.
Eccles. cap. 15.

EL MAESTRO FRAI LVIS DE LEON

28. FRANCISCO PACHECO, *Retrato de fray Luis de León*, ENGRAVING.
IN FRANCISCO PACHECO, *Libro de descripción de verdaderos retratos de
ilustres y memorables varones*, EDITED WITH AN INTRODUCTION BY
PEDRO M. PIÑERO RAMÍREZ AND ROGELIO REYES CANO (SEVILLE:
DIPUTACIÓN PROVINCIAL DE SEVILLA, 1985), 67.

5: ON THE STRATEGIES OF PORTRAITURE IN THE IMAGES AND TEXTS

brilliant cultural context that was that of Seville at a time when there were many artist-poets and poet-artists living in the city.

## Representing the Individual between Images and Texts

Given the close relationships that they knit with the contents of the books in which they appear, such engraved portraits form an important part of the book's paratextuality. They militate in favour of an efficient linkage between image and verbal discourse and, in this capacity, constitute a privileged site for the appearance of written culture. Nevertheless, the examples we have adduced thus far are not in any way cut off from the most common forms of visual culture, even less so from the art of portraiture within which engraved or sketched portraits enjoy an obvious legitimacy. In such instances, it is clear that painted pictures are not as far away from the universe of words as we are wont to believe. Here, we see much fluidity in the ways in which they function within the coherent system of reigning cultural values, of which they are of course an integral part. Several different conceptions of images emerge here, all of which suggest the need to read the painted portrait using methods that are deliberately open in their approach.

The four human effigies that we are about to produce in support of our claims are themselves various exemplifications of the ways in which the image as such relates to the almighty realm of religious thinking. Far from representing what Jean-Luc Nancy once called the "absolute portrait," each of our images can be seen to function like a veritable "staging" of what it meant at the time to translate a human being into the language of figures; such a language can be seen at work in the images provided of a preacher, a sinner, a saint, and a martyr. Being presented in succession, one after the other, the images allow for a demonstration of how the very status of the portrait can undergo certain variations, starting with what we might call the image of circumstance and moving towards the idealized image that bathes in a universal message. It is not merely the human face, all on its own, that counts, but more particularly the body in its entirety as it is implicated in a meaning process going well beyond the simple affirmation of a person's identity. Richly accompanied by texts and their words, these portraits are the works of painters who exercised their art in the specific ideological context that was that of Spain, a country that saw itself at the forefront of the triumphant Counter Reformation.

## The Preacher: El Greco's Hortensio Felix Paravicino (1609)

Part of the permanent collection housed in the Museum of Fine Arts of Boston, Massachusetts, the painting *Hortensio Felix Paravino* belongs to the last period in the career of the painter Domenikos Theotocopoulos, more commonly known as El Greco (Spanish for "the Greek"). This painting represents a preacher of Italian origin by the name of Hortensio Felix Paravicino, a man who enjoyed the favours of the court in Madrid and, for reasons of his personal charms and talents, went by the nickname "Pico de Oro" ("The Mouth of Gold").[20] In 1609, at the age of thirty, this young Trinitarian travelled all the way to Toledo in order to meet the old master of his religious order. No more information concerning the actual painting of this work is available than that concerning the subject himself, but we can surmise that the painting is much more a token of the friendship that existed between the monk and the painter than it is the result of any commission that a painter such as El Greco would normally receive to paint a portrait.[21]

The artist captured his model with his face turned toward the painter as he sits in a large armchair: all this is in conformity with the traditional ways of painting the portrait of a clergyman. Despite these traditional elements, the artist's decision to paint his subject according to a cruciform configuration gives the work an original flavour. The entire composition is structured by a number of inner tensions between geometrically straight lines and curves, between certain dark zones and

29. EL GRECO (DOMENIKOS THEOTOKOPOULOS), *Fray Hortensio Felix
Paravicino*, 1609, OIL ON CANVAS, BOSTON, MUSEUM OF FINE ARTS,
112.1 X 86.1 CM (PHOTOGRAPH © 2010, MUSEUM OF FINE ARTS, BOSTON).
(SEE ALSO P. 245 FOR COLOUR REPRODUCTION.)

other bright ones. On the one hand, we can speak of a relative instability in the way the subject is placed on the canvas (for example, there is a surprising diagonal line suggested by the back of the armchair); on the other, we witness the living presence of a figure who exposes himself to the beholder's view without any visible restraint. His head is turned ever so slightly to the left, a posture that highlights the salient features of his face, those that are brought to the fore by the harmonious spirals belonging to the hood worn by the painted subject. Turned in the direction of the viewer, the monk's gaze expresses the obvious strengths of his inner character. While grazing the chair's armrest, the fingers of his right hand might be the sign of a hidden feeling of impatience.

As if pulsating with life due to its many folds, the monk's habit is visually organized around the two-coloured cross, placed in the geometric centre of the composition. This is the cross worn by members of the Order of Trinitarians, and it occupies a highly significant space within the composition overall. We further notice two books, one a large in-folio, the other being of a much smaller format, both of them leaning against the left armrest of the chair. It is as if the artist had asked the monk to interrupt his reading (he was no doubt busy reading a religious work, maybe even a meditative text, as we might very well imagine). The monk responds to the artist's request by placing one of the fingers of his left hand at the spot in the small book where he had broken off his study. This gesture succeeds very well in suggesting a point in time immediately preceding the moment portrayed by the painter, just as it implicitly suggests the role to be played by the moment immediately following it. In addition, such a familiar gesture imparts a certain anecdotal quality to the composition; it highlights the spirit of complicity that appears to exist between the painter and his model.

When placed in the context of a highly uniform scale of colours, three exceptional zones of crimson red create a visible relationship among three symbolic elements present in the composition: first, there is the Trinitarian cross placed in the centre of the monk's habit; second, we see another cross partially represented on the arm whose hand is holding the book; and third we notice the preacher's mouth. Such a chromatic network is undoubtedly meant to be an integral part both of the subject's identity and of his normal activities as a Trinitarian,[22] not only his religious ones but also his intellectual and militant ones as well. This network further suggests that we should look for meaningful relationship between the words being read and the words to be said for the moral edification of the religious faithful with whom the monk is likely to deal.

Hortensio Felix Paravicino both wrote and delivered a large number of learned sermons; he also published many religiously inspired poems. As a form of homage intended for the artist who painted his portrait, Paravicino also composed a sonnet, for placement on this same canvas, whose title was, not insignificantly, *Al mismo Greco en un retrato que hizo del autor*, "for the same El Greco to be part of a portrait he painted of the author." In his poem, the monk speaks both about the actual painting of the portrait in which he is being represented and about the great admiration he feels for the artist's work. The fraternity between painting and poetry to which we earlier alluded could not possibly find a more pleasing legitimization than in the story of this extraordinary painting.

## The Sinner: *Don Miguel de Mañara Reading the Rule of the Holy Charity* by Juan de Valdés Leal (1681)

In 1681, the Sevillian painter Juan de Valdés Leal was charged with the mission of painting the portrait of the recently deceased Miguel de Mañara, the founder of the Hospital of Holy Charity in Seville.[23] It is not entirely meaningless to recall some of the facts relating to the life of this Sevillian nobleman. In his youth, De Mañara had led such a dissolute life that it was said that he may have been the real-life model for Tirso de Molina's *Don Juan*. However, the experience of his young wife's death during the plague epidemic of 1649 led to his radical conversion. From then on, Miguel de Mañara would dedicate his life to works of devotion: he logically became the zealous administrator of Seville's famous Hospital de la Caridad. Dressed in the gown of the Order of Calatrava, the

30. JUAN DE VALDÉS LEAL, *Don Miguel de Mañara Reading the Rule of the Holy Charity*, 1681, OIL ON CANVAS, SEVILLE, HOSPITAL DE LA CARIDAD, CHAPTER HOUSE, 196 X 225 CM. (SEE ALSO P. 246 FOR COLOUR REPRODUCTION.)

model of Juan de Valdes' portrait is sitting in a bench as he reads a book placed on the nearby lectern, a rule that he conceived for the Brothers of Charity. On a table covered by a rich velvet cloth decorated with ornate embroidery, we see a wooden cross that has been "planted" in a burning heart, the emblem of the Brotherhood. We also notice two urns that are used for holding the ballots cast by the members of the chapter, in addition to several books, amongst which we distinguish an ascetic treatise written by de Mañara himself, *Discorso de la verdad* ("The Discourse of Truth"), a work that deals with the necessity of penance.[24]

The founder of the Order is reading his text out loud for the benefit of his monks. In a grandiose gesture, he points in the direction of an allegorical painting hanging on the wall, which we can see on his right. The lower portion of this second composition shows a landscape with a rainbow; it also depicts a column of smoke rising towards the clouds, which are those of a heavenly Jerusalem. This image connoting the passage leading from our earthly existence towards eternal life is a symbol of the path of salvation accessible, according to Mañara, to all those who practice charity.[25] In the shadows forming the background of the main painting, placed on a luxurious desk, the careful viewer can distinguish several of the objects traditionally belonging to the *Vanitas* genre: books, a skull, a sand clock, a tulip placed in a crystal vase. In front of this desk, in full light, we see a child holding an open book on his knees: he addresses the viewer directly, indicating the need to remain silent.

The various portraits painted by Valdés Leal of Miguel de Mañara are very far indeed from representing an exercise in personal vanity because, quite to the contrary, they are an integral part of an overarching enterprise of exemplary humility. Due to the proliferation of representative details, the painting *Don Miguel de Mañara reading the Rule of the Holy Charity* points out all the clichés of the time concerning a system of cultural symbolism very much geared to moral edification. This clear goal on the didactic front turns the painting into a sort of visual sermon at the same time as it preaches in favour of penance, a life of asceticism, and the theological virtue of charity. The composition also aims to glorify books and writing. Thus the implicit discourse of the painting is that contained within the books represented therein: this is not only the discourse of the texts seen within an image but also that of an image as suggested by the text being read out loud.[26] The many books seen in this painting, both the open ones and the closed ones, are representative of an enterprise that seeks to make texts both visible and audible. This commemorative representation of Miguel de Mañara is constructed in the intersecting space that combines writing with spoken words: it is in this manner that it seeks to establish the best model possible for an idealized figure of the repenting sinner.

## THE SAINT: *SAINT TERESA WRITING WITH THE INSPIRATION OF THE HOLY SPIRIT* BY JOSÉ DE RIBERA (1644)

Living in Naples, the Spanish painter José de Ribera, painted a portrait of Saint Teresa of Avila, which he dated and signed in the year 1644.[27] While there are several slightly different versions of this same composition, in this work Ribera complies with an iconographic tradition that was particularly widespread at his time. He treats the theme of inspiration from the Holy Spirit with remarkable sobriety. Teresa is clearly visible against a dark background, uniform in colour; several essential elements of the composition are placed under an intense light: the dove, a pen and its ink jar, written pages, and a skull placed on top of a book (which makes for a traditional *memento mori*). In addition, our saint is represented without a halo, just as she has a face that is not in the least idealized. Given her energetic look, she possesses all the well-known characteristics of canonical portraits of Saint Teresa, traits that come from a life-like effigy painted in 1560 in the living presence of the model – almost despite the model's better wishes – by a certain Fray Juan de la Misería from Seville.[28]

The viewer's eye is struck by the geometric simplicity of the composition: first there is a triangle whose angles organize our understanding of the work; then there are two circular figures formed by two human heads as well as a series of parallel lines that form the basis of a particularly efficient symbolic network. The diagonal axis of the painting places three fundamental elements in a line of perfect continuity: the image of the Holy Spirit, the attentive gaze of the saint, and her quill, which refers to a process of writing still underway. The colour of the dove's wings is repeated in the white mantel worn by the Carmelite nun while the head of the saint seems to be repeated in the representation of a skull, all of which suggest the fugacity of our lives on earth. As Louis Marin once pointed out, behind every portrait there lurks the implicit image of a skull projecting an aura of death upon the painted model.[29] Finally, this painting shows a sheaf of paper, presumably texts that transcribe

31. JOSÉ DE RIBERA, *Teresa Writing with the Inspiration of the Holy Spirit*, 1644, OIL ON CANVAS, VALENCIA, MUSEO DE BELLAS ARTES DE VALENCIA, 129.5 X 104.4 CM.

the word of God, along with a printed book that serves as a source of inspiration for the saintly figure's meditations.

In this work, Ribera succeeds both in refining a particular representational type – with all its immediately legible codes – and in injecting deeper meanings into it. The rigour with which he composed the painting, along with the limited range of colours he uses, contributes to an overall impression of intensity within the painted scene. Everything reinforces the painting's value as a religious work of art.

Teresa was an extremely popular saint in Spain. Here she is presented to the religious faithful in her role as mediator between heaven and earth. But, more importantly, she is portrayed as a woman who writes. Her principal works, an autobiographical *Life of Teresa of Jesus* along with several mystical texts such as *The Way of Perfection* and the *Interior Castle,* enjoyed exceptionally wide circulation. Ribera's image of the saint thus appears to be inextricable from the representation of the book, which figures so prominently in the composition, and which further presides over a considerable number of its suggested meanings. The saint's inspired writing thus functions as an iconographic paradigm, one which commits the painter to depicting a scene that is both miraculous and profoundly human. It is not difficult to sense an active element of inter-iconicity in this painting, which calls upon many other canonical images of the time such as those depicting Saint Matthew the Evangelist who, like Teresa, wrote his Gospel while listening to the words dictated to him by an angel.

The painted scene has yet another direct textual source: Teresa's own written testimonies that were included in her autobiography. Our Saint vividly tells the story about a time when, as she remained intensely bent over her writing table, she was one day awakened by the fluttering sound of a dove's wings, directly above her head.[30] The divine vision celebrated in Ribera's painting of Saint Teresa is thus a scene that directly concerns the act of writing.

# The Martyr: *Saint Serapion* by Francisco de Zurbarán (1628)

Francisco de Zurbarán's work leads us to the very limits of what the portrait genre is able to accomplish. Painted in 1628 for the Convent of Mercy in Seville, the portrait he painted of Saint Serapion originally hung in the chamber known as *De profundis*, a room in which the corpses of deceased monks were exposed before burial.[31] Members of the Order of Mercedaries were specialists in the practice of paying ransom for the release of captives in danger of loosing their faith. For such missions, monks in the Order were required, if necessary, to sacrifice their own lives. This risk is vividly recalled by Zurbarán's painting, which represents the heroic death of Saint Serapion, one of the major figures in the rich martyrology preached by the Mercedaries. Serapion lived in the twelfth century: this imaginary portrait of an historically real model seeks to reveal a deep truth concerning the physical nature of a human body. With his hands attached by ropes, the monk is represented at the very moment of his death: his heavy head has fallen to one side, his face is swollen, and his mouth is slightly ajar. In all this, it is obvious that Zurbarán has no intention of insisting upon the horrors of martyrdom: not a single drop of blood is shown and all we see, in terms of a reminder of physical torture, is the expression of resigned exaltation belonging to a saintly Christian at the moment of his death.

The life story of this exemplary Mercedary was widely known in Spain due to a multiplicity of hagiographic narratives that were recounted throughout the land, popularized as they were by preachers. Three slightly variant versions of his story were diffused, which attributed the torturous acts either to Muslims from North Africa or to pirates coming from Marseilles. They were also at times said to be the work of heretics having arrived in Spain from faraway Scotland. In all of the extant versions of his story, Serapion invariably met with an extremely cruel death through disembowelment and a slit throat. For his painting, Zurbarán refuses to illustrate such anecdotes in order to give a sublime version of the saint's death. He does this by focusing on the martyr at close range

32. FRANCISCO DE ZURBARÁN, *Saint Serapion*, 1628, OIL ON CANVAS,
HARTFORD (CONNECTICUT), WADSWORTH ATHENEUM MUSEUM OF ART,
120 X 103 CM (THE ELLA GALLUP SUMNER AND MARY CATLIN SUMNER
COLLECTION FUND). (SEE ALSO P. 246 FOR COLOUR REPRODUCTION.)

and by the use of bright light. He takes particular care in painting the monk's habit: he limits himself to an almost abstract rendering of the fabrics of which it was composed; he stresses the flowing ups and downs of the garment with ample and solemn folds. The off-white colour of the garment is relayed by another dosage of a bright colour, that belonging to the Order's insignia, placed in the exact centre of the composition.[32] Let us recall for a moment that this painting is best interpreted in the context of the use to which it was officially dedicated, its role consisting in accompanying the funeral rites for fallen members of the convent. The painting thus presided over the prayers said over the body of the newly deceased, and it was during these funeral rites that texts were read out loud in special circumstances. The painting was also part of the moments of silence that followed any such readings, a time during which members of convent began to meditate upon the words they had just heard.

One important detail captures our attention: an unfolded, rectangular piece of white paper – with a tone of white different from the white of the Order's insignia – appears to be pinned to the canvas on the right side of the composition. This paper bears an inscription of the martyr's name: the letter "B" (for "Beatus," that is to say "Holy") is followed by his name *Serapio*. Barely legible, and placed just below this inscription, we can decipher the painter's signature, *Francisco de Zurbarán fecit*, along with the date of the composition, 1628. A similarly elaborate *mise-en-scène* used for placing a signature was often the practice of painters of the period[33]; by referring iconically in his painting to the Mercedaries' insignia, Zurbarán no doubt wished to comment upon the relationship between the artist and the patron who commissioned his work.

Zurbarán's brilliantly illusionary techniques invite the viewer to "detach" the piece of paper from the rest of the painting's represented objects. Appearing to have been superimposed upon the canvas, the paper gains an element of authority due to its outstanding position. At the same time, it reminds the reader that a martyr's portrait is still an image, still a painted work of art. Through this use of *trompe-l'oeil*, the painted subject's identity is associated with that of the painter himself, the deceivingly banal piece of paper thus becoming an astonishingly effective piece of metonymy. Once again, the conjunction of word and image is seen to be an integral part of the mission bestowed upon a religious work of art, the task of giving access to visibility by means of the sense of touch.

The four painted figures we have just seen were all captured in the midst of special circumstances, a context that allows the viewer to identify them. With the exception of the preacher, these images do not look back at us ["ne nous regardent pas"][34] but rather they exalt a given individual in order to transmit a much more universal message. Expressing either simple humility, the hidden presence of the divine, or even the resigned acceptance of our final hour, these images take part in the important functions of commemoration, edification and meditation. These "portraits" also make use of the implicit meanings of texts, meanings that precede the actual act of painting the image and which the image is destined to project. At the same time, these implicit meanings give legitimacy to the creative artist's work and create a setting that enables the painted work to make these meanings even more profound than they once were.

* * *

It is time to propose a few concluding remarks to this cursory examination of the Spanish portrait. Our survey has unfortunately taken on the appearance of an anthology. It is not easy to delineate all the major thrusts impelled by the strategies employed by portraitists: the observations we have just made often resemble variations on the same musical theme. The modalities of portraiture uncovered here are an integral part of what we might call the *complex legibility of the visible*, that is to say, they participate in our processes for apprehending images within a figurative network or, said in yet another way, they belong to a rich culture of interconnected signifying practices.

The progressive dilution of the academic principle known as *ut pictura poesis*, an aesthetic principle that encouraged emulation amongst the arts, has much to say, not only about the limits of what aesthetic codes can accomplish, but also about their vanity as part of a vanishing epiphenomenon. Gravitating around an individual figure, the ambiguity of the creative gesture is thus put into play. As an artist working with words, the case of a poet seen looking at the painter/engraver attempting to capture his identity is well worth a more thorough exploration. In the same way, one should be willing to delve more deeply into those numerous portraits that bring religious texts into their scope, texts that then reorganize the devotional image in such a way as to enable the all-important enterprise of making the faithful believe.

Words appearing inside the frame of a portrait (or even all around it) are inscribed into these relationships, both unstable and precarious ones that punctuate the entire history of the linkages forged between letter and image. Referring to the historian Marc Fumaroli, Michel Deguy once remarked that the real question is not one that requests *either* the word *or* the image: the real issues lie upstream of both words and images in a zone where, more or less in harmony, principles of energy and visual knowledge have borne both images and words together for such a very long time.[35]

## BIBLIOGRAPHY

Baticle, Jeannine, ed. *Zurbarán*. Paris: Réunion des Musées Nationaux, 1988.

Brown, Jonathan. *Images and Ideas in Seventeenth-Century Spanish Painting*. Princeton, NJ: Princeton University Press, 1979.

Butor, Michel. *Les Mots dans la peinture*. Paris: Flammarion, collection "Champs," 1969.

Caturla, María Luisa. *Francisco de Zurbarán*, ed. Odile Delenda. Paris: Wildenstein Institute, 1994.

Cerdan, Francis, ed. *Honras fúnebres y fama póstuma de Fray Hortensio Paravicino*. Toulouse: Hélios, 1994.

Chastel, André. *Mythe et crise de la Renaissance*. Geneva: Skira, 1989 (1st ed. 1969).

Civil, Pierre. "De l'image au texte: portrait de l'auteur dans le livre espagnol des XVIᵉ et XVIIᵉ siècles." In *Le livre et l'édition dans le monde hispanique, XVIᵉ–*

*XXᵉ siècles. Pratiques et discours paratextuels*, ed. Michel Moner and Michel Lafon, 45–62. Grenoble: Université Stendhal Grenoble III, 1992.

———. "Des mots dans la peinture espagnole du Siècle d'Or." In *Frontières éclatées. Peinture et écriture 3*, ed. Montserrat Prudon, 222–36. Paris: La Différence/Editions Unesco, 2000.

Damisch, Hubert. "La peinture prise au mot." In *Les Mots et les images*, by Meyer Shapiro, trans. Pierre Alferi, 5–27. Paris: Macula, 2000.

Deguy, Michel. "De l'image." In *La Pensée de l'image. Signification et figuration dans le texte et dans la peinture*, ed. Gisèle Mathieu-Castellani, 249–64. Paris: Presses Universitaires de Vincennes, 1994.

Fraenkel, Béatrice. *La Signature. Genèse d'un signe*. Paris: Gallimard, 1994.

Guinard, Paul. *Zurbarán et les peintres espagnols de la vie monastique*, Paris: Éditions du Temps, 1984 (1st ed. 1960).

Guttiérez Rueda, Laura. "Ensayo de iconografía teresiana." *Revista de espiritualidad* XXIII, no. 90 (1964): 5–168.

Hegel, G.W.F. *On the Arts: Selections from G.W.F. Hegel's Aesthetics, Or the Philosophy of Fine Art*, edited and trans. Henry Paolucci. Smyrna, DE: The Bagehot Council / Griffon House, 2001.

Holanda, Francisco de (Francisco d'Olanda). *Do Tirar Polo Natural* [1549], ed. José da Felicidade Alves, Lisbon, 1984 [in Spanish Francisco de Holanda, *Del sacar por el natural, De la pintura antigua, versión castellana de Manuel Denis* (1563), ed. Elías Tormo. Madrid, 1921].

John of the Cross (Saint). "L'iconographie de Thérèse de Jésus Docteur de l'Église." *Ephemerides carmeliticae, Sancta Teresia a Iesu Doctor Ecclesiae* XXI, no. 1–2 (1970): 219–60.

Lee, Rensselaer W. *Ut pictura poesis. The Humanist Theory of Painting*. New York: Norton, 1967 (1st ed. 1940).

Lope de Vega. *Laurel de Apolo con otras rimas*. Madrid: Juan González, 1630.

Marías, Fernando. *Greco, biographie d'un peintre extravagant*. Paris: Adam Biro, 1997.

Marin, Louis. "Masque et portrait: sur la signification d'une image et son illustration au XVIIᵉ siècle." In *Image et signification: Rencontres de l'École du Louvre*, 163–79. Paris: La Documentation française, 1983.

———. *Portrait of the King*, trans. Martha Houle. Minneapolis: University of Minnesota Press, collection "Theory and History of Literature," 1988.

———. *Des pouvoirs de l'image. Gloses*. Paris: Seuil, 1993.

Matilla, José Manuel. *La estampa en el libro barroco, Juan de Courbes*. Vitoria: EPHIALTE and Madrid: Real Academia de Bellas Artes de San Fernando, 1991.

Mexia, Pedro. *Silva de varia lección* [1570], ed. Antonio Castro. Madrid: Catedra, 1989.

Nancy, Jean-Luc. *Regard du portrait*. Paris: Galilée, 2000 (an excerpt of which is translated as "The Look of the Portrait". In *Multiple Arts: The Muses II*, by Jean-Luc Nancy, 220–47. Stanford, CA: Stanford University Press, 2006).

Pacheco, Francisco. *Libro de descripción de verdaderos retratos de ilustres y memorables varones*, ed. Pedro M. Piñero and Rogelio Reyes. Seville: Diputación Provincial de Sevilla, 1985.

Paravicino, Hortensio Felix. *Oraciones evangélicas y panegíricos funerales que a diversos intentos dixo el Rvmo. P. M. Fr. Hortensio Felix Paravicino*, ed. Cristóbal Núñez Osst. Madrid: María de Quiñones, 1641.

Pellicer de Salas y Tovar, José. *Lecciones solemnes a las obras de Don Luis de Góngora*. Madrid: Imprenta del Reino, 1630.

Portus, Javier. *The Spanish Portrait from El Greco to Picasso*. Madrid: Scala, 2004.

Schaub, Jean-Frédéric. *La France espagnole. Les Racines hispaniques de l'absolutisme français*. Paris: Seuil, 2003.

Serrera, Juan Miguel. "Alonso Sánchez Coello y la mecánica del retrato de corte." In *Alonso Sánchez Coello y el retrato en la corte de Felipe II*, 38–63. Madrid: Museo del Prado, 1990.

Shapiro, Meyer. *Words, Script and Pictures. Semiotics of Visual Language*. New York: George Braziller, 1996.

Spinosa, Nicola. *L'opera completa di Jusepe de Ribera*. Naples: Electa, 2006 (1st ed. 1978).

Teresa (Saint Teresa of Avila). *The Life of Teresa of Jesus: The Autobiography of Teresa of Avila*, trans. E. Allison Peers. New York: Doubleday, 1991.

———. *The Way of Perfection*, trans. E. Allison Peers. New York: Doubleday, 1991.

———. *Interior Castle*, trans. E. Allison Peers. New York: Doubleday, 1972.

Valdivieso, Enrique. *Juan de Valdes Leal*. Seville: Ediciones Guadalquivir, 1988.

———, ed. *Valdes Leal*. Madrid: Ministerio de Cultura / Seville: Junta de Andalucía, 1991.

Wethey, Harold Edwin. *El Greco and his School*, vol. II. Princeton, NJ: Princeton University Press, 1962.

# NOTES

1 André Chastel, *Mythe et crise de la Renaissance* [1969] (Geneva: Skira, 1989), 132.

2 Despite all these claims, portraiture was nevertheless seen as a minor genre. For this view to change, it would be necessary to wait until Hegel's *Lessons on Aesthetics*, which saw the portrait as representing the true and final development of painting. See on the this point G.W.F. Hegel, *On the Arts: Selections from G.W.F. Hegel's Aesthetics, Or the Philosophy of Fine Art*, ed. and trans. Henry Paolucci (Smyrna, DE: The Bagehot Council / Griffon House, 2001). For an overview of the history of portraiture, one of the best studies remains Édouard Pommier, *Théories du portrait de la Renaissance aux Lumières* (Paris: Gallimard, 1998).

3 Two prominent examples, amongst others, are Louis Marin, *Portrait of the King* (Minneapolis: University of Minnesota Press, 1988, collection "Theory and History of Literature") and Jean-Luc Nancy, *Regard du portrait* (Paris: Galilée, 2000), an excerpt of which is translated as "The Look of the Portrait," in Jean-Luc Nancy, *Multiple Arts: The Muses II* (Stanford, CA: Stanford University Press, 2006), 220–47.

4 The theoretical debates which raged in the Italo-Spanish context of the sixteenth and seventeenth centuries concerned the necessity for portraits to maintain the principles of mimesis, while at the same time advocating the idealization of the painted subject. The problems I propose to develop in this essay are thus those studied by cultural historians. It is from the point of view of an historian that I approach the relationship between texts and images, as they were developed in the art of the portrait that flourished in Spain during the seventeenth century. The practices I uncover here should be viewed not as mere examples but rather as instruments for comparison. We need to remember that, although by the seventeenth century a long historical process of political decline had already begun, Spain was still considered a major cultural model for the rest of Europe. France was particularly sensitive to Spain's literary works, to its religious thinking, and to the artistic productions of the Golden Age. See on this topic Jean-Frédéric Schaub, *La France espagnole. Les Racines hispaniques de l'absolutisme français* (Paris: Seuil, 2003).

5 In Portuguese, Francisco de Holanda (Francisco d'Olanda), *Do Tirar Polo Natural* [1549], ed. José da Felicidade Alves (Lisbon, 1984); in Spanish, Francisco de Holanda, *Del sacar por el natural, De la pintura antigua, versión castellana de Manuel Denis* [1563], ed. Elías Tormo (Madrid, 1921).

6 See Juan Miguel Serrera, "Alonso Sánchez Coello y la mecánica del retrato de corte," in *Alonso Sánchez Coello y el retrato en la corte de Felipe II* (Madrid: Museo del Prado, 1990), 38–63.

7 See on this point Pierre Civil, "De l'image au texte: portrait de l'auteur dans le livre espagnol des XVI^e et XVII^e siècles," *Le Livre et l'édition dans le monde hispanique, XVI^e-XX^e siècles. Pratiques et discours paratextuels*, eds. Michel Moner and Michel Lafon (Grenoble: Université Stendhal Grenoble III, 1992), 45–62.

8 For an excellent discussion of this painterly device, see Michel Butor, *Les mots dans la peinture* (Paris: Flammarion, 1969, collection "Champs"). For this topic, Meyer Shapiro's classical study is indispensable (Meyer Shapiro, *Words, Script and Pictures.*

*Semiotics of Visual Language* [New York: George Braziller, 1996]), including the insightful introduction written by Hubert Damisch to the French translation of this book (Hubert Damisch, "La peinture prise au mot," Meyer Shapiro, *Les Mots et les images*, trans. Pierre Alferi, [Paris: Macula, 2000], 5–27). I have published a study on this topic as it related to Spanish painting in "Des mots dans la peinture espagnole du Siècle d'Or," *Frontières éclatées. Peinture et écriture 3*, ed. Montserrat Prudon (Paris: La Différence/Editions Unesco, 2000), 222–36.

9    Barthélemy Aneau, *Imagination poétique (traduicte en vers François des Latins & Grecs, par l'auteur mesme d'iceux)* (Lyons: Macé Bonhomme, 1552), 6.

10   "You shall see how great Mexia was in his inner spirit, and here is how he appeared outwardly with his body." A similar device is present in a contemporary edition of Pierre de Ronsard's poetry. Here the poet is represented by a bust accompanied by the following quatrain:

"Tel fut Ronsard, autheur de cet ouvrage,

Tel fut son œil, sa bouche et son visage,

Portrait au vif de deux crayons divers:

Ici le corps et l'esprit en ses vers."

[Thus appeared Ronsard, the author of this work,

Thus appeared his eye, his mouth and his face,

A portrait painted as if from his living flesh using two different pencils:

Find here, in these verses, not only his body but also his mind].

11   Another issue at the heart of portraiture is the question of who can be the legitimate subject of an artistic portrait. Further, given that today we do no often know who these people were who sat before a portraitist, the collections of modern-day museums are filled with multiple portraits of unknown individuals.

12   Lope de Vega, *Laurel de Apolo con otras rimas* (Madrid: Juan González, 1630).

13   "Lope's sacred poetry is born of the Muses; while the latter may one day disappear, the former on the contrary will never die."

14   Concerning the work of this engraver, the reader should consult José Manuel Matilla, *La estampa en el libro barroco, Juan de Courbes* (Vitoria-Gasteiz and Madrid: Instituto de Estudios Iconográficos Ephialte / Real Academia de Bellas Artes de San Fernando, 1991).

15   José Pellicer de Salas y Tovar, *Lecciones solemnes a las obras de Don Luis de Góngora* (Madrid: Imprenta del Reino, 1630).

16   Velazquez (Diego Rodríguez de Silva y Velázquez), *Portrait of Luis de Góngora y Argote*, 1622, oil on canvas, Boston, Museum of Fine Arts, 50.2 x 40.6 cm.

17   "Of me there is no longer a copy than the one provided by my pen."

18   The best overview of this particular aspect is of course provided by Rensselaer W. Lee's classical study, *Ut pictura poesis. The Humanist Theory of Painting* [1940] (New York: Norton, 1967).

19   "He was corporally quite small but well proportioned; his large head, well shaped, was adorned by an abundance of curly hair; his forehead was broad, and his face more round than it was narrow; his skin was light in colour, his eyes particularly vivacious" (Francisco Pacheco, *Libro de descripción de verdaderos retratos de ilustres y memorables varones*, ed. Pedro M. Piñero and Rogelio Reyes [Seville: Diputación Provincial de Sevilla, 1985], 69).

20 Hortensio Felix Paravicino y Arteaga was also the author of *Oraciones evangélicas* ["Evangelical Prayers"], first written in 1635, which enjoyed a strong readership. On both this historical figure and his work, the reader can usefully consult Francis Cerdan, *Honras fúnebres y fama póstuma de Fray Hortensio Paravicino* (Toulouse: Ed. Hélios, 1994).

21 Information concerning this painting can be gleaned from Harold Wethey, *El Greco and his School*, vol. II (Princeton: Princeton University Press, 1962), illustration 153, and Fernando Marías, *Greco, biographie d'un peintre extravagant* (Paris: Adam Biro, 1997), 258–59.

22 For further information on this point, see Javier Portus, *The Spanish Portrait from El Greco to Picasso* (Madrid: Scala, 2004), 337.

23 About this admirable painting, still hanging in the chapter house of the hospital, see Enrique Valdivieso, *Juan de Valdes Leal* (Seville: Ediciones Guadalquivir, 1988), 196–97, and Valdivieso (ed.), *Valdes Leal* (Catalogue of an Exhibit at the Prado Museum, Madrid: Ministerio de Cultura, Seville: Junta de Andalucía, 1991), 250–51.

24 The spirit that presided over the composition of this text is directly related to de Mañara's decision to commission two other paintings from Valdés Leal, one entitled the *Hieroglyphics of Time*, the other, the *Hieroglyphics of Death*, both of which still hang on the walls of the Church which are part of the Hospital compound. For more details on these works, see Jonathan Brown, *Images and Ideas in Seventeenth Century Spanish Painting* (Princeton: Princeton University Press, 1979). For the decorations of the Hospital's church, Mañara also enlisted the help of Bartolomé Esteban Murillo.

25 In the preamble found at the beginning of the Brotherhood's Rule, Mañara refers to this visual device with the name of the *Monte de Dios*, the mountain of God.

26 We should mention, in addition, that the date of Valdes Leal's painting is inscribed on the bench where the child is seated. More importantly, one needs to decipher the crumpled piece of paper lying on the floor to the right: upon it are inscribed both the identity of the portrait's model and the titles of the books written by the latter.

27 On this particular painting, the reader should consult Nicola Spinosa, *L'opera completa di Jusepe de Ribera* [1978] (Naples: Electa, 2006), 136.

28 Laura Gutiérrez Rueda gives an informative overview of the rich iconography of Saint Teresa of Avila. See in particular her "Ensayo de iconografía teresiana," *Revista de espiritualidad* XXIII, 90 (1964): 5–168. A traditional source of information on this saint is of course Saint John of the Cross, "L'Iconographie de Thérèse de Jésus Docteur de l'Église," *Ephemerides carmeliticae, Sancta Teresia a Iesu Doctor Ecclesiae* XXI, 1–2 (1970): 219–60.

29 Louis Marin, "Masque et portrait: sur la signification d'une image et son illustration au XVIIe siècle," *Image et signification: Rencontres de l'École du Louvre* (Paris: La Documentation Française, 1983), 163–79.

30 In Spanish, this episode can be found in Teresa de Jesús, *Libro de la vida*, in *Obras completas*, eds. Efren de la Madre de Dios and Otger Steggink (Madrid: Biblioteca de Autores Cristianos, 1986, chapter 38–100), 209.

31 On this particular painting, see Jeannine Baticle, ed., *Zurbarán* (Catalogue of the exhibited organized at the Grand Palais in Paris, Paris: Réunion des Musées Nationaux, 1988), 124; Paul Guinard, *Zurbarán et les peintres espagnols de la vie monastique*

[1960] (Paris: Éditions du Temps, 1984), 94–95; and María Luisa Caturla, *Francisco de Zurbarán*, ed. Odile Delenda (Paris: Wildenstein Institute, 1994), 55.

32   It is impossible at this point to resist the temptation of quoting the following words about Saint Matthew's Gospel on the Transfiguration as written by Louis Marin: "[S]eeing the figure of Light, the blinding whiteness of the Image, has something to do with death itself, with the experience of 'tasting' its sweetness. It is as if this extreme image, this ultimate image, that of an absolutely white figure, could do no more, and no less, than to anticipate the taste of an exquisite death" (Louis Marin, *Des pouvoirs de l'image* [Paris: Seuil, 1993], 239). The

contemporary poet Michel Deguy is also enchanted by this same passage. See the latter's "De l'image," ed. Gisèle Mathieu-Castellani (Paris: Presses Universitaires de Vincennes, 1994), 258.

33   See on this point Béatrice Fraenkel, *La Signature. Genèse d'un signe* (Paris: Gallimard, 1994), 168–74.

34   Translator's note: in an oblique reference to Jean-Luc Nancy's essay entitled the *Regard du portrait*, Pierre Civil plays with the double meaning of the French verb "regarder." The words "ne nous regardent pas" can either mean "do not look back at us" or "do not concern us."

35   See Deguy, "De l'image," 249.

# 6

# THE INVENTION OF PREHISTORIC ROCK ART: A VISUAL EXPERIENCE[1]

*Béatrice Fraenkel*

In July 1906, the Anthropological Society of Paris published an article written by one of its most eminent members, Félix Regnault.[2] In this publication, Regnault announced the discovery of human hand-prints painted on the wall of the cave at Gargas, France. Although this cave had already been known for several decades, both by geologists and by prehistorians, it was now about to become, from this moment forward, a star-cave. What earned the Gargas cave such notoriety was, first and foremost, the extraordinary number of negative hand-prints that it contained, that is to say, nearly two hundred of them, a number since confirmed by various efforts to catalogue them. In addition, the hands in question appear in groups and are organized along long panels whereas, in other caves – for example Altamira, Castillo, or Tibiran – the hands one sees are almost always associated with other figures. The Gargas hands also possess another quality, one that is both essential and singular: silhouettes of hands are incomplete in that their fingers lack joints.

All of these factors combine to make Gargas the sole cave of human prehistory to be dedicated primarily to the production of negative images of hands. But they also present us with a number of enigmas, the first of which is the question of how to read these hands. Were these silhouettes made from perfectly normal hands whose fingers were simply

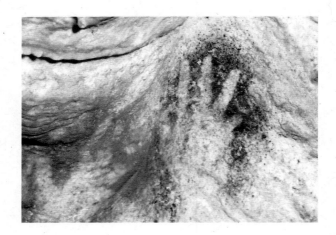

33. PANEL OF NEGATIVE HANDS IN THE GARGAS CAVE, PHOTOGRAPH BY BÉA-
TRICE FRAENKEL.

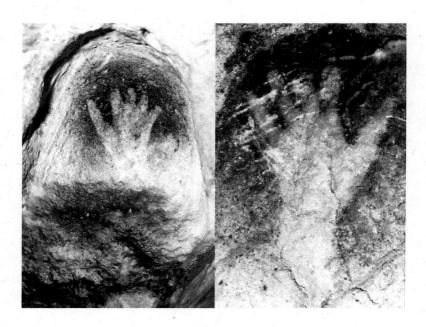

34. INCOMPLETE NEGATIVE HANDS IN THE GARGAS CAVE, PHOTOGRAPHS BY
BÉATRICE FRAENKEL.

bent inwards, or were they rather sick hands whose finger-joints had broken off? Or were these silhouettes perhaps made from healthy hands whose fingers had been purposely cut? Controversies surrounding these visible hands have never ceased to rage: the debate has been simplified somewhat by the appearance of two contradictory hypotheses, which give voice to two separate schools of interpretation. Ever since a study first published in 1967 by André Leroi-Gourhan,[3] it would seem that the majority of prehistorians follow their master in considering that the Gargas hand-prints were made by hands with folded fingers, while other scholars favour a different hypothesis, one postulating sick hands with mutilated fingers. We are faced here with a typical problem of interpretation since, according to whether one opts for the hypothesis concerning the model-hand as being sick and/or deformed or whether one postulates a healthy or normal hand, the meanings one attributes to the Gargas paintings entail opposing conjectures. For the one case, we witness prophylactic readings; for the other, cynegetic ones.[4] Many hypotheses, founded on diverging interpretations of what could well be named a symptom (missing joints on the fingers), have been proposed ever since 1906, that is to say, since the time when the first serious analyses of prehistoric rock paintings were being developed. The big names of the nascent discipline of prehistory, Henri Breuil and Émile Cartailhac, wrote several articles about Gargas.

## FÉLIX REGNAULT: A READER'S GAZE

The main point of the present study does not, however, concern this particular controversy. We prefer instead to establish a clear distinction between, first, the problem of interpreting negative images of hands and, second, a very different issue involving certain other thorny questions. This second problem has to do with perception itself, that is, how we perceive these figures today. Our point of departure concerns the moment when these hands were first discovered in the Gargas cave: we would do well to call this moment a "destination point" rather than a point of departure, a *terminus a quo* rather than a *terminus ad quem*. The problem of how to perceive these hands correctly is sketched out in the very first lines of Félix Regnault's text, words written by the cave's discoverer. His paper begins as follows: "Since the hand-prints from the Altamira and Marsoulas caves, as pointed out by Cartailhac and Breuil, had captured my interest, I took great care in examining the Gargas cave where I found myself on June 11 of this year."[5]

It is worth pausing for a moment at the words "captured my interest," which seem to present an immediate problem. One needs to know that, at the time of his writing, Regnault was already familiar with the Gargas cave, and indeed for quite a long time. He had already written a dozen or more papers on his digs in Gargas between 1873 and 1906. After more than thirty years of work at the site, he had uncovered a vast amount of anthropological and palaeontological material. In 1878 he put together a plan for cutting two cross-sections in the cave[6]; in 1883 he published a study on "fossiliferous deposits"[7]; and during the following year he undertook an exploration of the "secret dungeons of Gargas,"[8] a project that led to the exceptional uncovering of a hyena skeleton, almost intact.[9] And then, in 1895, after having dug a tunnel in order to pursue further digs, he discovered several human graves and other Palaeolithic deposits in an upper chamber.[10]

It therefore seems reasonable to assume that by 1906 Regnault knew the cave rather well, even if it is also true to say that he had not always participated personally in all the digs. During a period of over thirty years, he must have visited the cave on numerous occasions without ever having seen any hand-paintings. On June 11, 1906, once his interest had been "captured," to re-use his words, he decided to examine the cave's walls with great care and now, finally, he "saw" the hands. We could of course conclude that Regnault must have been particularly inattentive on previous occasions, that his blindness vis-à-vis the cave walls was part of a personal problem. At first blush, then, the history of his gaze appears rather simple. Up until then, his attention in the Gargas cave had been monopolized by his search for bones and stones: Regnault was a man of the ground, not one of the walls. The only thing he needed to do was to read an article and suddenly he raises his eyes: he looks and he discovers.

Far from representing anything very original, a similar scenario appears in the accounts written by numerous other prehistorians of the time. It would seem that a common narrative pattern regulated the stories told by our "discoverers." According to this pattern, discoveries appear to have been prompted by the reading of texts that announced in advance these same discoveries, so much so that a causal chain of events appears to be in operation whereby readings and earlier digs dictate what the current scholar is going to see. In such a scenario, the actual act of seeing is inseparable from the decision to have a look. The discoverer is a well-informed person who follows the instructions suggested in his readings. It is therefore difficult to retain the earlier hypothesis which purported that Regnault was just a bit too inattentive during his earlier digs, unless of course one postulates that all of the discoverers of his time were just as inattentive as he, all being (like him) totally dependent on the visual examinations undertaken by their predecessors. But I wish to suggest here that the history of the discipline of prehistory is on the contrary punctuated by epistemological breaks, unexpected discoveries, and the recurrent need to confront newly uncovered objects.

As far as cave painting is concerned, one asks whether it is even possible to establish a firm point of departure, an absolute beginning that would characterize a new discovery, that is to say, a beginning without precedent, a new type of gaze that, at the moment of its encounter with the "never-yet-seen," would be dependent on no previous reading.

## WALLS, SUPPORTS, FIGURES, AND SIGNS

Let us therefore take a second look at the texts written by Cartailhac and Breuil to which Regnault gives credit for having piqued his interest. Is it possible to insert these articles, all of which point to the existence of negative hands in the Altamira and Marsoulas caves, into the same narrative skeleton that we just described? Or do they have a different status? Is it the case that their discovery of hands was itself conditioned by something they had previously read? Was it conditioned by a similar capturing of their interest? Or is it preferable to view these texts as being captivating in their own right, having themselves produced the first impulses that led to a whole flurry of other discoveries?

Indeed, the articles published by Cartailhac and Breuil between 1904 and 1905 are almost universally acclaimed by historians of prehistory as being endowed with a special epistemological force, even if these texts do not themselves recount any new discoveries. Written by recognized authorities in the field, these articles tolled the knell for an entire era during which scholars had expressed serious doubts concerning the wall paintings that had been discovered in a number of caves in southwestern France and in Spain. The papers presented the results from attempts to catalogue the paintings and engravings that had been found in the Altamira and Marsoulas caves during expeditions undertaken as early as 1902 by Cartailhac and his younger colleague Breuil. For the first time, they presented an ambitiously systematic analysis of "cave art." Rather than representing the discovery of any new signs and figures, however, these texts mark the end of an era. They must be understood as if they constituted the ultimate certificates of authenticity needed for prehistoric wall painting, while at the same time they open up a new era of research through the transformation they allow of the scientific status one gives to the caves at issue. From now on, excavators must take a careful look at ceilings, walls, façades, nooks and crannies. It no longer sufficed to dig holes in the ground and to sift through the uncovered debris: indeed such an operation, as Leroi-Gourhan would not fail to point out, leads to the destruction of the very document that had just been discovered.[11] Henceforth, the important thing was to scan visually, to scrutinize, and to examine the available surfaces without looking for objects that could be extracted, as if the latter constituted trophies for the discoverers. Pickaxes are replaced by pencils, charcoal crayons, and pastels; stratigraphers are replaced by painters and draughtsmen.

It is difficult to overestimate the extent to which these changes in scientific conduct are part and parcel of a veritable cognitive revolution.

The search for knowledge no longer applies to the same objects as before: the implied subjects, actors, and addressees have all been modified. When Palaeolithic rock painting becomes a field of investigation of its own, it thereby displaces the existing epistemic framework. The cave has become a new space for reading and all the signs that it contains will now be seen in a different manner.

As a consequence, we understand that, for Regnault to have noticed these negative hands, it was first necessary that the cave's wall be re-qualified as potential supports for Palaeolithic works. Regnault's purported blindness had therefore nothing to do with any so-called inattentiveness on his part; if he had literally seen nothing at Gargas during his thirty years of archaeological digs, this is because cave walls had nothing of value to offer to his expert gaze. The history of the invention of cave-wall paintings illustrates perfectly well the role played by the material support not only in the interpretation of these signs but also in their actual perception. The status one grants to the cave walls constitutes a veritable frame of experience, in the sense that Erving Goffman attributes to this term.[12] In order for Palaeolithic cave wall painting to exist, first a change in the frame needed to occur: how could such a change occur?

## AN ACCIDENTAL LOOK: THE MARCHIONESS OF SAUTUOLA AT ALTAMIRA (1878)

When Cartailhac and Breuil travel to Altamira in 1902 in order to undertake a catalogue of the cave's contents, they are not about to discover anything new. All they are going to do is to *rediscover* a number of paintings that had already been heralded in 1878, paintings which, by 1880, had already been the subject of a publication written by the Marchioness of Sautuola. In fact, at that time (1902), the existence of these very works had been stubbornly refuted for over twenty years by the exact same Cartailhac, as well as by the scientific community at large.

As a consequence, the history of Regnault's looking at the cave walls at Gargas and his discovery of negative hands therein first had to come across the publications written by Cartailhac and Breuil. But still, these latter texts are not in themselves any true point of departure. The two latter prehistorians did nothing other than to align themselves with the visual examination that, more than twenty years earlier, the Marchioness of Sautuola had herself made of the ceiling in the Altamira cave. At first censored, disqualified, even belittled, this old sighting begins to take on a new importance at the beginning of the twentieth century. What could have happened in Altamira? Would we be correct to say that, without his knowledge, the history of Regnault's look at the cave walls began in Spain in the year 1879?

There are obviously certain persons who discover important deposits by accident, as is the case of Mademoiselle Sautuola in Altamira [...] This little girl was the first to see the paintings in the caves of Altamira in Spain. While her father, the Marquee of Sautuola, was digging in the floor of the cave, his little Spanish daughter was meanwhile looking up at the ceiling. She had no problem in discerning a host of animals painted polychromatically in many different positions.[13]

Whereas, in the first lines of his text, Regnault presented his own discovery as being dependent on other previously published works and thus was an integral part of the scholarly collective, this second narrative about Altamira gives the model for recounting an accidental discovery. Here, the observer's innocence – she was after all a child –, her naïve ignorance and her lack of prejudices all compel the scholar, absorbed by his excavation work, to take notice of a new object of knowledge. Although Señor Sautuola's subsequent look at the wall is in no way connected to any previous reading of a text, it does not in itself represent any new beginning because it is dependent on the pointing finger of a child, that is, on someone else's chance gaze, a look that was external to the frame of reference shared by prehistorians. This canonical story, reprinted in virtually in every textbook on prehistory – with a few variants[14] – often resembles a founding event, the moment that led prehistoric science to a spectacular epistemological leap, i.e., the discovery of prehistoric painting. To this extent, it is a welcome addition to the still rather thin anthology of scientific miracles, which includes both Newton's apple and the famous children from Lascaux.

If the discovery can readily be construed as the result of what happens when reasoned intuition (for example how one chooses the spot for an archaeological dig) combines with luck, theatrical turns of events of a grandiose scale can never be excluded. The discipline of prehistory, exactly like traditional history, works on traces from the past, on the hidden vestiges of a lost world: anyone taking a walk in nature is thus able to find a treasure. As is well known, the world's most famous Palaeolithic site, Lascaux, was only discovered due to the curiosity of a few teenagers. However, at the time when Lascaux was discovered, that is, in September 1940, scientists had already studied a large number of other caves. It was already known that prehistoric man had made paintings on cave walls. The children of Lascaux organized watch shifts at the mouth of the cave until official representatives of the scientific community could arrive: fully aware of the value of what they had found, they were also afraid of potential pillages. But, in 1879, the story of the Altamira cave was totally different.

## A Censored Gaze: Altamira Refused

After the charming episode featuring Señorita de Sautuola had occurred, more than twenty years would pass before the reality of prehistoric paintings would finally be accepted. There was no need to post guards at the entrance to the Altamira cave because no one would have thought of going into the cave in order to pillage its treasures. This is why the moment when the story of the Marquee's discovery would be recognized as a foundational moment could only occur once the scientific discourse of prehistory would itself, at long last, be ready to rethink its own past and to rationalize its beginnings *après coup*. This twenty-year interval, as is well known, was not exactly characterized by critical debates within the discipline; in fact there was, simply stated, no ongoing debate at all during which the partisans of prehistoric painting would one day gain the upper hand. Rather these twenty years represent a period of consensus within the scientific community, whose members unanimously agreed that the hypothesis of prehistoric paintings was inadmissible.[15]

Such a consensus was maintained thanks to the authoritarian structure of the scientific community in France at the time, a phenomenon that Nathalie Richard describes, not without skilful litotes, as the "weight of personalities." Men such as Mortillet,[16] who was in control of the research institutes of Paris, or Cartailhac, who reigned supreme in Toulouse, refused outright the idea of prehistoric painting. As early as 1880, at the time when a professor from the University of Madrid, Vilanova, is getting ready to present a paper to the Anthropological Congress of Lisbon on the cave paintings found in the Altamira cave, he decides on his own accord – or perhaps due to the pressure exerted by certain "personalities" – to remain silent. During the same year, Cartailhac sends an emissary to the site, the palaeontologist Édouard Harlé. The latter submits a report that confirms the inauthenticity of the paintings in the cave. And when, at the congress of the Association pour l'Avancement des Sciences held at La Rochelle in 1883, the same Madrid professor Vilanova once again attempts to defend the authentic nature of the paintings against the conclusions reached by Harlé in his report, Cartailhac and Harlé get up and leave the room. The professor from Madrid will of course denounce this "inextricable spirit of opposition,"[17] but in vain.

Even if Altamira had already been discovered, it was still undiscovered. As Félix Regnault walks up and down the corridors of the Gargas cave, excavating the ground surface, constructing a tunnel, exploring dungeons, he passes and re-passes in front of the cave wall where hundreds of human hands had been painted, and he doesn't notice a thing. These hands are invisible for him because prehistoric rock painting does not yet exist. By the end of the nineteenth century, the knowledge acceptable to prehistorians was predicated on the study of objects made from bones or ivory, objects such as needles, scrapers, handles, etc. Placed in enormous collections, some of these items were even sculpted or engraved. For several decades already, scientists were aware that prehistoric man adorned his personal objects with sculpted or engraved images of mammoths, bison, deer, or fish.[18] The prehistoric artist was said to be a skilful craftsman who adorned his tools during his moments of leisure, much like a bored shepherd biding his time. The idea that artistic activity could exist independently of a purely technical culture was not compatible with the dominant way of representing "antediluvian" man, the latter being seen as an unsophisticated being overdetermined for the most part by his primary needs. And this is why, even though the frescos in the Altamira cave presented creatures that were similar to those found in the adornments of personal tools, even though they were perfectly coherent in the context of then-accepted knowledge, the discovery of rock painting was nevertheless unacceptable. Inasmuch as it comprised paintings and frescos, and not sculptures and tools, the art from the Altamira cave conflicted with the dominant picture of how human evolution must have occurred, that is to say, with the vision of mankind presented by Auguste Comte who asserted that sculpture *preceded* painting.[19] On the other hand, the discovery made in the Altamira cave occurred in a truly exceptional site. Containing a space familiar to excavators, the cave had always been interpreted as a primitive space for habitation, but in this instance the cave had also become the place where monumental works of art were exhibited. Such a scenario contradicted every accepted theory as it suggested, with these paintings, that prehistoric man was able to engage in contemplative activities. The opinion concerning the aberrant nature of these frescos was reinforced by the fact that, at the time, there were no solid criteria available for the authentication of artefacts. In 1880, accepting the discovery of prehistoric paintings meant accepting simply to "believe" in them without the slightest proof.[20] No expedition is therefore organized to catalogue the paintings after Sautuola's publication and indeed Altamira will soon be entirely forgotten. The published text that announces this discovery would seem to be totally bereft of any communicational savvy: it does not manage to insert itself into any known chain of scientific operations and it does not lead to any further discoveries.

Earlier, we asked a simple question: where does the story of Regnault's gaze at the cave wall really begin? Our question still remains without an answer. Even if, chronologically, the visual discovery made by Sautuola, the text he subsequently published and the drawings produced therein were objectively the "first" events, these things did not possess in and of themselves enough power to become the originary moment in the historical discovery of prehistoric cave-wall painting. For indeed it is not enough simply to notice paintings of bison, even exceptional bison, nor is it enough to notice negative images of hands, even enigmatic ones, for any such noticing to constitute a "discovery." The gap between perception, recognition, and discovery is clearly illustrated by this particular story. What could the felicity conditions have been that led to the epistemological break that did indeed occur, as we well know? What was it that led to a change in the framework of experience? How did scientists finally admit to the existence of wall painting? What was the accident that allowed people to see these figures and signs, even the caves themselves, in a different light?

## THE FELICITY CONDITIONS OF VISUAL EXAMINATIONS: BISON IN THE LA MOUTHE CAVE (1895)

The first actual visual experience involving prehistoric wall painting could be situated in 1895 when the geologist, Rivière, was studying various archaeological layers present in the cave of La Mouthe. There, after clearing off a section of a wall, Rivière discovered the engraving of a bison. The fact that over time this engraving had been covered over by several archaeological layers provided irrefutable proof of the engraving's authenticity since the latter could only have been executed at a time that corresponded with the geological layer in which it was found, that of the layer on the floor that the archaeologist had reached in his digging and clearing away. Rivière's discovery was quite literally based on an uncovering. Having received an invitation to visit the site, Cartailhac immediately accepted to come and see things for himself. He will always remember that precise moment in time when he came to a new realization, despite his personal scepticism:

> Monsieur Rivière was graceful in allowing me to pursue every one of my queries. As best as I could, I examined his discovery, scrutinizing its circumstances, the images he had uncovered, every imaginable detail. New digs had just begun. Only part of the cave had been cleared; beyond that point, we came across an embankment; it was possible to go even further by crawling over it. *I personally cleared away part of the totally untouched floor of the cave, and uncovered the foot of a represented animal.* Thus I had the pleasure of recognizing that Monsieur Rivière had not been confused by what he found.[21]

The cave at La Mouthe has now become the site of a veritable struggle for the truth: Cartailhac is personally placed in the position of the discoverer, he is able to appraise the quality of the site with a single glance ("totally untouched"), he executes the appropriate gestures himself ("I personally cleared away …"), and in the very movement by which he perceives the object he also sees the proof of its authenticity. The series of gestures executed by Cartailhac, consisting of clearing away part of the stone engraving, represents nothing short of the typical act executed by a stratigrapher of his time, and this act embodies the entire body of knowledge possessed by his profession. From an empirical point of view, the scientist reaches a state of total certainty concerning the object's authenticity. He does this on the basis of observations made *de visu* and *de manu*. The represented figure was situated in a context that allowed for its authentication, that is, it was couched in a geological layering whose identification was dependent on another science the accuracy of which was itself beyond all doubt: geology. Cartailhac's experience in the cave is not only determined by an exceptional situation; it is also shaped by familiar ways of conducting business. His current experience is based on experience from the past that is both practical and cognitive in nature. Cartailhac clears away debris in order to create the environment capable of accommodating an event so strange that it necessitates enhanced validation procedures. The discovery in which he wishes to participate personally is both a perceptual experience and an embodied act of reasoning.

Yet another discovery will have a lasting effect in this context, one occurring in the cave of Font-de-Gaume, France,[22] where a "certain number of figures (with lines and colours) are covered over by a stalagmitic coating, which in places is nearly two centimetres thick."[23] A layer of calcite guarantees the authenticity of the figures that it covers; it also enables the discoverer to date these figures. In this instance too, the object of knowledge made available to the prehistorian's gaze incorporates that same evidence that can be used to authenticate it. To this extent, the presence of geological concretions is not in itself sufficient for authenticity, but such concretions can nevertheless constitute strong evidence when combined with other factors.[24] Once again, the archaeological site provides the locus where various elements favouring the recognition of authentic wall paintings come together: these are exemplary cases of situated cognition.[25] Here, the determining factors are the circumstances created by the physical environment – the fact that engravings were buried in La Mouthe or covered over by a calcareous deposit in Font-de-Gaume – as well as situational factors – the fact that recognized scientists from different but complementary disciplines were able to collaborate in their analysis of the site.

# A Picnic and a *mea culpa*: The Permission to View the Site Dating from 1902

Regnault's visual discovery is therefore not only dependent on the data provided by Cartailhac and Breuil. It further incorporates the heterogeneous elements we have just mentioned: the clearing away of a bison in the La Mouthe cave, the calcite covering the aurochs found in Font-de-Gaume, Mademoiselle de Sautuola's index finger pointing to the cave ceiling, the censorship and processes of forgetting imposed by certain "personalities," and the rediscovery of Altamira. To this list of factors we should also add the large body of papers delivered during colloquia, congresses and other professional meetings whose importance in the ongoing elaboration of knowledge relevant to the science of caves was enhanced due to the fact that the discipline was itself only loosely structured. Two public events from 1902 should be highlighted, events that led to the official recognition of cave painting: first, the solemn act of contrition published by Cartailhac, and second, an act, ceremonial in nature, that occurred during a picnic organized during the Congress of Prehistorians held in Montauban, France. As these two events are relatively well known, we will concentrate here on their performative dimension.

Cartailhac's *mea culpa* forms a typical speech act, one uttered in the first person singular and in the present tense: "I am the accomplice of an error perpetrated more than twenty years ago," he writes, "an act of injustice which it is now necessary both to confess and to repair." While this utterance is an act of contrition pronounced in proper form, its force as a confession is somewhat diminished due to the fact that, as an autocratic figure, Cartailhac not only confesses his wrongdoing, but he also judges and absolves himself. Furthermore, we should not forget that, from the time, at La Mouthe, when he first reached his personal conviction regarding cave painting, to that moment in time when he finally made a public confession concerning his former errors, a period of no less than seven years had already passed.

35. PHOTOGRAPH FROM IN FRONT OF THE LA MOUTHE CAVE, DURING AN
EXCURSION ORGANIZED FOR THE CONGRESS OF THE FRENCH ASSOCIATION
FOR THE ADVANCEMENT OF SCIENCE HELD AT MONTAUBAN, AUGUST 4,
1902. FROM LEFT TO RIGHT: FÉLIX REGNAULT (4TH PERSON), ÉMILE
CARTAILHAC (5TH PERSON), FRANÇOIS DALEAU (7TH PERSON, SEATED),
HENRI BREUIL (13TH PERSON), ÉMILE RIVIÈRE (14TH PERSON), SAINT-
GERMAIN-EN-LAYE, ARCHIVES OF THE MUSÉE D'ARCHÉOLOGIE NATIONALE
(FONDS BREUIL, ALBUM #1).

In addition, the public and collective nature of the 1902 picnic held
in Montauban, followed by the excursion to the caves in La Mouthe
et Font-de-Gaume, bestows a truly performative dimension upon this
speech act. On this particular day in history, an official ceremony was
organized in order to recognize the arrival of cave painting into the scientific field of study known as prehistory. It was a matter of staging a
collective act of recognition whose aim consisted in cementing the acceptance of the scientific community at large. Prehistorians gather at the
two sites where the reversal of scientists' beliefs had first occurred. The
result of such an experience of "conversion" is that these scientists have
now become both witnesses and guarantors of a new truth. After this

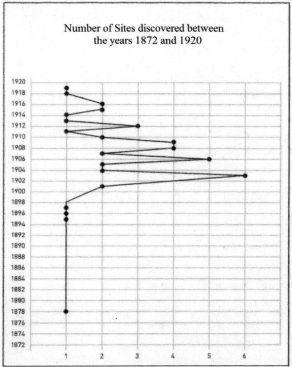

Number of Sites discovered between
the years 1872 and 1920

Number of sites discovered per year (according to the
chronology established by Marc Groenen [1994])

excursion has taken place and after Cartailhac's *mea culpa* has been duly published, it now becomes possible to "see" either painted or engraved works of art executed by Palaeolithic artists. From now one, all such discoveries are authorized. The effectiveness of this authorization is surprising: the greater part of the now-known sites containing prehistoric paintings were discovered almost as if they were part of an assembly line, occurring one after the other in quick succession either in that very year or in the years immediately following[26] (see **Table 5**).

Beyond the symbolic nature of the 1902 excursion, the main thing that is confirmed by this event has to do with the material nature of the rock support where the paintings were found, that is to say, with the very walls of the cave. From now on, caves would become the place where such works were on exhibit; they would also be the locus where a new field of perception is legitimized, one filled with many new signs and figures that now need to be read. All these changes transformed cave walls into a site where inscriptions could be found. Up until this point in time, prehistorians were much more concerned with finding material evidence for determining the authenticity of discovered works than they were with the actual works themselves. This is why it was necessary that a layer of earth should cover over the engravings in the La Mouthe cave or that an envelope of calcite should veil the aurochs of Font-de-Gaume: they needed to be validated as authentic works. From 1902 onwards, figures and signs found on the walls of caves, either painted or engraved, were now all possible prehistoric objects, even when they were directly visible to the naked eye, even when they were not accompanied by material clues pointing to their authenticity. New authenticating processes would quickly be established, most notably those having to do with judgments based on the formal similarities discovered amongst various sites. The time had come when it became necessary to conduct an inventory of the works discovered, and also to classify them. Such enterprises would allow for comparison between various sites.

## NEVER BEFORE SEEN, ALREADY SEEN: THE QUESTION OF MNESIC TRACES

It therefore comes as no surprise if a certain number of the cave-wall sites "discovered" in the following years had in fact already been known, and even exploited, as sites for earlier digs. More than actual discoveries, what occurred was a new way of seeing things, a new way of examining the available evidence or of paying careful attention to it. Before anyone else, after the Congress held in Montauban, Cartailhac and Breuil rush to the caves in Altamira in order to *rediscover* the cave. It almost seems as if the cave had never really disappeared from their personal memories, or had at least remained there in a repressed form. A little while later, after learning of the artefacts documented by Cartailhac and Breuil in their work, Regnault embarks upon an expedition intended to find "negative" hands, traces he will now be able to "recognize" on the walls of the Gargas cave. Such events confirm the theoretical observation according to which human "[a]ttention first of all presupposes a transformation of the mental field, a new way for consciousness to be present to its objects."[27]

There still remains, however, a final series of facts that was part of the way in which this particular episode in the history of science was constructed. A careful analysis can establish the appropriate profile these facts deserve. We are thinking here of the many testimonials that attest to discoveries that had no doubt been made "ahead of their time." For indeed it would not only seem that prehistorians such as Breuil, Cartailhac, and Regnault revisit their sites, look at them for a second time, thereby lending new attention to them, but it would also seem that many scholars now began to remember having seen something in such and such a cave, sometimes many years ago. We are blessed with a rich set of recollections whose details about how such and such a find was discovered are remarkably different from the accounts we have examined up until now.

The stories told of discoveries made "ahead of their time" constitute a neatly circumscribable corpus. Considered from a chronological point of view, the oldest of these narratives concerns the discovery of paintings made at Niaux. Well before the discoveries made in the Altamira cave, in 1866, Félix Garrigou explores a cave near his home and discovers a number of drawings on the walls. These are the words he writes in the logbook he kept of his expeditions: "A secondary corridor on the left and, on the right, a large corridor leading to a circular chamber. The walls are covered with strange drawings of oxen and horses????." During another visit he writes the following words: "A large circular chamber containing strange drawings. What is this? Amateur artists who drew animals. But why? Already seen this before." Forty years later, in 1906,

36. DRAWINGS BY BREUIL FROM THE ALTIMARA CAVE, 1902–1903,
PENCIL, SANGUINE AND PASTEL ON PAPER, 36.5 X 54 CM, PARIS,
MUSÉE NATIONAL D'HISTOIRE NATURELLE, MAIN LIBRARY (FONDS
ICONOGRAPHIQUE BREUIL, NO. 54 1933BIS).

people came to call on Garrigou after excursionists had discovered the famous "black chamber" of the cave, a space adorned with a multitude of images, all drawn in black, depicting deer, horses, and bison. And Garrigou suddenly remembers the notes he had taken so long ago and decides to validate the visual discovery he had made at the time.

Between 1871 and 1873, Jules Ollier de Marichard conducts an excavation in the caves of Ebbou in the Ardèche region of France. Even though he speaks in his notebooks of "animal silhouettes sketched on the walls of a large corridor," he does not think anything of them at the time.

In 1878, Léopold Chiron is at work in another cave of the Ardèche region, that of Chabot. Here he notices a series of lines deeply engraved in the surface of the cave's walls. Upon careful inspection of these walls,

BÉATRICE FRAENKEL

he believes he has seen representations of birds with open wings as well as five or six human figures mixed in with them. He places these engravings in the Quaternary period. Speaking to no one about what he found, it is only ten years later that he feels that the time is right to write about them.

The man who, in 1896, discovered the Pair-Non-Pair caves situated in the Department of the Gironde, François Daleau, presents a case that is worth examining in greater detail. The notes he wrote in his notebook are eloquently detailed:

> August 31, 1896. When entering the cave I fortuitously noticed several engravings on the East wall (I first noticed these drawings on December 19, 1883. See "Excursions.") I see, or at least believe I've seen, a four-legged creature whose poorly drawn head is covered by a sort of harness? I take my pencil and try to draw what I've seen in my notebook (fig. 373). In order better to understand what I've seen, I slide the tip of my fingers along the engraved lines and am thus able to follow the contours by touch. Muddy earth is pushed into the engraved lines and I don't think I have damaged anything. I have often attempted to draw these engravings or just to understand them. Never have I seen them as clearly as I did today. Is this just a question of light, or am I actually seeing things better? I'm reminded of a riddle from a few years back: "Can you see the cat?"

Daleau's story is significantly different from the one told by Garrigou. His gaze only came across the engravings "fortuitously." But this fortuitous glance is nevertheless guided by what he remembered from earlier expeditions. The engravings function like mnesic traces and quickly remind him of a sighting he had made in 1883. But he writes this in 1896, precisely at a time when the existence of prehistoric cave-wall painting is only beginning to be accepted by a handful of scholars. The lines seen by Daleau are thus given renewed attention, in the sense described by

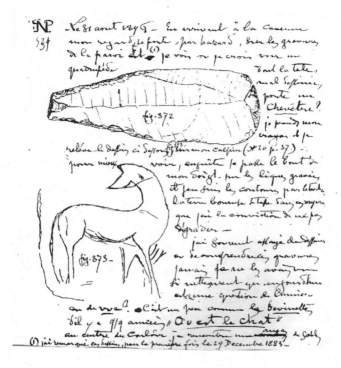

37. A PAGE FROM THE NOTEBOOKS OF FRANÇOIS DALEAU, REPRODUCED
IN MARC GROENEN, *Pour une histoire de la préhistoire*, GRENOBLE:
JÉRÔME MILLION, 1994.

Merleau-Ponty: "To pay attention is not merely further to elucidate pre-
existing data, it is to bring about a new articulation of them by taking
them as figures."[28] We notice, however, that he does not immediately
recognize any figures: Daleau first needs to find a method for reading
what he has seen, one that is appropriate for the surfaces he is examining.
Above all else, he needs a "handle." The drawing itself is not enough; he
also needs to follow the contours of what he has seen with his fingertips.
Only then is he able to decipher the graphic enigma before him, only
then is he able to pass from the simple perception of lines to the recognition of a specific form.

In his published *mea culpa*, Cartailhac comments upon these discoveries reported by Daleau:

> I never had any specific doubts about the accuracy of Daleau's observations; and yet on seeing these curious drawings I had the distinct impression that, since my attention had never been caught by such works, that is, by such decorative spaces, I may have passed them by without ever noticing them. And this is perhaps what had happened both to me and to several of my colleagues. We need to go back to our caves; that was the conclusion I reached.[29]

Cartailhac contrasts two modes of existence for signs: they can either be visible and recognized or they can be invisible and "likely to go unnoticed." It is remarkable that the narratives told by Daleau, Garrigou, or others – even Rivière claims to have noticed engravings in the La Mouthe cave before 1896 – all show that many scholars had seen either signs, drawings, or engravings of this nature without ever having actually "discovered" them. The signs were, as it were, "in waiting," visible but impossible to suspect. The wall of a cave can indeed offer a number of features that are curious enough to find their way into someone's notebook, even if these same features have not yet been integrated into a relevant epistemological framework.[30]

The narratives told of discoveries occurring "before their time" thus allow us to see, in a much broader light, the positive effects accruing to the official permission issued in 1902 by the scientific community allowing researchers to go and view the actual sites. What these narratives tell us is that, beyond the recognition of such and such a figure, beyond the process of deciphering during which the moment of perceiving a line becomes the moment of distinguishing a figure, there always remains – lurking in the background – the ambiguous presence of something that had been perceived in the past, something that, stocked in our memory, we might call the limbo of perceptual consciousness. That which – as in the case of Altamira – prehistorians had excluded from their specific field of inquiry, that is to say that which had been banished from everyone's attention – as was the case for Daleau and Garrigou – was now about to return with a vengeance and thereby to attest to the existence of a certain type of memory which, although involuntary in nature, is nevertheless active. The initially tacit recognition of cave art, later becoming official, thus appears to have paved the way for the resurfacing of certain censored memories.

## THE GREAT TIME OF INVENTION

It is no doubt time to return to the question we posed at the start of our query: in the case of the man who discovered negative hands in the Gargas cave, Félix Regnault, where does his gaze actually begin? The first reaction to this question consisted in asking a second one: when was prehistoric cave-wall painting first discovered? By following the announcements of discoveries as told in one text and then in another, we showed the impossibility of giving any "first" date or any "first" sighting, a single identifiable event that would have determined all the others coming later on. Once it has been described with the same careful detail as that used in describing an actual birth, every discovery thereby appears to have been preceded by an earlier, even more foundational event, which it then takes as an inspiration. One hesitates between several competing facts, each one of which, some more directly than others, could presumably constitute an acceptable origin for the event mentioned at the onset of this query, i.e., the discovery of hands made by Regnault in the Gargas cave.

The very process of discovery thus comes into view under several different lights, sometimes contradictory ones. Regnault's discovery provides an excellent example of informational processing. He reads, he examines, he discovers. The discovery made by Sautuola confirms the importance, not only of fortuitous accidents, but also of changes in our horizon of expectations. Without prior knowledge there can be no discoveries: this is a comforting point for phenomenological theories of perception. The details of how, in the history of science, the existence of cave-wall painting was recognized also show the influential role played by authoritative figures, social hierarchies and the intricacies of censorship, even self-censorship, in the constitution of a person's perceptual field. In the opposite sense, the collaborative efforts amongst scholars also exerted a decisive influence at several key moments of this story. In the case of the La Mouthe cave, the work undertaken together at a single site led to irreversible changes. However, from a completely different theoretical point of view, there are decisive episodes that show how much a discovery is dependent on the physical environment, on the resources this environment makes available to the scholar, and on the special features that are prominent at a given site. Daleau's story about the moment when he finally managed to distinguish a figure amongst the scrambled lines and curves he saw ends with a simple question, one that is much more important than what at first meets the eye: "Is this just a question of light, or am I actually seeing things better?" Saying that a discovery depends on the light available in a cave or on the quality of the researcher's eyesight already constitutes a correct response, even if, as such, it is insufficient. In particular, as we have already seen, we also need to wait for great time to follow its course, that is to say time that is open to multiple events, which is precisely the time of discovery.

## BIBLIOGRAPHY

Cartailhac, Émile. "Les cavernes ornées de dessins. La grotte d'Altamira, Espagne. 'Mea-culpa' d'un sceptique." *L'Anthropologie* XIII (1902): 348–54.
———. "Les mains inscrites de rouge et de noir de Gargas." *L'Anthropologie* XVII (1906): 624–25.
———, and Henri Breuil. "Les peintures et gravures murales des cavernes pyrénéennes." *L'Anthropologie* XV (1904): 625.
Cheynier, André. *Comment vivrait l'homme à l'âge des cavernes*. Paris: R. Arnoux, 1967.

Cohen, Claudine, and Jean-Jacques Hublin. *Boucher de Perthes. Les origines romantiques de la préhistoire*. Paris: Belin, 1989.

Comte, Auguste. *Système de politique positive*, vol. I. Paris: Carillan-Goery et Dalmont, 1851.

Coye, Noël. *La Préhistoire en paroles et en actes. Méthodes et enjeux de la pratique archéologique (1830–1950)*. Paris: L'Harmattan, 1997.

Foucher, Pascal, Cristina San Juan-Foucher, and Yoan Rumeau. *La Grotte de Gargas, un siècle de découvertes*. Communauté des communes du canton de Saint-Laurent-de-Neste, 2007.

Fraenkel, Béatrice. "Les empreintes." In *La Signature. Genèse d'un signe*, 205–22. Paris: Gallimard, 1992.

Freeman, Leslie G., and Joaquin Gonzalez Echegaray. *La Grotte d'Altamira*. Paris: Seuil/La Maison des Roches, 2001.

Gaudry, Albert. "Note sur les hyènes de la grotte de Gargas découvertes par M. Félix Regnault." *Comptes rendus hebdomadaires des séances de l'Académie des sciences*, vol. C (1885, meeting held on February 9, 1885): 325–28.

Gibson, James Jerome. *The Ecological Approach to Visual Perception*. Boston: Houghton Mifflin, 1979.

Goffman, Erving. *Frame Analysis: An Essay on the Organization of Experience*. Cambridge, MA: Harvard University Press, 1974.

Groenen, Marc. *Pour une histoire de la préhistoire*. Grenoble: Éditions Jérôme Million, 1994.

Koffka, Kurt. "Perception: An introduction to the *Gestalt-theorie*." *Psychological Bulletin XIX* (1922): 531–85.

Lartet, Édouard, and Henri Christy. "Sur des figures d'animaux gravés ou sculptés et autres produits d'art et d'industries rapportables aux temps primordiaux de la période humaine." *Revue anthropologique* IX (New Series) (1864): 233–67.

Leroi-Gourhan, André. "Les mains de Gargas. Essai pour une étude d'ensemble." *Bulletin de la Société préhistorique française* 64, no. 118 (1967): 107–22.

———. *Les Religions de la préhistoire*. Paris: Presses Universitaires de France, 1983 [1st ed. 1964].

Merleau-Ponty, Maurice. *Phenomenology of Perception*, trans. Colin Smith. London: Routledge, 2004 (1st ed. 1945).

Regnault, Félix. "Empreintes de mains humaines dans la grotte de Gargas (Hautes-Pyrénées)." *Bulletin et Mémoires de la Société d'anthropologie de Paris* VII (5th series) (1906): 331–32.

————. "La Grotte de Gargas." *Bulletin de la Société historique nationale de Toulouse* XII (1878).

————. "La Grotte de Gargas. Origines de cavernes, études des dépôts fossilifères." *Bulletin de la Société historique nationale de Toulouse* XVII (1883): 237–58.

————. "Un Repaire de hyènes dans la grotte de Gargas." *Bulletin de la Société historique nationale de Toulouse* XIX (1885): 30–35.

————. *Sépulture dans la grotte supérieure de Gargas*, vol. II. Bordeaux: Association française pour l'avancement des sciences, 1895.

Richard, Nathalie. *L'Invention de la préhistoire. Textes choisis, préfacés et commentés.* Paris: Presses Pocket, 1992.

————. "L'institutionnalisation de la préhistoire." In *Les Débuts des sciences de l'homme*, 89–207. Paris: Seuil, 1992.

Rouillon, André. "Au gravettien, dans la grotte de Cosquer (Marseille, Bouches-du-Rhône), l'homme a-t-il compté sur ses doigts?" *L'Anthropologie* CX, 4 (2006): 500–509.

Sanz de Sautuola, Marcelino, *Breves Apuntes sobre algunos objetos prehistóricos de la Provincia de Santander.* Santander, 1880.

Suchman, Lucy. *Plans and Situated Action: The Problem of Human/Machine Communication.* Cambridge: Cambridge University Press, 1987.

## NOTES

1   Building on previously published work from 1992, preliminary versions of the present contribution were presented in 2002 during a colloquium organized at the University of Paris VII and in 2005 at the École des Hautes Études en Sciences Sociales in the context of the graduate seminar given by Professors Jean-Louis Fabiani and Noël Barbe. I wish to extend a special thanks to Yann Pottin and Claudine Cohen, who carefully re-read the current version of my text and offered many comments and suggestions for improvement (The French version of this text appears in *Gradhiva* 6 [2007]: 18–31).

2   Félix Regnault, "Empreintes de mains humaines dans la grotte de Gargas (Hautes-Pyrénées)," *Bulletin et Mémoires de la Société d'anthropologie de Paris*, VII (5th Series, 1906), 331–32.

3   André Leroi-Gourhan, "Les mains de Gargas. Essai pour une étude d'ensemble," *Bulletin de la Société préhistorique française* 64, 118 (1967): 107–22.

4   The recent discovery, in the Cosquer cave, of negative hands with incomplete fingers has re-ignited the entire debate. New hypotheses have been put forward, including one

concerning an arithmetic meaning for these figures (see André Rouillon, "Au gravettien, dans la grotte de Cosquer (Marseille, Bouches-du-Rhône), l'homme a-t-il compté sur ses doigts?," *L'Anthropologie* CX, 4 [2006]: 500–509).

5   Regnault, "Empreintes de mains humaines," 331.

6   Félix Regnault, "La grotte de Gargas," *Bulletin de la Société historique nationale de Toulouse*, t. XII (1878).

7   Félix Regnault, "La grotte de Gargas. Origines de cavernes, études des dépôts fossilifères," *Bulletin de la Société historique nationale de Toulouse*, t. XVII (1883): 237–58.

8   Félix Regnault, "Un repaire de hyènes dans la grotte de Gargas," *Bulletin de la Société historique nationale de Toulouse*, t. XIX (1885): 30–35.

9   Albert Gaudry, "Note sur les hyènes de la grotte de Gargas découvertes par M. Félix Regnault," *Comptes rendus hebdomadaires des séances de l'Académie des sciences*, t. C (1885), meeting held on February 9 (1885), 325–28.

10  Félix Regnault, *Sépulture dans la grotte supérieure de Gargas*, t. II. Bordeaux, Association française pour l'avancement des sciences (1895).

11  "The main difference between the prehistorian's sources and those of the historian lies in the fact that the former destroys his document while excavating it." (André Leroi-Gourhan, *Les Religions de la préhistoire* [Paris: Presses Universitaires de France, 1983, first edition in 1964], 7).

12  See on this point Erving Goffman, *Frame Analysis: An Essay on the Organization of Experience* (Cambridge, MA: Harvard University Press, 1974).

13  André Cheynier, *Comment vivrait l'homme à l'âge des cavernes* (Paris: R. Arnoux, 1967).

14  This is why we are not surprised to find, in the illustrated work on the Gargas cave recently published by Leslie G. Freeman and Joaquin Gonzalez Echegaray (*La Grotte d'Altamira* [Paris: Seuil/La Maison des Roches, 2001]), the following sentence, which presumably could be attributed to the little girl Maria: "Look Dad, painted bulls!" (p. 14). Other versions give basically the same phrase with a bit more local colour: "¡Torros, torros!"

15  Marc Groenen shows that such was the situation for "fossilized men" whose very existence was in dispute for the longest of time. Discoveries of human bones and skeletons simply went unnoticed. In scientific publications, they earned only negligence (Groenen, *Pour une histoire de la préhistoire* [Grenoble: Éditions Jérôme Million, 1994]).

16  Nathalie Richard, "L'Institutionnalisation de la préhistoire," *Les Débuts des sciences de l'homme* (Paris: Seuil, 1992), 198.

17  Noël Coye, *La Préhistoire en paroles et en actes. Méthodes et enjeux de la pratique archéologique (1830–1950)* (Paris: L'Harmattan, 1997), 243.

18  In 1860 Lartet and Christy discover the image of a mammoth engraved in a piece of ivory, a discovery that proved the existence of prehistoric art for personal objects. Up until this time, it was believed that these objects came from Celtic cultures (Lartet and Christy, "Sur des figures d'animaux gravés ou sculptés et autres produits d'art et d'industries rapportables aux temps primordiaux de la période humaine," *Revue anthropologique* IX, [1864]).

19  See Auguste Comte, *Système de politique positive*, vol. I (Paris: Carillon-Goery et Dalmont, 1851).

20  In such an intellectual context, those who, like Édouard Piette, recognized

the authenticity of the Altamira paintings were rare.

21 Émile Cartailhac, "Les cavernes ornées de dessins. La grotte d'Altamira, Espagne. 'Mea-culpa' d'un sceptique," *L'Anthropologie* XIII (1902): 348–54.

22 This discovery, made by Denis Peyroni, Louis Capitan and Henri Breuil, occurred in 1901.

23 Henri Breuil and Louis Capitan (in 1901) as quoted by Nathalie Richard, *L'Invention de la préhistoire. Textes choisis, préfacés et commentés*m (Paris: Presses Pocket, 1992), 322.

24 Groenen (*Pour une histoire de la préhistoire*) points out that, despite the limestone concretions discovered in 1830 by Schmerling, which covered over human skeletal remains, no scientist from this period was willing to consider them as being "antediluvian."

25 These cases are both exemplary and atypical because classical texts on acts of situated cognition deal more often with routine acts than they do with exceptional discoveries. See on this point Lucy Suchman, *Plans and Situated Action: The Problem of Human/Machine Communication* (Cambridge: Cambridge University Press, 1987).

26 A similar discovery process occurred in the 1860s after Jacques Boucher de Perthes had delivered his famous lecture entitled "De l'homme antédiluvien et de ses œuvres" ["Concerning antediluvian man and his works"] to the *Société impériale d'émulation* of Abbeville. This event marked, as it were, the official recognition of the discipline of prehistory. The lecture was followed by a tidal wave of archaeological digs: "Everywhere in Europe scholars began to turn over the ground in order to find these famous axes" and other tools cut from stone (Claudine Cohen and Jean-Jacques Hublin, *Boucher de Perthes. Les origines romantiques de la préhistoire* [Paris: Belin, 1989], 195).

27 Maurice Merleau-Ponty, *Phenomenology of Perception*, trans. Colin Smith (London: Routledge, 2004), 33.

28 Ibid., 35. In this instance, Merleau-Ponty is referring to the gestaltist psychologist Kurt Koffka, in particular to his article "Perception, an introduction to the Gestalt Theorie" published in 1922 in the *Psychological Bulletin*.

29 Cartailhac, "Les cavernes ornées de dessins. La grotte d'Altamira, Espagne. 'Mea-culpa' d'un sceptique," 328.

30 From this point of view, the entire narrative told by Daleau could be analyzed using the theory of *affordances* as sketched by James Jerome Gibson in *The Ecological Approach to Visual Perception* (Boston: Houghton Mifflin, 1979). It is useful to remember that the notion of *affordance* relies heavily on the work published by Koffka.

# 7

# Word-and-Image Studies in France: A Bibliographical Essay

For the past twenty-five years or more, and on a vast international scale, the field of "word-and-image" studies has represented a prominent zone of innovative inquiry in a number of academic disciplines. It has also been resolutely interdisciplinary in the best sense of the term. Including not only the humanities and the social sciences, it has also expanded during the past decade, via the cognitive sciences, into areas explored by neural scientists, psychologists and psycholinguists, and even computer scientists. Related to the humanities, it has spawned, amongst other things, semiotic research, investigations in the philosophy of art, work related to anthropology and the invention of writing, innovative work on theories of metaphor, new theories of representation and depiction, research into bilingualism, film studies, and much interpretive work both in literary studies and in art history. In the social sciences, it has become a prominent feature of the constellation of disciplines now known as "Communication Studies," where it figures heavily in contemporary work done by sociologists as well as by scholars working in the area of cultural studies. Nowhere better than in France has such interdisciplinary inquiry been actively present in the articles and books that the country's academics have produced.

Concerning the vibrant field of "word-and-image" studies, it would of course be impossible to discuss each and every one of the books that have been published in France and other French-speaking countries over the past twenty-five years. Rather than merely mentioning in a sentence or two the most important of the several hundred French-language books that are part of the "word-and-image" field documented here, the following bibliographical essay adopts a different approach. To give the English-speaking reader an informative overview of some of the most important strands of research that have emerged during the past two and a half decades, three very recent books have been chosen for particular attention, two of which were written by widely published authors (both with strong philosophical backgrounds), the third published by a lesser known writer stemming from the venerable tradition of rhetorical studies. In this choice of books, three considerations took strong prominence: (1) the authors presented here should be relatively unknown to the English-speaking world (and indeed as indicated further on, all of these authors fall into this category, albeit to greater or lesser degrees); (2) the books presented here should come from different schools of thought, optimally from competing traditions (a surprising feature of these three authors is that they rarely, if ever, quote from one another's work); and (3) the books should be broad enough in scope to give a good glimpse either of the author's broader corpus of works or at least of the intellectual tradition within which these works are a part.

The three works in question are:

(I)    Georges Didi-Huberman, *L'Image ouverte*, Paris: Gallimard, collection "Le Temps des images," 2007, 401p.

(II)   Marie-José Mondzain, *Homo spectator*, Paris: Bayard, 2007, 271p.

(III)  Anne Surgers, *Et que dit ce silence? La rhétorique du visible*, Paris: Presses de la Sorbonne Nouvelle, 2007, 372p.

# I. Georges Didi-Huberman

A fervent and unorthodox reader of Freud and Lacan, Georges Didi-Huberman is above all a flamboyant art historian. He is also a provocative thinker in the field of cultural studies. Even if he is not a philosopher by trade – that is, in the academic sense of someone who teaches in a philosophy department –, he is indeed a philosopher in the broader sense of the term, i.e., that of someone who widely reads and uses philosophy in his work. Concerning word-and-image studies, Georges Didi-Huberman is undoubtedly one of France's most prolific academic writers. Surprisingly enough, of the vast corpus of works he has published during the past twenty-five years or more,[1] only three (considerably older) books have been translated into English.[2] Since virtually nothing of his recent (and always stimulating) writing has appeared in English, and given the richness of the topics with which they deal, it is entirely fitting that his work be given a strong profile in the overview proposed here of work published in France, which is part of the field of "word-and-image" studies.

In many ways, *L'Image ouverte* is an unusual book. At first glance, it might be considered to be a simple compendium of much of what Didi-Huberman had written in earlier years, but which had never become part of a book volume. Indeed, the core of *L'Image ouverte* consists of eight hitherto separate essays, all of which had first appeared in the late 1980s or early 1990s. Any impression of *déjà vu* as derived from this fact is nevertheless somewhat misleading because it does not deal with the reality that the juxtaposition of these essays often attains salutary results because strange, new connections often give rise to fruitful new suggestions. There is a remarkable unity of focus in these slightly reworked essays from the past; there is also a surprising lack of repetition from one essay to the next. And when repetition does occur – as with the distinction of the visual and the visible (the former being an interruptive force at work within the latter) – it arrives in entirely different contexts, not unlike what happens in some of the great Dostoevsky novels where similar scenes repeat themselves in the lead-up to an epileptic fit.

It is impossible, when reading Didi-Huberman, not to be impressed by his intimate knowledge of Sigmund Freud's vast writings or by the unexpected ways in which he uses Freud's thought throughout his essays (Freud no doubt represents the most extensively quoted figure of the volume). While deeply informed by Freud, and to a lesser extent by Jacques Lacan, Didi-Huberman's reflections and musing are anything but purely psychoanalytical. Dealing in the first instance with artistic languages, and with mediaeval and Renaissance art in particular, these essays could be described as *both* psychoanalytical *and* non-psychoanalytical, that is, both at the same time. Frequent references to the logic of dreams, as exposed by Freud, all lead to a way of discussing the semantic possibilities possessed by images, powerful suggestions that are inherent in their fundamental ways of making meaning, which include, of course, the constant combining of contradictory elements. Didi-Huberman makes frequent use and mention Hegel's concept of the *Aufhebung* in the way he discusses images' abilities to incorporate conflicting elements; he is interested in understanding how contradictory forces meet up with one another and make images work in subtle ways.

Indeed, the book displays a veritable love for contradiction. The fact of using the title *L'Image ouverte* while claiming that it has nothing to do with Umberto Eco's famous work *L'Œuvre ouverte* is but one in a long series of paradoxes, oppositions, and contradictions in which Didi-Huberman will invest heavily. This he does with a relatively wide choice in the particular topics he places at the heart of the eight essays composing this volume (eight, that is, if we exclude the extensive and previously unprinted introduction of forty pages): (1) Apelle and the impossibility of painting "foam," (2) the contradictions surrounding imagery in the early-Christian writings of Tertulian, (3) blood in Christian painting, (4) a general rhetoric of imagery, (5) the secret "stains" on the Shroud of Turin, (6) hysterical convulsionaries of the eighteenth century and self-crucifixion, (7) dermographism, and (8) Georges Bataille.

One gathers from such a cursory glance at the table of contents that Didi-Huberman is anything but a classical art historian, even if in this book, as in much of his other writings, his credentials as an incredibly curious and knowledgeable art historian cannot be denied. His knowledge and deftness as both an art historian and a theoretician of visual languages are wide: he wishes to lead us away from a narrow semiotic vision of images and their inner functioning toward a much wider view that construes them not as signs *but as symptoms*, not as representation *but as "re-presencing,"* not as statements *but as collocations of oftentimes competing elements*, as depicting not a single event *but complex acts and processes* as occurring in and over time. Didi-Huberman is not just interested in the image – or in the history of images – he is also very curious about their interplay with other contemporary cultural phenomena and, in particular, with words and literature. Besides the fifteen beautifully reproduced plates with which the book opens (all of which are referred to, sometimes on numerous occasions), the book contains eighty-five other black and white illustrations. While this book is literally steeped in imagery, these same images are also intimately connected to the etymology of key words in the history of Western culture (hypostasis, exegesis, figure, drama, intelligence as "the gift of someone knowing how to read between the lines"). They are furthermore placed in the context of close textual analyses of Greek and Latin texts from antiquity, which in turn are meticulously dissected. The original ancient words from Latin or Greek which he quotes often accompany the detailed glosses he provides in French. Didi-Huberman is no name-dropper: when he mentions an important thinker from the past, he also gives an abundance of incisive – and oftentimes extensive – quotations that give the reader a definite feel for the text from which he is culling a notion – and he will also provide an extensive secondary bibliography in his generous notes. Even though the bulk of the book was written in the late 1980s, these essays still have a surprising now-ness to them. The reader cannot do without psychoanalysis and needs to be cognizant of visual semiotics, literary theory, anthropology, classical philology and mythology, twentieth-century literature (Bataille and Kafka), twentieth-century philosophy, Christian theology (both from Late Antiquity and the Middle Ages), and mysticism (mediaeval as well as contemporary).

Along with the shadow of Erwin Panofsky, which hovers over most of what Didi-Huberman wrote as a young scholar, his writing in this book displays an astonishingly deep familiarity with German theory (which of course makes his use and understanding of Freud all the more convincing). He quotes not only from Freud but also from other important Germanic thinkers such as Aby Warburg, Hans Belting, Werner Ehlich, Horst Bredekamp, Gerhard Wolf, Erich Auerbach, Götz Lahusen, and many others. Didi-Huberman's Freud is therefore not a thinker narrowly attached to the production of images in dreams and the unconscious; the French theoretician's writing helps us appreciate to the fullest some of the Viennese thinker's greatest insights concerning the secret workings of human culture. What we witness is much less Freud the reader of the unconscious than Freud the penetrating analyst of culture (both high and low); Freud the philosopher will contribute to a better understanding of Bataille, Tertullian, Charcot, Saint Augustine, and Saint Paul, to name but a few of the cultural icons covered in this challenging book. The meaning of the phrase "the open image" is often prodded: images that pull the reader/spectator into them, images of open wounds, images that point to what they cannot figure themselves. This is above all else a book about the Christian mystery of Incarnation, a mystery explored from a multiplicity of angles. Questioning Kantian principles of aesthetics – even though Didi-Huberman is specifically intent on studying religious images – the author wishes to underscore the *interestedness* of images of incarnation – from both the metapsychological and the anthropological points of view.

> You cannot pry the *visual object* (this concrete piece made of wood, canvas and pigments which is hanging on the walls of a museum, for example) away from the *subject of the gaze* (that of the painter, the patron or the connoisseur who follow one another in placing themselves in front of the work, and even our own gaze today). Nor can you pry the *image* from *imagination* or the latter from networks of psychic economies where they come to play. (p. 34)

In the same ways in which the visual disturbs the visible, the symptom disturbs the sign and exegesis disturbs reading. This is a book about words and images which, for various reasons, open themselves up to their exact opposites, and even incorporate them. A method must be devised for seeing this invisible realm and for reading these illegible signs. Just as the foetal Christ clings to the walls of Mary's uterus, hidden – essential – meanings cling to the insides of images and words; we must become sensitive not only to their very existence but also to what they are trying to say. Like the mystical Catherine of Sienna dreaming of entering Christ's body through the wounds of his crucified body, we must learn to envisage a multiplicity of indirect routes for arriving at those hidden languages of which the surface leaves only traces, hints, or symptoms. This is the fascinating language of figures of which the artists of Christianity, despite this religion's original hatred of images, inherited from Moses; it is the language of icons which, in general if not in principle, will eventually become the undisputed masters of Christian thinking. The model for understanding imagery, devised by Christian theologians and artists alike, is far from that developed by Greco-Roman theories of the sign, which presupposed the absence of the thing signified: in the Eucharist, that epitome of mysterious images, the referent – Christ's body – is said to be present in the very sign (bread) with which it subsists. Here too one is struck – and not only by this particular example – by the absolute non-resemblance between the visible signifier (the host) and the signified (Christ's body), as if for an adequate understanding of these languages of sacred art and early Christian theology it were necessary to remember that, ever since Adam and Eve's sin in Paradise, mankind has been excluded from the realm of likeness, that original resemblance that united the Creator with his creatures (mankind created as an image of God). Mankind therefore had to learn to live in the realm of differences. And in these languages of dissemblance one can perhaps discern the principal reason why, for studying the history of Incarnation, it is impossible to dissociate verbal from visual languages: one understands that, in the workings of figures, there is a profoundly verbal *and* iconic basis. The ambiguities inherent in a figure's meanings are not to be disentangled –

this is a region of human meaning-making where contradiction can be neither "undone, resolved nor suppressed" (p. 198) – for what is interesting, as in the language of dreams, is to observe (if not to comprehend) how the one and the other, in all their differences *and despite these differences,* work together in strange relationships of mutual convertibility.

## II. Marie-José Mondzain

A Director of Research at France's prestigious CNRS, as well as a philosopher in the professional sense of the word, Marie-José Mondzain's intellectual career has always been characterized by a provocatively formulated set of inquiries concerning the complicated connection, both in the West and the Near East, between images and icons. Originally a translator of Nicephorus, and soon to become an expert writer on the history of iconoclasm both in Ancient Byzantium and in the West, Mondzain has always sought, with intimate knowledge of ancient theology and philosophy, to uncover the extreme importance of notions of imagery, all of which are deeply rooted in our modern-day culture. Her work has thus brought her to explore the prominence of imagery in contemporary society, the intimate link between political philosophy and the history of images, and lately to the study of films. Bearing the Latin title of *Homo spectator,* Mondzain's 2007 book starts with several anthropological facts concerning the painting of hands on cave walls over thirty-thousand years ago. She reinterprets these facts as the "beginning of mankind" in the social sense of the term, a beginning that occurs through and in spectatorship. She then follows several crucial turns in the history of human spectatorship, including fascinating readings of Saint Paul, and works her way up to the present day in which we witness a much-mutilated spectator in relation to the one with which humanity began.

Of the many volumes published in French by Marie-José Mondzain (see the bibliography at the end of this essay), only one has been translated into English[3] and very few articles have appeared in English as journal entries or book chapters. Her book discussed here contains a multi-dimensional reflection on the philosophical and anthropological meanings that can be attributed to the gestures of those prehistoric humans who, in a cave such as Chauvet in France, but also in many other caves in Europe, began over thirty thousand years ago to paint their hands on the walls and ceilings of the hidden and dark sites they were visiting. Their paintings were achieved by holding a hand on the cave wall or ceiling, spitting paint and pigments both on the hand and all around it, and then by removing the hand, thus leaving a "negative" imprint on the rock's surface.

Following up on (and vastly augmenting) an incisive article first published in 2006, Mondzain interprets this creative gesture as constituting the very first semiotic and artistic gesture of mankind. As such, the negative images of human hands should be differentiated from images of bison and other animals. Moreover, the special creativity of these hand-signs can only be interpreted in the context of the corporeal gestures of which they are the result. More specifically, this creativity must be linked to the fact that the hand-sign as such can only appear in its entirety when the hand is physically removed from the cave's wall where it has just been painted. Without ever presenting the necessity of absence in the birth of humanity's first signs, that is to say, without interpreting these signs as belonging uniquely to a psychoanalytical reading of desire and lack, Mondzain's writing is not entirely bereft of psychoanalytical tones nor is she disinterested in the fact of physical separation that characterizes this founding gesture of humanity. More than anything else, what guides Mondzain's thinking can be seen in the multiple links she explores between the birth of truly human signs (the image of a hand that must have been held at a distance from its bearer), the fact of physical separation (this image of the hand can only become a sign once its owner has removed it from the spot where it was painted), and human language in general (that is, "language" in the broadest of senses).

Recalling, near the end of the book, the famous allegorical fable, as told by Diogenes Laertius, which describes human life as a game or struggle attended by three classes of men – competitors, vendors, and spectators – Marie-José Mondzain's *Homo Spectator* emphasizes the importance of spectatorship in both the philosophical constitution and the anthropological development of humanity. The full-fledged human is born at that crucial moment in time when the humanoid begins to show his or herself to someone else *precisely as someone in the act of showing something*. Humanity's humanness is born when more than one subject recognizes the other at a distance, and in a complicated dialectical relationship. In other words, humanity is born at the moment when more than one being exchanges signs in a place where it was also necessary to overcome fear and darkness. Human language is born alongside humanity. The birth of language is seen as occurring within the dynamic connection specifically related to visual signs, that is to say, between a first person's desire to show something and a second one's willingness to witness this same showing. This moment of shared spectatorship is thus considered to be at the heart of human language. As she writes in reference to André Leroi-Gourhan's famous work on human gestures:[4] "It was necessary to give a certain freedom to human thinking on the body, but not by transforming thought into an entity that would exist outside and independently of the body. On the contrary, it was by placing thought within the body, and in bodily gestures, that mankind, at the moment of its birth into humanity, will invent the life of things in their absence" (p. 11).

We thus understand the primordiality of absence in the constitution of humanity *per se* and we also see that language (*logos*) is first of all born of a relationship between a first person who sees and a second person who signals what he or she sees. The moment of spectatorship is an empowering one: it implies a surmounting of fear and darkness, a moment of sharing the experience of what is being shown, an event shared by the person who has shown his or herself showing and all the other persons in attendance. "Creating an image amounts to giving birth to the human being as a spectator. Being human amounts to producing the trace of one's absence on the world's walls and constituting oneself as a subject" (p. 37). Any such human subject will not be seen by others as just another object in the world, because such a subject is showing to others what it is that they can share: signs, traces, gestures, withdrawal. The sign of the hand is seen as having been desired to be seen, and the owner of the hand, as subject, shows his or her own fragility in the very sign that demonstrates its own distinctiveness from all other objects. This distinctiveness derives from the fact that it belongs to a newly born human subject.

The dimensions of absence and separateness play a crucial role in Mondzain's vision of the birth of human language. In this context, she later provides yet another interesting re-reading, this time of the Tower of Babel. It is near the middle-point of her rich book where she discusses this story in detail, linking it specifically to that ancient founding gesture of the prehistoric human placing his or her hand on the cave wall and then withdrawing it. In this same gesture, it is important not to forget the blowing of pigments all over the hand from the mouth. The multiplication of languages in the story of the Tower of Babel is a figure of the need of humans to deal with differences amongst one another, of the need to mature beyond an undifferentiated and undifferentiable semiotic mass. "Speaking together is a means of regulating disagreement, a politics of translation and misunderstanding" (p. 133): it has no other purpose than to constitute, over and over again, a fragile sharing of space and time. Indeed, as Mondzain writes, the inhabitant of language has no fixed address and the site of human subjectivity has no fixed locus. "What is qualified by an image is the nature of the gaze that the subject bears upon it" (p. 82).

This book is difficult reading. It combines semiotics and psychoanalysis, political theory and theology. Mondzain's reader is challenged by a rich panorama of thinking about language and images which includes insightful analyses of the role of hands and pointed discussions concerning idols within religious thinking (as well as the attempts to abolish these idols within that same thinking), the place of images in the thinking of the early Christian Church as compared both to Jewish and Islamic thinking. It stresses the forever shifting historical boundaries between what is visible and what is invisible just as it brings out the necessarily political nature of the visual sign and all the human gestures that ground it. In short, Mondzain's book is an unusual history of the nature of human spectatorship, beginning with that founding moment when prehistoric beings painted their hands on cave walls (and brought themselves to humanity), to the present period characterized by the spectacular productions of audio-visual industries. In between, we find bold uses of the imagery of the Pietà in Christian culture, we find the story of the gift of languages and how this story changed the politics of imagery and language, and we also discover the role of film in the midst of manipulative modern imagery as well as the role of images in the history of modern propaganda.

Her wish is that we never forget that empowering, humanizing moment that those precious early occurrences of painted-painting hands must have incorporated. The current danger is that the link with images, which characterized the birth of humanity, may now also become the cause of humanity's death. Aesthetics and politics are inherently intertwined both in their philosophical bases and in their technical make-up. One can see this in the ways in which human spectators – the contemporary citizens of Western societies – are becoming less and less owners of their spectatorship and more and more subjected to a constant downgrading of an all-important part of humanity, that part that derives from the originary moment when one person first showed his or her self to someone else in the act of showing. All this, along with the cynical attitudes of what Adorno called the cultural industry, is part of a regrettable tendency in contemporary societies to mistreat spectators-citizens by equivocating them with passive receivership.

If one agrees that, in many ways, this book functions as a summary of much of Mondzain's previous work, one must also observe that it does this summarizing with many new twists and turns. Further, the ways in which it summarizes her previous work are entirely different from those seen in Didi-Huberman's book, which literally contains articles having formerly appeared in article form. Here the "status of summary" is achieved through a provocative return to issues broached in her earlier work, each time by adding new developments to these problems and by including thought-provoking references to the current political climate in France (the discussions where Mondzain analyzes the politics of fear – and how these politics are part of a long tradition in the West – are nothing short of fascinating). Her book comprises bold ventures into the field of film studies, and incisive parallels are established between thinking on images and twentieth-century political philosophy, especially that of Hannah Arendt.

## III. ANNE SURGERS

Anne Surgers has been actively involved, over the past two decades, in the French theatre and has published a number of academic articles in this area of study. Through her work on the history of theatre, she became interested in the multi-medial area of theatrical décor, exploring extant sets and engravings from the sixteenth and seventeenth centuries in addition to studying the written testimonies about the stage décor of famous plays.[5] From this work stems the current, beautifully illustrated book, which combines her interest in "theatrical art" with two other long-standing lines of inquiry, that of the history of rhetoric and that of art history.

The words in the book's title *Et que dit ce silence?* ["And what does this silence mean?"] come from the end of the second act in Jean Racine's *Bérénice*, at that crucial moment when the ever-loving Bérénice is left breathless by the brusque departure of Titus, the man who dramatically leaves both the stage and her life. Anne Surger's book postulates that, before the dominance of writing had established itself in the West over oral forms of communication, rhetoric – as an expressive tool conceived for attaining conviction – was the implicit model not only for verbal forms of expression but for non-verbal means of expression as well, including in particular images. "Amongst the hypotheses which inspired the present work lies a question: why would the realm of the visible, at a time when rhetoric was still the only means of transmitting one's thought, not have been constructed with rhetorical tools, considering that the visible too is laden with the responsibility of conviction?" (p. 47)

The core of Anne Surgers' book is thus dedicated to resurrecting one of the facets of rhetoric that, very early in our modern period, the cultural history of the West had unfortunately forgotten, before having discarded rhetorical theory in its entirety as something artificial and contrived: this facet is known as *"elocution*," that is rhetoric as action, as bodily movement, as bodily attitudes and physical production.

This book is part of the grand and venerable tradition of rhetorical studies in the French-speaking world, a tradition that can be seen in Perelman's and Olbrecht-Tyteca's ground-breaking work of the post-war period in Belgium[6] and which was perpetuated in the contemporary period by such prominent French writers as Marc Fumaroli, Georges Vignaux, Alain Michel, Roland Barthes and Gérard Genette.[7] Surgers explicitly compares her approach to the study of "pictorial rhetoric" with that adopted by the now-famous group of researchers from Liège known as the Group μ.[8] Whereas the Liège scholars, Surgers claims, proceed from a generalist point of view, developing first a theoretical framework with which the researcher can then turn to specific works as illustrations of their theory, Surgers wishes to adopt a much more inductive approach, taking a number of significant visual works and then discerning which rhetorical tools can be seen to be working within their hidden structures. Twenty-seven visual works are chosen for illustrations (for the most part beautifully reproduced) and they are each analyzed in detail with a view to uncovering the rhetorical devices that are part of their deep structure (very often these illustrations are accompanied by a detail or by an analytical view, which can include a visualized dissection of the image). The works explored (with the exception of Jan van Eyck's *Marriage of the Arnolfi*) all stem from the long period of European cultural history stretching from the invention of the printing press in 1440 to the publication in France of the first serious monolingual dictionary (1660).

After its opening chapters consisting of general presentations of the work, the book then proposes a loosely-knit dictionary of some twenty-two rhetorical terms (replete with synonyms for each relevant entry). Every "definition" is accompanied by a comparative look at several other definitions, sometimes competing ones, written by prominent rhetoricians. Each definition is also accompanied by at least one visual example that "illustrates" (although Surgers is scrupulous in avoiding use of the word "illustrate") the device being explored. Such a method provides an insightful reading of the famous allegorical portrait of Elizabeth I known as the "rainbow portrait" just as it provides useful tools for reading Nicolas Poussin's *Judgment of Solomon*. Unfortunately, it is less convincing for seeing the paintings involved as more than an excuse for illustrating one or two devices; and it is not apt at bringing the single painting into "dialogic contact" with other contemporary paintings dealing with the same subject matter nor with verbal discourses about that particular painting, either contemporary with the painting itself or with our viewing of it today. This fault is especially true of competing interpretations concerning a given work and how discourses about painting also try to be convincing in relation to one another. Unfortunately, the method developed cannot account either for the inclusion of the "sublime" as a rhetorical device nor can it explain the uncharacteristically incomplete analysis of metaphor (which does not even earn a single illustration within the book).

Much indebted to valuable work on the history of rhetoric, in particular to Marc Fumaroli's books on the history of rhetoric and to Kandinsky's writings on art,[9] and entirely familiar with contemporary semiotic thinking on the theory of dictionaries, Anne Surgers' work provides a valuable corrective to approaches to the word-and-image nexus that often place words ahead of images and neglect the highly rhetorical nature of silently visible languages. In its own way, it attempts to give back to images the powers that the history of the printing press and the historical emphasis on perspective led us to lose.

* * *

In the following bibliography, the reader will mainly find, with only a few exceptions, works printed in France from 1993 to the present (i.e., the last sixteen years). Exceptions concern significant re-editions of important works from the not-too-distant past, influential translations into

French from either English or German (i.e., works that have left a lasting mark on the French-speaking community), and several important publications written in French-speaking countries other than France. Concerning the dates of publication, all books written by the three authors featured in the present bibliographical essay (even those printed before 1993) have been included in the list that follows. Otherwise, the bibliography presented here limits itself to works published since, and including, that year (1993).

## BIBLIOGRAPHY

Abramovici, Jean-Christophe, Pierre Frantz, Jean-Marie Goulemot, and Frédéric Calas. *Diderot, Salons*. Paris: Éditions Atlande, 2007.

Agamben, Giorgio. *Image et mémoire*. Paris: Hoëbeke, 1998.

Albertan-Coppola, Sylviane, ed. *La Philosophie en images*. Valenciennes: Presses Universitaires de Valenciennes, 2004.

Alibet, Jean-Louis. *Le Son et l'image*. Grenoble: Presses Universitaires de Grenoble, 2008.

Arasse, Daniel. *L'Ambition de Vermeer*. Paris: Adam Biro, 1993.

———. *Le Détail. Pour une histoire rapprochée de la peinture*. Paris: Flammarion, collection "Champs," 1996 (1st ed. 1992).

———. *Le Sujet dans le tableau. Essais d'iconographie analytique*. Paris: Flammarion, 1997.

———. *Léonard de Vinci. Le Rythme du monde*. Paris: Hazan, 1997.

———. *L'Annonciation italienne. Une histoire de perspective*. Paris: Hazan, 1999.

———. *On n'y voit rien. Descriptions*. Paris: Denoël, 2000.

———. *Histoires de peintures*. Paris: Denoël, 2004.

———. *Anachroniques*. Paris: Gallimard, 2006.

Armengaud, Françoise, Marie-Dominique Popelard, and Denis Vernant, eds. *Du Dialogue au texte: autour de Francis Jacques*. Paris: Éditions Kimé, 2003.

Arnheim, Rudolf. *La Pensée visuelle*, translated from the English by Claude Noel and Marc Le Cannu. Paris: Flammarion, 1999.

Aubral, François, and Dominique Château, eds. *Figures, figural*. Paris: L'Harmattan, 1999.

Aumont, Jacques. *L'image*. Paris: Armand Colin, 2005.

Auraix-Jonchière, Pascale, ed. *Écrire la peinture entre les XVIIIᵉ et XIXᵉ siècles*. Clermont-Ferrand: Presses de l'Université Blaise-Pascal, 2003.

Baillaud, Bernard, Edmond de Gramond, Jérôme de Gramond, and Denis Hüe, eds. *Images et Encyclopédies*. Rennes: Presses Universitaires de Rennes, 2004.

Bailly, Christophe. *L'Apostrophe muette. Essai sur les portraits du Fayoum*. Paris: Hazan, 2005.

Barreto, Joana, Jérémie Cerman, and Gilles Soubigou, eds. *Visible et lisible*: *Confrontations et articulations du texte et de l'image*. Paris: Éditions Nouveau Monde, 2007.

Bartholeyns, Pierre, Olivier Dittmar, and Vincent Jolivet. *Images et transgression au Moyen Âge*. Paris: Presses Universitaires de France, 2008.

Bégin, Richard, ed. *La Circulation des images: médiation des cultures*. Paris: L'Harmattan, 2006.

Béguin-Verbrugge, Annette. *Images en texte, images du texte*. Lille: Presses Universitaires du Septentrion, 2006.

Bellour, Raymond. *L'Entre-images*, Paris: POL, 1999.

Belting, Hans. *Pour une anthropologie des images*, translated from the German by Jean Torrent. Paris: Gallimard, 2004.

———. *La vraie image*, translated from the German by Jean Torrent. Paris: Gallimard, 2007.

Bergez, Daniel. *Littérature et peinture*. Paris: Armand Colin, 2004.

Berthet, Dominique. *Les Défis de la critique d'art*. Paris: Kimé, 2006.

Beyaert-Geslin, Anne, ed. *L'Image entre sens et signification*. Paris: Publications de la Sorbonne, 2007.

Besançon, Alain. *L'Image interdite. Une histoire intellectuelle de l'iconoclasme*. Paris: Fayard, collection "L'Esprit de la Cité," 1994.

Bocquillon, Michèle. "La Métamorphose (ou la vision) de Denis Diderot." *Tangence* 73 (2003): 117–35.

Boissier, Jean-Louis. *La Relation comme forme. L'interactivité en art*. Geneva: Musée d'art moderne et contemporain (MAMCO), 2004.

Bonfait, Nicolas, ed. *Peinture et rhétorique*. Paris: Réunion des Musées Nationaux, 1994.

Bonfait, Olivier, ed. *La Description de l'œuvre d'art*. Paris: Somogy, 2004.

———, et al., eds. *Curiosité. Études d'histoire de l'art en l'honneur d'Antoine Schnapper*. Paris: Flammarion, collection "Écrits d'artistes," 1998.

Bonfand, Alain. *Le Cinéma saturé: Essais sur les relations de la peinture et des images en mouvement*. Paris: Presses Universitaires de France, 2007.

Bonnefoy, Yves. *Lieux et destins de l'image*. Paris: Seuil, 1999.

———. *L'Arrière-Pays*. Paris: Gallimard, 2003.

Boulnois, Olivier. *Au-delà de l'image: Une archéologie du visuel au Moyen Âge*. Paris: Seuil, 2008.

Bourriaud, Nicolas. *Esthétique relationnelle*. Paris: Les Presses du réel, 1998.

Bouvier, Pascal. *L'image en politique: Théâtralité et réputation*. Chambéry: Presses universitaires de Savoie, 2008.

Brogniez, Laurence. *Préraphaélisme et symbolisme. Peinture littéraire et image poétique*. Paris: Champion, 2003.

Bukdahl, Else-Marie. "Diderot et l'art – éducateur de la société." *Orbis litterarum* 58, no. 1 (2003): 30–43.

Calabrese, Omar. *L'Art de l'autoportrait. Histoire et théorie d'un genre pictural*, translated from the Italian by Odile Menegaux and Reto Morgenthaler. Paris: Citadelles et Mazenod, 2006.

Caliandro, Stefania. *Images d'images: Le métavisuel dans l'art visuel*. Paris: L'Harmattan, 2008.

Castellani, Jean-Pierre, and Monica Zapata, eds. *Texte et image dans les mondes hispanique et hispano-américain*. Tours: Université François-Rabelais, 2007.

Castenet, Hervé. *Entre mot et image*. Nantes: Éditions Cécile Defaut, 2006.

Castillo-Durante, Daniel. *Les Dépouilles de l'alterité*. Montréal: XYZ Éditeur, 2004.

Chambat-Houillon, Marie-France, and Anthony Wall. *Droit de citer*. Paris: Bréal, 2004.

Chassay, Jean-François, and Bertrand Gervais, eds. *Paroles, textes et images. Formes et pouvoirs de l'imaginaire*, 2 vols. Montreal: Presses de l'Université du Québec à Montréal, collection "Figura," 2008.

Chastel, André. *Le Geste dans l'art*. Paris: Éditions Liana Levi, 2001.

———. *Histoire du retable italien des origines à 1500*. Paris: Éditions Liana Levi, 2005.

Château, Dominique. *À propos de "La Critique."* Paris: L'Harmattan, 1995.

———. *Sémiotique et esthétique de l'image*. Paris: L'Harmattan, 2007.

Chauviré, Christiane. *Voir le visible: La seconde philosophie de Wittgenstein*. Paris: Presses Universitaires de France, 2003.

Christin, Anne-Marie. *L'Image écrite ou la déraison graphique*. Paris: Flammarion, collection "Champs," 1995.

Clair, Jean. *Éloge du visible*. Paris: Gallimard, 1996.

Clémens, Éric. *Façons de voir*. Paris: Presses Universitaires de Vincennes, 1999.

Clüvel, Claus, Véronique Plesch, and Leo Hoek, *Orientations. Space/Time/Image/Word*. Amsterdam: Rodopi, 2005.

Coblence, Florence. *Les Fables du visible*. Bruxelles: La lettre volée, 2004.

Cometti, Jean-Pierre. *Art, modes d'emploi*. Bruxelles: La lettre volée, 2000.

Cousinié, Frédéric. *Beautés fuyantes et passagères*. Paris: Gérard Montfort Éditeur, 2005.

Croizy-Naquet, Catherine, ed. *Texte et image*. Villeneuve-d'Ascq: Publications de l'Université Charles de Gaulle-Lille 3, 2003.

Cullin, Olivier. *L'Image musique*. Paris: Fayard, 2006.

Curnier, Jean-Paul. *Montrer l'invisible: Écrits sur l'image*. Paris: Éditions Jacqueline Chambon, 2009.

Dagron, Gilbert. *Décrire et peindre. Essai sur le portrait iconique*. Paris: Gallimard, 2007.

Damisch, Hubert. "La peinture prise au mot." In *Les Mots et les images*, by Meyer Schapiro, 5–27. Paris: Macula, 2000.

Darras, Bernard, ed. *Images et sémiotique (Sémiotique pragmatique et cognitive)*. Paris: Publications de la Sorbonne, 2007.

Déan, Philippe. *Diderot devant l'image*. Paris: L'Harmattan, 2000.

Dekoninck, Ralph. *Ad Imaginem: statuts, fonctions et usages de l'image dans la littérature jésuite du XVII<sup>e</sup> siècle*. Geneva: Droz, 2005.

———, Agnès Guiderdoni-Bruslé, and Nathalie Kremer. *Aux limites de l'imitation. L'Ut pictura poesis à l'épreuve de la matière (XVI<sup>e</sup>-XVIII<sup>e</sup> siècles)*. Amsterdam: Rodopi, 2009.

Delon, Michel. *L'Invention du boudoir*. Cadeilhan: Zulma, 1999.

———. *Album Diderot*. Paris: Gallimard, collection "Pléiade," 2004.

Delporte, Christian. *Images et politiques en France au XXe siècle*. Paris: Éditions Nouveau Monde, 2006.

Démoris, René. "Peinture et science au Siècle des Lumières. L'invention d'un clivage." *Dix-Huitième Siècle* 31 (1999): 45–60.

———, and Florence Ferran, *La Peinture en procès. L'Invention de la critique d'art au siècle des Lumières*. Paris: Presses de la Sorbonne Nouvelle, 2001.

Denis, Michel. *Image et cognition*. Paris: Presses Universitaires de France, 2007.

Desgoutte, Jean-Paul. *Le Verbe et l'image. Essais de sémiotique audiovisuelle*. Paris: L'Harmattan, collection "Champs visuels," 2003.

Desjardins, Lucie. *Le Corps parlant*. Québec: Presses Universitaires de Laval, collection "La République des letters," 2001.

Dethurens, Pascal. *Écrire la peinture de Diderot à Quignard*. Paris: Citadelles & Mazenod, 2009.

"Devant la peinture. Daniel Arasse," special issue of *Esprit* 325, no. 6 (2006).

Didi-Huberman, Georges. *Invention de l'hystérie. Charcot et l'iconographie photographique de la Salpêtrière*. Paris: Macula, 1982.

———. *Mémorandum de la peste. Le fléau d'imaginer*. Paris: Christian Bourgois, 1983.

———. *La peinture incarnée*. Paris: Éditions de Minuit, 1985.

———. *Devant l'image. Question posée aux fins d'une histoire de l'art*. Paris: Éditions de Minuit, 1990.

———. *Fra Angelico – Dissemblance et figuration*. Paris: Flammarion, 1990.

———. *Ce que nous voyons*. Paris: Éditions de Minuit, 1992.

———. *Le Cube et le visage. Autour d'une sculpture d'Alberto Giacometti*. Paris: Macula, 1993.

———, R. Garbetta, and M. Morgaine. *Saint Georges et le dragon. Versions d'une légende*. Paris: Éditions Adam Biro, 1994.

———. *La Ressemblance informe, ou le gai savoir visuel selon Georges Bataille*. Paris: Macula, 1995.

———. *L'Empreinte*. Paris: Éditions du Centre Georges Pompidou, 1997.

———. *Phasmes. Essais sur l'apparition*. Paris: Éditions de Minuit, 1998.

———. *L'Étoilement. Conversation avec Hantaï*. Paris: Éditions de Minuit, 1998.

———. *La Demeure, la souche. Apparentements de l'artiste*. Paris: Éditions de Minuit, 1999.

———. *Ouvrir Venus. Nudité, rêve, cruauté (L'image ouvrante, 1)*. Paris: Gallimard, 1999.

———. *Devant le temps. Histoire de l'art et anachronisme des images*. Paris: Éditions de Minuit, 2000.

———. *Être crâne. Lieu, contact, pensée, sculpture*. Paris: Éditions de Minuit, 2000.

———. *L'Homme qui marchait dans la couleur*. Paris: Éditions de Minuit, 2001.

———. *Génie du non-lieu. Air, poussière, empreinte, hantise*. Paris: Éditions de Minuit, 2001.

———. *L'Image survivante. Histoire de l'art et temps des fantômes selon Aby Warburg*. Paris: Éditions de Minuit, 2002.

———. *Ninfa moderna. Essai sur le drapé tombé*. Paris: Gallimard, 2002.

———. *Images malgré tout*. Paris: Éditions de Minuit, 2003.

———, and Laurent Mannoni. *Mouvements de l'air. Étienne-Jules Marey, photographe des fluides*. Paris: Gallimard-Réunion des Musées nationaux, 2004.

————. *Gestes d'air et de pierre. Corps, parole, souffle, image*. Paris: Éditions de Minuit, 2005.

————. *Le Danseur des solitudes*. Paris: Éditions de Minuit, 2006.

————. *Ex voto. Image, organe, temps*. Paris: Bayard, 2006.

————. *L'Image ouverte*. Paris: Gallimard, collection "Le temps des images," 2007.

————. *La Ressemblance par contact: archéologie, anachronisme et modernité de l'empreinte*. Paris: Éditions de Minuit, 2008.

————. *Quand les images prennent position*. Paris: Éditions de Minuit, collection "Paradoxe," 2009.

————. *Survivance des lucioles*. Paris: Minuit, 2009.

————, ed. *À visage découvert*. Paris: Flammarion, 1992.

————, ed. *Empreinte du ciel*, edition of C. Flammarion's *Caprices de la foudre*. Paris: Antigone, 1994.

————, and F. Fédida, eds. *Les Démoniaques dans l'art* suivi de *La foi qui guérit* de J.-M. Charcot et P. Richer. Paris: Macula, 1984.

Doguet, Jean-Paul. *L'Art comme communication. Pour une re-définition de l'art*. Paris: Armand Colin, 2007.

Dosse, François, and Jean-Michel Frodon. *Gilles Deleuze et les images*. Paris: Cahiers du Cinéma, 2008.

Dubus, Pascale. *Qu'est-ce qu'un portrait ?*. Paris: L'Insolite, 2006.

Escoubas, Éliane. *L'Espace pictural*. Paris: Encre marine, 1995.

Fraenkel, Béatrice. *La Signature. Genèse d'un signe*. Paris: Gallimard, 1994.

Frantz, Pierre, and Élisabeth Lavezzi, eds. *Les Salons de Diderot. Théorie et écriture*. Paris: Presses de l'Université Paris-Sorbonne, 2008.

Fresnault-Deruelle, Pierre. *L'Éloquence des images*. Paris: Presses Universitaires de France, 1993.

Fumaroli, Marc. *L'École du silence. Le Sentiment des images au XVII^e siècle*. Paris: Flammarion, collection "Champs," 1994.

Gagnebin, Murielle, ed. *Les Images parlantes*. Seyssel: Champ Vallon, collection "L'Or d'Atalante," 2006.

————, and Christine Savinel, eds. *Le Commentaire et l'art abstrait*. Paris: Presses de la Sorbonne Nouvelle, 1999.

————, and Christine Savinel, eds. *L'Image récalcitrante*. Paris: Presses de la Sorbonne Nouvelle, 2001.

————, and Julien Milly, eds. *Les images-limites*. Seyssel: Champ Vallon, collection "L'Or d'Atlande," 2008.

Gaillard, Aurélia. *Le corps des statues – Le vivant et son simulacre à l'âge classique (de Descartes à Diderot)*. Paris: Honoré Champion, 2003.

———, ed. *Pour décrire un Salon. Diderot et la peinture*. Bordeaux: Presses de l'Université de Bordeaux, 2007.

Genin, Christophe, ed. *Images et esthétique*. Paris: Publications de la Sorbonne, 2007.

Gens, Jean-Claude, and Pierre Rodrigo, eds. *Puissances de l'image*. Dijon: Éditions de l'Université de Dijon, 2007.

Godeau, Florence, ed. *'Et in Fabula Pictor.' Peintres-écrivains au XX$^e$ siècle: des fables en marge de tableaux*. Paris: Éditions Kimé, 2006.

Gratton, Johannie. *L'Œil écrit: études sur les rapports entre image et texte*. Geneva: Slatkine, 2005.

Guénon, Denis. *L'Exhibition des mots (et autres idées du théâtre et de la philosophie)*. Paris: Circé, 1998.

Guerena, Jean-Louis, ed. *Image et transmission des savoirs dans les mondes hispanique et hispano-américain*. Tours: Université François-Rabelais, 2007.

Guillemet, Morgane. "Tableaux enchanteurs. Peintures et images de boudoir dans le roman libertin du XVIII$^e$ siècle." In *À l'œil. Des interférences textes/images en littérature*, ed. Jean-Pierre Montier, 169–85. Rennes: Presses Universitaires de Rennes, 2007.

Hamon, Philippe. *Imageries, littérature et images au XIX$^e$ siècle*. Paris: José Corti, 2001.

Haquette, Jean-Louis, and Emmanuelle Hénin, eds. *La Scène comme tableau*. Poitiers: La Licorne, 2004.

Havelange, Carl. *De l'Œil au monde. Une histoire du regard au seuil de la modernité*, Paris: Fayard, 1998.

Hébert, Louis. *Dispositifs pour l'analyse des textes et des images*. Limoges: Presses Universitaires de Limoges, 2007.

Heck, Christian. *Lecture, représentation et citation: l'image comme texte et l'image comme signe (XI$^e$–XVII$^e$ siècles)*. Lille: Université Charles-de-Gaulle, 2007.

Henry, Michel. *Voir l'invisible. Sur Kandinsky*. Paris: Presses Universitaires de France, 2005.

Herschberg-Pierrot, Anne. *Le Style en mouvement. Littérature et art*. Paris: Belin, 2005.

Heuser, Martin, Michèle Hannosch, Eric Haskell, Leo Hoeck, David Scott, and Peter de Voogd, eds. *On Verbal/Visual Representation*. Amsterdam: Rodopi, 2005.

Hoek, Leo H. and Kees Meerhoff, eds. *Rhétorique et image. Textes en hommage à A. Kibéda Varga.* Amsterdam: Rodopi, 1995.

"Images en textes," special issue of *Romantisme* 118, no. 4 (2004).

*Image[&]Narrative* (on-line journal available at http://www.imageandnarrative. be)

Jacob, Stéphane. *La Curiosité. Éthologie et psychologie.* Bruxelles: Mardaga, 2002.

Jacques, Francis, and Jean-Louis Leutrat. *L'Autre visible.* Paris: Klincksieck / Presses de la Sorbonne Nouvelle, 1998.

Jacquot, Dominique, and Sophie Join-Lambert, eds. *L'Apothéose du geste. L'esquisse peinte en France au siècle de Boucher et Fragonard.* Paris: Hazan, 2003.

Jakobi, Marianne. *Jean Buffet et la fabrique du titre.* Paris: CNRS Éditions, 2006.

Joly, Martine. *L'Image et son interprétation.* Paris: Nathan, 2002.

———. *L'Image et les signes.* Paris: Nathan, 2004.

———. *Introduction à l'analyse de l'image.* Paris: Nathan, 2004.

Jullien, François. *Le Nu impossible.* Paris: Seuil, 2005.

———. *Si parler va sans dire. Du logos et d'autres ressources.* Paris: Seuil, 2006.

Klossowski, Pierre. *Tableaux vivants: essais critiques 1936–1983.* Paris: Gallimard, collection "Le Promeneur," 2001.

Kramer, Nathalie. *Préliminaires à la théorie esthétique du XVIII^e siècle.* Paris: Kimé, 2008.

Labarthe-Postel, Judith. *Littérature et peinture dans le roman moderne. Une rhétorique de la vision.* Paris: L'Harmattan, 2002.

La Font de Saint-Yenne, Étienne de. *Œuvre critique,* ed. Étienne Jollet. Paris: École Nationale Supérieure des Beaux-Arts, 2001.

Lageira, Jacinto. *L'Image du monde dans le corps du texte,* 2 vols. Bruxelles: La Lettre volée, 2003.

———, ed. *Du Mot à l'image et du son au mot.* Marseille: Le Mot et le reste, 2006.

Landowski, Éric. *Présences de l'autre.* Paris: Presses Universitaires de France, collection "Formes sémiotiques," 1997.

Landry, Jean-Pierre, and Pierre Servet, eds. *Le Dialogue des Arts, 1: Littérature et peinture du Moyen Âge au XVII^e siècle.* Lyons: CEDIC, 2001.

Lavaud, Laurent, ed. *L'Image.* Paris: GF-Flammarion, 1999.

Lavezzi, Elizabeth. *Diderot et la littérature d'art. Aspects de l'intertexte des premiers Salons.* Orleans: Paradigme, 2007.

Le Cercle, François. "Le regard dédoublé." *Nouvelle Revue de psychanalyse* 44 (1991): 101–28.

Legendre, Pierre. *Dieu au miroir. Étude sur l'institution des images.* Paris: Fayard, 1994.

Le Guern-Forel, Odile. "Dire le visible: à la recherche de correspondances visuelles pour des systèmes de catégories visuelles." *Visio* 4, no. 3–4 (2002–2003): 17–23.

Lenain, Thierry. *L'Image : Deleuze, Foucault, Lyotard.* Paris: Vrin, 1997.

Le Rider, Jacques. *Les Couleurs et les mots,* Paris: Presses Universitaires de France, 1997.

Lévi-Strauss, Claude. *Regarder, écouter, lire.* Paris: Plon, 1993.

Lièvre-Crosson, Élisabeth. *Comprendre la peinture.* Toulouse: Les Essentiels Milan, 1999.

Lilti, Antoine. *Le Monde des salons. Sociabilité et mondanité à Paris au XVIII^e siècle.* Paris: Fayard, 2005.

"L'Image et la poésie," special issue of *Poésie* 47 (2006).

"Littérature et peinture," special issue of *Europe* 933–934 (2007): 1–508.

Lojkine, Stéphane. "De l'écran classique à l'écran sensible: le *Salon de 1767* de Diderot." In *L'Écran de la représentation,* 292–346. Paris: L'Harmattan, 2001.

———. "De la figure à l'image: l'allégorie dans les *Salons* de Diderot." *Studies on Voltaire and the Eighteenth Century* 2003 : 07 (2003): 343–70.

———. *Image et subversion.* Nîmes: Éditions Jacqueline Chambon, collection "Rayon Philo," 2005.

———. *L'Œil révolté.* Nîmes: Jacqueline Chambon, 2007.

Louvel, Liliane. "La Description 'picturale.' Pour une poétique de l'iconotexte." *Poétique* 112 (1997): 475–90.

———. *L'Œil du texte.* Toulouse: Presses de l'Université Mirail, 1998.

———. "Nuances du pictural." *Poétique* 126 (2001): 175–89.

———. *Texte/Image. Images à lire, textes à voir.* Rennes: Presses Universitaires de Rennes, collection "Interférences," 2002.

———, and Henri Scepi, eds. *Texte / Image: nouveaux problèmes,* Rennes: Presses Universitaires de Rennes, 2005.

Lucbert, Françoise. *Entre le voir et le dire.* Rennes: Presses Universitaires de Rennes, 2005.

Magritte, René. *Les Mots et les images,* ed. Éric Clémens. Bruxelles: Éditions Labor, 1994.

Marion, Jean-Luc. *La Croisée du visible.* Paris: La Différence, 1991 (2nd ed., Paris: Presses Universitaires de France, 1996).

Marin, Louis. *Opacité de la peinture. Essais sur la représentation au Quattrocento.* Paris: Casa Usher, 1989 (2nd ed. prepared by Cléo Pace, Paris: Éditions de l'École des Hautes Études en Sciences Sociales, 2006).

———. *Des Pouvoirs de l'image. Gloses.* Paris: Seuil, 1993.

———. *De la représentation.* Paris: Gallimard / Seuil, 1994.

———. *De l'Entretien.* Paris: Éditions de Minuit, 1997.

———. *Détruire la peinture.* Paris: Flammarion, 1997.

———. *Politiques de la représentation.* Paris: Kimé, 2005.

Martin, Christophe. *Dangereux Suppléments. L'Illustration du roman en France au XVIIIᵉ siècle.* Paris/Leuven: Peeters, 2005.

Martin-Haag, Éliane. *Lettre sur les aveugles. Diderot.* Paris: Ellipses, 1999.

Massin, Robert. *La Lettre et l'image.* Paris: Gallimard, 1993.

Massing, Jean-Michel. *La Calomnie d'Apelle et son iconographie. Du texte à l'image.* Strasbourg: Presses Universitaires de Strasbourg, 1995.

Mathet, Marie-Thérèse, ed. *La Scène: littérature et arts visuels.* Paris: L'Harmattan, collection "Champs visuels," 2001.

———, ed. *L'Incompréhensible. Littérature, réel, visuel.* Paris: L'Harmattan, collection "Champs visuels," 2003.

Mathieu-Castellani, Gisèle, ed. *La Pensée de l'image. Signification et figuration dans le texte et la peinture.* Paris: Presses Universitaires de Vincennes, 1994.

Melot, Michel. *Une brève histoire de l'image.* Paris: L'Œil Neuf Éditions, 2007.

Michaud, Philippe-Alain. *Aby Warburg et l'image en mouvement.* Paris: Macula, 1998.

Michon, Pierre. *Corps du roi.* Paris: Verdier, 2002.

Milner, Max. *L'Envers du visible. Essai sur l'ombre.* Paris: Seuil, 2005.

Milly, Jullien, and Mirielle Gagnebin, eds. *Les images limites.* Seyssel: Champ Vallon, 2008.

Modica, Massimo. "Diderot philosophe et critique d'art." *Recherches sur Diderot et sur l'Encyclopédie* 33 (2002): 73–95.

Mondzain, Marie-José. Translation, notes and presentation of Nicephoros. *Discours contre les iconoclastes.* Paris: Klincksieck, 1989.

———. "L'Image mensongère." *Rue Descartes* 8–9 (1993): 11–26.

———. *L'Image naturelle.* Paris: Nouveau commerce, 1995.

———. *Van Gogh ou la peinture comme tauromachie.* Paris: Éditions de l'Épure, 1996.

———. *Cueco. Dessins.* Paris: Cercle d'art, 1997.

———. *Image, icône, économie.* Paris: Seuil, 1998.

———. *Transparence, opacité ?* Paris: Cercle d'art, 1999.

———. *L'Image peut-elle tuer ?* Paris: Bayard, 2002.

———. *Le Commerce des regards.* Paris: Seuil, 2003.

———, ed. *Voir ensemble.* Paris: Gallimard, 2003.

———. "Les Images parlantes." In *Les Images parlantes,* ed. Murielle Gagnebin, 13–28. Seyssel: Champ Vallon, collection "L'Or d'Atalante," 2005.

———. *L'Arche et l'arc-en-ciel. Michel-Ange – la voûte de la chapelle Sixtine.* Paris: Le Passage, 2006.

———. *Qu'est-ce que tu vois?.* Paris: Gallimard, 2007.

———. *Homo spectator.* Paris: Bayard, 2007.

———. *La Mode.* Paris: Bayard Centurion, 2009.

Mons, Alain. *La Traversée du visible.* Paris: Les Éditions de la passion, 2002.

Montandon, Alain, ed. *Iconotextes.* Clermont-Ferrand: Presses Universitaires Blaise-Pascal, 2002.

Montier, Jean-Pierre. *À l'oeil: interférences textes/images en littérature.* Rennes: Presses Universitaires de Rennes, 2007.

———, ed. *Mots et images de Guillevic.* Rennes: Presses Universitaires de Rennes, 2007.

Morizot, Jacques. *La Philosophie de l'art de Nelson Goodman.* Nîmes: Éditions Jacqueline Chambon, collection "Rayon Art," 1996.

———. *Interfaces: Texte et image. Pour prendre du recul vis-à-vis de la sémiotique.* Rennes: Presses Universitaires de Rennes, 2004.

———. *Qu'est-ce qu'une image ?.* Paris: Vrin, 2005.

Moser-Verrey, Monique, Lucie Desjardins, and Chantal Turbide, eds. *Le Corps romanesque: Images et usages topiques sous l'Ancien Régime.* Quebec City: Presses de l'Université Laval, collection "La République des Lettres. Symposium," 2009.

Nancy, Jean-Luc. *Le Regard du portrait.* Paris: Galilée, 2000.

———. *À l'écoute.* Paris: Galilée, 2002.

———. *Au fond de l'image.* Paris: Galilée, 2003.

———, and Federico Ferrari. *Iconographie de l'auteur.* Paris: Galilée, 2005.

Née, Patrick. *Yves Bonnefoy.* Paris: Ministère des Affaires étrangères, 2005.

———. *Yves Bonnefoy penseur de l'image ou les Travaux de Zeuxis.* Paris: Gallimard, 2006.

Neyrat, Frédéric. *L'Image hors-l'image.* Paris: Éditions Léo Scheer, 2003.

Noudelmann, François. *Image et absence: essai sur le regard.* Paris: L'Harmattan, 1998.

Ortel, Philippe. *La Littérature à l'ère de la photographie. Enquête sur une révolution invisible.* Nîmes: Éditions Jacqueline Chambon, 2002.

Ouellet, Pierre. *Voir et savoir. La perception des univers du discours.* Montréal: Éditions Balzac, 1993.

——, and Simon Harel, eds. *Quel Autre? L'Altérité en question.* Montréal: VLB éditeur, 2007.

Paillard, Marie-Christine, ed. *Le roman du peintre.* Clermond-Ferrant: Presses Universitaires Blaise-Pascal, 2008.

Pavis, Patrice. *Vers une théorie de la pratique théâtrale. Voix et images de la scène.* Lille: Presses Universitaires du Septentrion, 2007.

Peñuela Cañizal, Eduardo. "La voix dans le miroir: le dialogisme métaphorique." *Recherches sémiotiques / Semiotic Inquiry* 18, no. 1–2 (1998): 205–16.

Péquignot, Bruno. *Recherches sociologiques sur les images.* Paris: L'Harmattan, 2008.

Peyré, Yves. *Peinture et poésie. Le dialogue par le livre.* Paris: Gallimard, 2001.

Piret, Pierre. *La literature à l'ère de la reproductibilité technique.* Paris: L'Harmattan, 2007.

Popelard, Marie-Dominique. *Moi Gabriel, vous Marie. L'Annonciation: une relation visible.* Paris: Bréal, 2002.

——. *Ce que fait l'art. Approche communicationnelle.* Paris: Presses Universitaires de France, 2002.

——, and Anthony Wall. *Des Faits et gestes.* Paris: Bréal, 2003.

——, and Emmanuele Banfi. *Peindre les idées? Sur la calligraphie chinoise.* Paris: Presses Universitaires de France, 2007.

——, ed. *Moments d'incompréhension. Une approche pragmatique.* Paris: Presses de la Sorbonne Nouvelle, 2007.

Preiss, Nathalie, and Joëlle Raineau, eds. *L'Image à la lettre.* Paris: Éditions des Cendres / Paris-Musées, 2005.

Prudon, Montserrat, ed. *Peinture et écriture, 1.* Paris: La Différence-Éditions Unesco, 1996.

——, ed. *Peinture et écriture, 2: Le livre d'artiste.* Paris: La Différence-Éditions Unesco, 1997.

——, ed. *Peinture et écriture, 3: Frontières éclatées.* Paris: La Différence-Éditions Unesco, 2000.

Quenot, Michel. *Du Visible à l'invisible.* Paris: Éditions du Cerf, 2008.

Quignard, Pascal. *Le Nom sur le bout de la langue.* Paris: P.O.L., 1993.

——. *Rhétorique speculative.* Paris: Éditions Calmann-Lévy, 1995.

————. *Georges de La Tour*. Paris: Galilée, 2005.

Rancière, Jacques. *Le Destin des images*. Paris: La Fabrique, 2003.

Recht, Roland, ed. *Le Texte de l'œuvre d'art: la description*. Strasbourg: Presses Universitaires de Strasbourg, 1998.

Rey, Jean-Michel. *Le Tableau et la page*. Paris: L'Harmattan, 1997.

Richer, Laurence, ed. *Le Dialogue des Arts, 2: Littérature et peinture aux XIXᵉ et XXᵉ siècles*. Lyons: CEDIC, 2002.

Ricœur, Paul. *La Métaphore vive*. Paris: Seuil, collection "Points Essais," 1997 (1st ed. 1975).

Rochlitz, Rainer. *L'Art au banc d'essai. Esthétique et critique*. Paris: Gallimard, 1998.

————, and Pierre Rusch, eds. *Walter Benjamin: critique philosophique de l'art*. Paris: Presses Universitaires de France, 2005.

Ropars-Wuilleumier, Marie-Claire. *L'Idée d'image*. Paris: Presses Universitaires de Vincennes, 1995.

Rosso, Jeanette Geffriaud. *Diderot et le portrait*. Pisa: Editrice Libreria Golardica, 1998.

Rougé, Bertrand, ed. *L'Index*. Pau: Presses de l'Université de Pau, collection "Rhétorique des arts," 2008.

Rykner, Arnaud. *Paroles perdues. Faillite du langage et représentation*. Paris: José Corti, 2000.

————. *Pans. Liberté de l'œuvre et résistance du texte*. Paris: José Corti, 2004.

Sahut, Marie-Catherine, and Nathalie Volle, eds. *Diderot et l'art de Boucher à David*. Paris: Éditions de la Réunion des Musées nationaux, 1984.

Saint-Martin, Fernande. *Le Sens du langage visuel*. Montréal: Presses de l'Université du Québec, 2007.

Saouter, Catherine. *Le Langage visuel*. Montréal: XYZ éditeur, 2000.

————. *Images et sociétés*. Montréal: Presses de L'Université de Montréal, 2003.

Schefer, Jean-Louis. *Du monde et du mouvement des images*. Paris: Essais-Cahiers du Cinéma, 1997.

Schmitt, Jean-Claude. *Le Corps des images. Essai sur la culture visuelle au Moyen Âge*. Paris: Gallimard, 2002.

Schnell, Alexandre. *L'Image*. Paris: Vrin, 2007.

Segalen, Victor. *Peintures*. Paris: Gallimard, collection "L'Imaginaire," 1996.

Séguin, Jean. *Images et corps*. Saint-Étienne: Presses Universitaires de Saint-Étienne, 2008.

Sierek, Karl. *Images oiseaux*. Paris: Klincksieck, 2008.

Starobinski, Jean. *L'Invention de la liberté, 1700–1789* suivi de *Les Emblèmes de la Raison*. Paris: Gallimard, 2006.

Stoichita, Victor. *L'Instauration du tableau*. Geneva: Droz, 1999.

Surgers, Anne. *La Comédie française. Un théâtre au-dessus de tout soupçon*. Paris: Hachette, 1982.

———. *Introduction à la scénographie du théâtre*. Paris: Dunod, 1999.

———. *Scénographies du théâtre occidental*. Paris: Nathan Université, 2000 (2nd ed., Paris: Armand Colin, 2006).

———, and Christine Hamon-Siréjols, eds. *Théâtre: espace sonore, espace visuel*. Lyons: Presses Universitaires de Lyon, 2003.

———. *Et que dit ce silence? La rhétorique du visible*. Paris: Presses de la Sorbonne Nouvelle, 2007.

Symington, Micéala. *Écrire le tableau. L'Approche poétique de la critique d'art à l'époque symboliste*. New York: Peter Lang, 2006.

Szendy, Peter. *Écoute: une histoire de nos oreilles*. Paris: Éditions de Minuit, 2001.

———. *Sur Écoute. Esthétique de l'espionnage*. Paris: Éditions de Minuit, 2007.

*Textimage* (on-line journal available @ http://www.revue-textimage.com).

Thélot, Jérôme. *Les Inventions littéraires de la photographie*. Paris: Presses Universitaires de France, 2003.

Tiercelin, Claudine. *La pensée-signe. Études sur Peirce*. Nîmes: Jacqueline Chambon, collection "Rayon Philo," 1998.

Tilleul, Jean-Louis, ed. *Théories et lectures de la relation image-texte*, Fernelmont (Belgium): Éditions Modulaires Européennes, 2005.

———, and Myriam Wattée-Delmotte. *Texte, image, imaginaire*. Paris: L'Harmattan, 2007.

Tripet, Arnaud. *Poétique du secret*. Paris: Honoré Champion, 2007.

Turcot, Laurent. *Le Promeneur à Paris au XVIII$^e$ siècle*. Paris: Gallimard, collection "Le promeneur," 2007.

Vaugeois, Dominique, ed. *L'Écrit sur l'art: un genre littéraire?*. Pau: Publications de l'Université de Pau, 2005.

Vettraino-Soulard, Marie-Claude. *Lire une image*. Paris: Armand Colin, 1993.

Virilio, Paul. *L'Art du moteur*. Paris: Galilée, 1993.

Vogel, Christina. *Diderot : L'Esthétique des Salons*. Berne: Peter Lang, 1993.

Vouillloux, Bernard. "La Description du tableau dans les *Salons* de Diderot. La figure et le nom." *Poétique* 73 (1988): 27–50.

———. *La Peinture dans le texte: XVIII$^e$–XX$^e$ siècles*. Paris: CNRS Éditions, 1994.

——. *Langages de l'art et relations transesthétiques*. Paris: Éditions de l'Éclat, 1997.

——. "*L'Impressionnisme littéraire*: une révision." *Poétique* 121 (2000): 61–92.

——. "Discours du collectionneur, discours de la collection au xix^e siècle." *Poétique* 127 (2001): 301–12.

——. *Le Tableau vivant: Phryné, l'orateur et le peintre*. Paris: Flammarion, 2002.

——. *Tableaux d'auteurs: Après l'*Ut pictura poesis. Paris: Presses Universitaires de Vincennes, 2004.

——. "Du Figural iconique." *Poétique* 146 (2006): 131–46.

Wahl, François. *Introduction au discours du tableau*. Paris: Seuil, 1996.

Wall, Anthony. "Le Vocatif des textes écrit et visuel." In *Du Dialogue au texte: autour de Francis Jacques*, ed. Françoise Armengaud, Marie-Dominique Popelard and Denis Vernant, 171–84. Paris: Kimé, 2003.

——. *Ce Corps qui parle: pour une lecture dialogique de Denis Diderot*. Montréal: XYZ Éditeur, collection "Théorie et littérature," 2005.

Watthée-Delmotte, ed. *Art de lire, art de vivre*. Paris: L'Harmattan, 2008.

Winkelvoss, Karine. *Rilke, la pensée des yeux*. Paris: Presses de la Sorbonne Nouvelle, collection "Institut d'allemand d'Asnières," 2004.

Wunenburger, Jean-Jacques. *La Vie des images*. Strasbourg: Presses Universitaires de Strasbourg, 1995.

——. *Philosophie des images*. Paris: Presses Universitaires de France, collection "Thémis Philosophie," 1997.

Zimmermann, Laurent, ed. *Penser par les images*. Nantes: Éditions Cécile Defaut, 2006.

# Notes

1    See the bibliography at the end of this Bibliographical Essay.

2    See *Confronting Images* [French original 1990], trans. John Goodman (University Park: Penn State University Press, 2005); *Invention of Hysteria* [French original 1982], trans. Alisa Hartz (Cambridge, MA: MIT Press, 2004); *Fra Angelico* [French original 1990], trans. Jane Marie Tood (Chicago: University of Chicago Press, 1995). Surprisingly few of his numerous journal articles have found their way into English-language publications.

3    *Image, Icon, Economy: The Byzantine Origins of the Contemporary Imaginary* [French original 1997], trans. Rico Frances (Stanford: Stanford University Press, 2004).

4    André Leroi-Gourhan, *Le Geste et la parole*, 2 vol. (Paris: Albin Michel, 1964).

5    None of Anne Surgers's works (see the accompanying bibliography) has been translated into English.

6    Chaim Perelman and Lucie Olbrecht-Tyteca, *La Nouvelle Rhétorique. Théorie de l'argumentation* (Paris: Presses Universitaires de France, 1958); Chaim Perelman and Lucie Olbrecht-Tyteca, *Traité de l'argumentation* (Bruxelles: Éditions de l'Université de Bruxelles, 1959); Chaim Perelman, *L'Empire rhétorique* (Paris: Vrin, 1977).

7    Marc Fumaroli, *L'Âge de l'éloquence. Rhétorique et "res literara" de la Renaissance au seuil de l'époque classique* (Paris: Albin Michel, 1994); Marc Fumaroli (ed.), *Histoire de la rhétorique dans l'Europe moderne 1450–1950* (Paris: Presses Universitaires de France, 1999); Georges Vignaux, *Le Discours, acteur du monde. Énonciation, argumentation et cognition* (Paris: Ophrys, 1988, collection "L'Homme dans la langue"); Georges Vignaux, *L'Argumentation: du discours à la pensée* (Paris: Hatier, 1999); Alain Michel, *Rhétorique et philosophie chez Cicéron* (Paris: Presses Universitaires de Paris, 1960); Alain Michel, *La Parole et la beauté. Rhétorique et esthétique dans la tradition occidentale* (Paris: Les Belles Lettres, 1982), Gérard Genette, *Figures I* (Paris: Seuil, 1966); Gérard Genette, *Figures II* (Paris: Seuil, 1969); Gérard Genette, *Figures III* (Paris: Seuil, 1972); Roland Barthes, "Rhetoric of the Image," *Image, Text, Music*, trans. Stephen Heath (New York: Hill and Wang, 1977), 32–51; Roland Barthes, "L'ancienne rhétorique. Aide-mémoire," *Communications* 16 (1970): 172–223.

8    Groupe μ, *Rhétorique générale* (Paris: Seuil, 1982, collection "Points"); Groupe μ, *Rhétorique de la poésie: lecture linéaire, lecture tabulaire* (Paris: Seuil, 1990, collection "Points"); Groupe μ, *Traité du signe visuel. Pour une rhétorique du signe visuel* (Paris, Seuil, 1992).

9    Kandinsky, *Du spirituel dans l'art et dans la peinture en particulier*, trans. Philippe Sers (Paris: Gallimard, 1989, collection "Folio Essais"); Michel Henry, *Voir l'invisible: sur Kandinsky* (Paris: Presses Universitaires de France, 1988).

# 8

# OTHER CITED (BUT UNILLUSTRATED) WORKS OF ART

Auguste, Bernard (also known as Bernard d'Agesci). *Lady Reading the Letters of Heloise and Abelard*, ca.1780, oil on canvas, The Art Institute of Chicago, 81.3 x 64.8 cm.

Bellini, Giovanni. *Sacra Conversazione*, 1505, oil on canvas transferred from a wood panel. Venice, Church of San Zaccaria, 402 x 273 cm.

Benson, Ambrosius. *Young Woman Reading a Prayer Book*, ca. 1520–1530, oil on wood panel, Paris, Louvre, 75 x 55 cm.

Bourdon, Sébastien. *The Brigands*, middle of the 17th Century, oil on canvas, Lyons, Musée des Beaux-Arts, 38 x 59.5 cm.

Bronzino, Agnolo. *Portrait of Ugolino Martelli*, ca. 1535, oil on wood panel, Berlin, Gemäldegalerie, 102 x 85 cm.

Cano, Alonso. *Noli me tangere*, ca. 1640, oil on canvas, Budapest, Szépmûvészeti Múzeum, 141.5 x 109.5 cm.

Caravaggio. *Narcissus*, ca. 1594–1599, oil on canvas, Rome, Galleria Nazionale d'Arte Antica, 110 x 92 cm.

———. *The Supper at Emmaus*, 1606, oil on canvas, Milan, Pinacoteca di Brera, 141 x 175 cm.

Carpaccio, Vittore. *The Legend of Saint Ursula*, cycle of nine large canvasses in Venice, Gallerie dell'Accademia, 1490–1495.

Champaigne, Philippe de. *The Supper at Emmaus*, ca. 1656, oil on canvas, Angers, Musée des Beaux-Arts, 137.5 x 179.5 cm.

Correggio. *Noli me tangere*, ca. 1525, oil on canvas, Madrid, Museo del Prado, 130 x 103 cm.

Courbet, Gustave. *L'Atelier de l'artiste*, 1855, oil on canvas, Paris, Musée d'Orsay, 361 x 598 cm.

Dürer, Albrecht. *Erasmus of Rotterdam*, 1526, engraving, Amsterdam, Rijksmuseum, 24.9 x 19.3 cm.

Fragonard, Jean-Honoré. *Coresus Sacrificing Himself for Callirhoé*, 1765, oil on canvas, Paris, Louvre, 309 x 400 cm.

———. *Don Quixote Reading*, ca. 1780–81, black chalk and bistre on paper, Winterthur (Switzerland), Oskar Reinhart Museum, *Am Römerholz*, 41 x 27.5 cm.

———. *Education of the Virgin Mary*, ca. 1772–1773, oil on canvas, Fine Arts Museum of San Francisco, 84 x 115 cm.

———. *Education of the Virgin Mary*, ca. 1772–1778, oil on wood panel, Los Angeles, Armand Hammer Foundation, 28.8 x 23.2 cm.

———. *Education of the Virgin Mary*, ca. 1775, oil on canvas, Amiens, Musée de Picardie, 92.1 x 73.1 cm.

———. *Education of the Virgin Mary* [tableau de Bérard], ca. 1772–1778, oil on canvas, Paris, private collection, 90 x 72 cm.

———. *Les progrès de l'amour* or *Les Quatre âges de l'amour* (*L'Amour couronné*), ca. 1771–1772, New York, Frick Collection, 317.8 x 243.2 cm.

Greuze, Jean-Baptiste. *The Young Reader*, ca. 1763, oil on canvas, Paris, Musée Cognacq-Jay, 46.5 x 36 cm. (anonymous copy).

———. *The Little Reader* (*Young Girl Reading the Cross of Jesus*), originally painted in 1763 (and since then lost), engraving by Marie L. Boizot from 1780, Tournus, Musée Greuze, 23.5 x 19.2 cm.

Guido Reni. *Cleopatra with the Asp*, ca. 1630, oil on canvas, Windsor Castle, Royal Collection, 113.7 x 94.9 cm.

———. *Cleopatra*, ca. 1635–1640, oil on canvas, Florence, Galleria Palatina, Palazzo Pitti, 122 x 96 cm.

Hagesandrus, Polydorus and Athenodorus. *Laocoon and his Two Sons*, 1st Century A.D., sculptural group in marble, Vatican City, Museo Pio Clemintino, 224 cm in height.

Holbein, Hans (the Younger). *Portrait of a Young Merchant*, 1541, oil on wood panel, Vienna, Kunsthistorisches Museum, 46.5 x 34.5 cm.

Lagrenée, Louis-Jean-François. *The Death of Cleopatra*, 1755, oil on canvas, Paris, École Nationale Supérieure des Beaux-Arts.

Le Sueur, Eustache. *Jesus Christ Appearing to Mary Magdalene*, ca. 1651, oil on canvas, Paris, Louvre, 145 x 129 cm.

Magritte, René. *La Trahison des images* (*Ceci n'est pas une pipe*), 1929, oil on canvas, Los Angeles, Los Angeles County Museum of Art, 49.5 x 80 cm.

Mignard, Pierre. *Madame de Maintenon (Françoise d'Aubigné) en Sainte Françoise Romaine*, 1694, oil on canvas, Versailles, Musée national du Château et de Trianon, 128 x 97 cm.

Poussin, Nicolas. *Landscape of a Man Killed by a Snake*, ca. 1648, oil on canvas, London, National Gallery, 118.2 x 197.8 cm.

———. *Landscape with Pyrame and Thisbe*, 1651, oil on canvas, Frankfurt, Städelsches Kunstinstitut, 192 x 273.5 cm.

———. *Esther before Ahasuerus*, ca. 1654, oil on canvas, Saint Petersburg, State Hermitage Museum, 119 x 155 cm.

Reynolds, Joshua. *Boy Holding a Pen* (*The Studious Boy*), ca. 1747–1748, oil on canvas, South Africa, private collection, 76.2 x 63.5 cm.

———. *Boy Reading*, 1747, oil on canvas, private collection, 78.7 x 63.5 cm.

———. *Boy Reading*, 1777, oil on wood panel, private collection (sold by Sotheby's, London, November 29, 2001), 76 x 63 cm.

———. *Boy Reading*, oil on canvas, Buenos Aires, Museo Nacional de Bellas Artes, 77 x 64.5 cm (this is an earlier version of the painting sold by Sotheby's in 2001).

———. *Portrait of a Young Boy*, oil on canvas, private collection (sold by Sotheby's, London, November 10, 1993), 83 x 69 cm.

———. *Portrait of Anthony Chamier*, ca. 1762–1764, oil on canvas, Houston, Museum of Fine Arts, 125 x 100 cm.

———. *Portrait of Dorothy, Countess of Lisburne*, ca. 1771–1777, oil on canvas, private collection (sold by Sotheby's, New York, January 12, 1989), 123.2 x 100.3 cm.

———. *Portrait of Emma, Countess of Mount Edgcumbe*, 1762, 127 x 101 cm (work since destroyed).

———. *Portrait of John Mudge*, ca. 1752, oil on canvas, private collection of Arthur Mudge Cardale, 77.5 x 66 cm.

———. *Portrait of Mary Isabella, Duchess of Rutland*, ca. 1784–1787, oil on canvas, private collection, 127 x 101 cm.

———. *Portrait of Miss Emily Wynyard*, 1766, present location unknown, engraving by Samuel William Reynolds housed in London, National Portrait Gallery, 20.1 x 12.8 cm.

———. *Portrait of Miss Popham*, 1765, oil on canvas, private collection (sold by Sotheby's, London, November 15, 1989), 75 x 62 cm.

————. *Portrait of Miss Sophia Hoare*, 1783, oil on canvas, Rochester (New York), Memorial Art Gallery, University of Rochester, 91.4 x 71.1 cm.

————. *Portrait of Mrs. Edmund Burke*, ca. 1767–1773, oil on wood panel, private collection (sold by Sotheby's, New York, May 27, 2004), 76.2 x 61.6 cm.

————. *Portrait of Mrs. Charles Symmons*, 1771, oil on canvas, private collection (sold by Christie's, London, June 16, 2005), 128.5 x 102.8 cm.

————. *Portrait of Mrs. William Johnson*, 1763, oil on canvas, private collection, 72.6 x 63.6 cm.

————. *Portrait of Mrs. Yates reading*, 1774, oil on canvas, present location unknown, 127 x 102 cm.

————. *Portrait of Richard Robinson*, 1763, oil on canvas, Christ Church, Oxford, 124 x 99 cm.

————. *Portrait of Samuel Johnson* (*Blinking Sam*), ca. 1775, oil on canvas, San Marino (California), Huntington Galleries (on loan from Frances and Laurent Rothschild), 75.3 x 62.4 cm.

————. *Portrait of Theophilia Palmer reading Clarissa Harlow*, ca. 1771, oil on canvas, private collection (sold by Sotheby's, London, November 24, 2005), 76 x 63 cm.

————. *Portrait of Reverend Thomas Stuart*, 1735, oil on canvas, private collection, 67.5 x 57.2 cm.

————. *Portrait of William Baker*, ca. 1761–62, oil on canvas, The Provost and Fellows of Eton College, 91 x 71 cm.

————. *Portrait of William Hamilton*, 1757 (or perhaps 1772), oil on canvas, Toledo (Ohio), Toledo Museum of Art, 76.8 x 63.8 cm.

————. *Portrait of William Hamilton*, ca. 1776–1777, oil on canvas, London, National Portrait Gallery, 255.3 x 175.2 cm.

————. *Self-Portrait as a Deaf Man*, ca. 1775, oil on wood panel, London, Tate Britain, 79.9 x 62.2 cm.

———— (attributed). *Presumed Portrait of James Boydell*, oil on canvas (sold by Christie's, London, December 21, 1921), 59.7 x 48.3 cm.

Sirani, Elisabetta. *Cleopatra*, ca. 1650, oil on canvas, Flint (Michigan), Flint Institute of Arts, 99.7 x 75.6 cm.

Solario, Andrea. *Cleopatra*, ca. 1514, oil on canvas, private collection.

Subleyras, Pierre. *Artist's Studio*, ca. 1747–1749, oil on canvas, Vienna, Akademie der bildenden Künste, 130.5 x 101 cm.

Titian. *The Empress Isabel of Portugal*, 1548, oil on canvas, Madrid, Museo del Prado, 117 x 98 cm.

Turchi, Alessandro. *The Death of Cleopatra*, ca. 1631, oil on canvas, Paris, Louvre, 267 x 255 cm.

Valdés Leal, Juan de. *Hieroglyphics of Time* (*Finis Gloria Mundi*), ca. 1670–1672, oil on canvas, Seville, Church of the Hospital de la Caridad, 220 x 216 cm.

———. *Hieroglyphics of Death* (*In ictu oculi*), ca. 1670–1672, oil on canvas, Seville, Church of the Hospital de la Caridad, 220 x 216 cm.

Velazquez (Diego Rodríguez de Silva y Velázquez), *Portrait of Luis de Góngora y Argote*, 1622, oil on canvas, Boston, Museum of Fine Arts, 50.2 x 40.6 cm.

———. *The Supper at Emmaus*, ca. 1622–1623, oil on canvas, New York, Metropolitan Museum of Art, 123.2 x 132.7 cm.

Vermeer, Johannes. *Woman in Blue Reading a Letter*, ca. 1662–64, oil on canvas, Amsterdam: Rijksmuseum, 46.5 x 39 cm.

Vernet, Joseph. *Occupations of the Riverbank*, 1766, oil on canvas, Paris, private collection, 49 x 39 cm.

———. *Occupations of the Riverbank*, ca. 1767, oil on canvas, Saint Petersburg, State Hermitage Museum, 47.5 x 37.5 cm (no doubt a copy of the latter).

———. *A Storm*, 1769, oil on canvas, private collection (once the personal property of Denis Diderot).

Vien, Joseph-Marie. *Saint Denis Preaching the Faith in France*, 1767, oil on canvas, Paris, Church of Saint Roch, 665 x 393 cm.

Vignon, Claude. *Cleopatra's Suicide*, ca. 1640–1650, oil on canvas, Rennes, Musée des Beaux-Arts, 95 x 81 cm.

# COLOUR PLATES

Passant,
regarde ce grand arbre
et à travers lui
il peut suffire.

Car même déchiré, souillé,
l'arbre des rues,
c'est toute la nature,
tout le ciel,
l'oiseau s'y pose,
le vent y bouge, le soleil
y dit le même espoir malgré
la mort.

Philosophe,
as-tu chance d'avoir l'arbre
dans ta rue,
tes pensées seront moins ardues,
tes yeux plus libres,
tes mains plus désireuses
de moins de nuit.

Pierre Alechinsky          Yves Bonnefoy

THE ALECHINSKY-BONNEFOY WALL, 40 RUE DESCARTES, PARIS (CLOSE-UP).

LAURENT LA HYRE, *Noli me tangere*, 1656, OIL ON CANVAS, GRENOBLE, MUSÉE DE GRENOBLE, 162 X 175 CM.

LAURENT LA HYRE, *The Appearance of Christ at Emmaus*, 1656, OIL ON CANVAS, GRENOBLE, MUSÉE DE GRENOBLE, 162 X 165 CM.

HANS HOLBEIN THE
YOUNGER, *Noli me
tangere*, CA. 1524,
OIL ON
OAK PANEL, HAMP-
TON COURT (ENG-
LAND), THE ROYAL
COLLECTION
(© 2010, HER
MAJESTY QUEEN
ELIZABETH II), 76.7
X 95.8 CM.

PIERRE SUBLEYRAS, *Presumed Portrait of Giuseppe Baretti*, CA. 1745, OIL ON CANVAS, PARIS, LOUVRE, 74 X 61 CM. (ERICH LESSING/ART RESOURCE, NY).

JEAN-FRANÇOIS GILLES COLSON, *Portrait of a Young Girl Reading*, SECOND
HALF OF THE EIGHTEENTH CENTURY, OIL ON CANVAS, MORLANNE (PYRÉNÉES-
ATLANTIQUES, FRANCE), MUSÉE DU CHÂTEAU, 58 X 48 CM (PHOTOGRAPH BY
JEAN-MARC DECOMPTE, CONSEIL GÉNÉRAL DES PYRÉNÉES-ATLANTIQUES).

ANNIBALE CARRACCI, *Hercules at the Crossroads*, CA. 1595–1596, OIL ON CANVAS, NAPLES, MUSEO E GALLERIA NAZIONALI DI CAPODIMONTE, 237 X 167 CM.

EL GRECO (DOMENIKOS THEOTOKOPOULOS), *Fray Hortensio Felix Paravicino*, 1609, OIL ON CANVAS, BOSTON, MUSEUM OF FINE ARTS, 112.1 X 86.1 CM (PHOTOGRAPH © 2010, MUSEUM OF FINE ARTS, BOSTON).

JUAN DE VALDÉS LEAL,
*Don Miguel de Mañara
Reading the Rule of the
Holy Charity*, 1681, OIL
ON CANVAS, SEVILLE,
HOSPITAL DE LA CARI-
DAD, CHAPTER HOUSE,
196 X 225 CM.

FRANCISCO DE ZURBA-
RÁN, *Saint Serapion*,
1628, OIL ON CANVAS,
HARTFORD (CONNECT-
ICUT), WADSWORTH
ATHENEUM MUSEUM
OF ART, 120 X 103 CM
(THE ELLA GALLUP
SUMNER AND MARY
CATLIN SUMNER COL-
LECTION FUND).

# INDEX

## A

absorption, 65–66, 76, 84, 86, 178
Agamemnon, 109, 110, 117–18
Alechinsky, Pierre, vii, 2–3, 6–9, 11,
    14–15, 18–19, 22, 239
Altamira, 171, 174, 175, 176, 177–78,
    179–81, 185, 194, 199
Apollinaire, Guillaume, 9, 21, 23
Arasse, Daniel, xviii, 46, 58, 60, 80, 87,
    92, 216, 220
Aretino, Pietro, 47, 58, 60
Aristotle, 104, 107
Arnheim, Rudolf, 10–11, 12–13, 21,
    23–24, 216
art history, xvii–xviii, xx, 20, 201, 203–4,
    213
Augustine (Saint), 26–29, 58, 59, 206

## B

Babel (Tower of), 211
Baretti, Giuseppe, viii, xxi, 68–70, 71, 78,
    80–86, 87, 89, 90, 92, 242
Barthes, Roland, 126, 132, 214, 231
Baudelaire, Charles, 76
belief, xxiii, 11, 24, 26–27, 28–29, 41, 164,
    181, 186
Bérulle, Pierre de, 25, 30, 34–35, 36–37,
    54–55, 58, 59, 60
Bible, 25, 37, 56, 58, 65, 75, 89, 97–98,
Bonnefoy, Yves, vii, 1–2, 6–9, 14–15, 19,
    23, 218, 226, 239
Boucher, François, vii, 66–67, 76
Bourdaloue, Louis, 39, 58, 59
Bourdon, Sébastien, 45, 60, 233
brochure/booklet, 61, 63, 71, 120, 153
Byzantium, 1, 208, 231

## C

calligraphy, 12, 21, 24, 148, 227
Cano, Alonso, 50, 60, 233
Caravaggio, 56, 57, 60, 233
Cardinal de Retz, 93–94, 133, 134
Cartier-Bresson, Henri, 93–94, 126, 132,
    134
Carpaccio, Vittore, 12, 24, 233
Carracci, Annibale, ix, xxi, 113–16, 244
Challe, Charles Michel-Ange, ix, xxi,
    123–25, 127, 136
Champaigne, Philippe de, 56, 60, 134,
    233
Chardin, Jean-Baptiste-Siméon, viii, 72,
    80, 81, 136
Chardon, Louis, 36, 41–42, 58, 59, 60, 78
Chartier, Pierre, 61, 87–88
Chastel, André, 139, 164, 167, 218
Chauvet cave, 209
Cleopatra, ix, 123–26, 127, 136, 234, 236,
    237
Clytemnestra, 109, 111, 117
composition, xxii, 66, 71, 95–96, 98–99,
    107–9, 118, 121, 123, 127, 131, 135,
    153, 157, 162
Comte, Auguste, 181, 196, 198
contradiction, 30, 34–35, 36, 41, 66, 98,
    104, 116, 124, 127, 173, 181, 204,
    207–8
*Conversation Piece*, 65–66, 75
Correggio, 50–51, 60, 233
Council of Trent, 28–29, 50
Counter Reformation, 46, 151
Courbet, Gustave, 76, 91, 234

# D

Dagron, Gilbert, 1, 7–8, 21, 23, 219
decisive moment, , xxi, 93–131, 133, 135
depiction, xix–xx, 2–4, 7–8, 22, 23, 24,
    63, 65, 72, 105, 113, 116, 120,
    147–48, 201, 205
dialogism, 1–2, 18, 65, 86, 215, 216, 227,
    230
Diderot, Denis, xxi, 5–6, 8, 11, 13–14, 21,
    22, 23, 24, 72, 84, 86–87, 89–90,
    92, 103, 105–27, 129–31, 132, 133,
    134, 135–36, 137, 216, 217, 218,
    219, 220, 221, 222, 223, 224, 225,
    228, 229, 230, 237
Dido, 117
Didi-Huberman, Georges, 20, 21, 24,
    202, 203–8, 220–21, 231
Diogenes Laertius, 209
disbelief, 28, 30, 39
disfigurement, 108–11, 116, 118, 120,
    122–23, 131
disguise, 41–42, 47, 50, 100, 114, 163, 207
Don Quixote, 78, 92, 234

# E

Education of the Virgin, 65, 74–75, 89, 234
eikonismos, 7–8
Emmaus (supper at Emmaus), vii, xx, 25,
    29, 31–32, 37–42, 45–46, 54–57, 59,
    60, 233, 237, 240
engraving, xxii, 1, 106, 113, 136, 141–46,
    150, 164, 176, 181–83, 188, 191,
    193, 213,
fiction, 4, 70, 73, 80, 115, 143, 153, 160
film, 18, 201, 208, 212, 213, 217
Fontana, Lavinia, vii, 47–49
Foucault, Michel, xxii, 224
Fragonard, Jean-Honoré, 65, 67, 72, 74,
    78, 89, 92, 115, 135, 223, 234
Francisco de Holanda, 140, 165, 167
French theory, xvii–xviii
Frege, Gottlob, 9, 11, 21
Fried, Michael (absorption), 65, 87, 89
Fumaroli, Marc, 164, 214, 215, 221, 231

# G

Gagnebin, Mireille, xviii, 87, 92, 221,
    225–26
Gargas, x, 171–74, 177–78, 180, 189, 194,
    196, 197, 198
gaze, 9, 14–15, 17, 35, 72, 78, 83–84,
    120, 136, 153, 157, 163, 164, 166,
    167, 170, 173–75, 177–81, 182–84,
    189, 191, 194, 198, 206, 208, 210,
    211–12
genre/genre painting, 14, 34, 63, 65, 70,
    72, 74–75, 88, 89, 90, 100, 127, 128,
    140–41, 156, 160, 167, 218, 229,
gesture, 15, 34, 40, 50, 52, 57, 82, 93, 108,
    153, 155–56, 164, 171–73, 178–79,
    183, 185, 192, 209, 210–14
Goethe, Johann Wolfgang von, 5–6, 8, 11,
    13, 22, 23, 24, 90
Golden Legend, 44, 59, 60
Golgotha, 34, 42, 46
Góngora, Luis de, ix, 145–46, 166, 168,
    237,
Greco (El Greco) or Doménikos
    Theotokópoulos, x, 151–54, 165,
    166, 169, 245
Greuze, Jean-Baptiste, ix, xxi, 65, 72, 76,
    78, 89, 91–92, 120–22, 126–29,
    234,

# H

hair, 53–54, 55, 84, 168
Hercules, ix, 113–17, 133, 135, 244
hesitation, 112–13, 116–18, 131
history, 30, 80, 86, 93–95, 98–100, 102,
    126, 129, 131, 140, 160, 175, 177,
    179, 189, 195, 208, 212, 214
Holanda, Francisco de Holanda, 140, 163,
    167
Holbein, Hans (the younger), vii, 46,
    52–53, 88, 234, 241
Horace, ut pictura poesis, 94, 147, 163, 165,
    168, 230

## I

iconic language, xx, 2, 5, 7–8, 9–13, 16,
   20, 37, 42, 46, 47, 50–52, 58, 94–95,
   101–3, 111–12, 115, 120, 129, 140,
   156, 159, 163, 205, 207, 211, 214
index/indexicality, 7–8, 9, 23, 78–79, 143,
   153, 185, 228
invisible, xx, 123, 180, 193, 207, 211, 219,
   222, 227

## J

Johnson, Samuel, 71, 82, 90, 236

## K

Kant, Immanuel, 18, 22, 24, 206

## L

La Hyre, Laurent de, vii, xx, 30, 42–45,
   52–58, 240
Lafon, Guy, 37, 58, 59, 60, 165, 167
language (birth of), xxiii, 182, 209–10,
   211, 212
Largillierre, Nicolas de, 70
Lascaux, 179
La Tour, Maurice Quentin de, 74, 86
Le Brun, Charles, xxi, 95–102, 104–6,
   107–9, 111–12, 128, 132
Leroi-Gourhan, André, 173, 176, 196,
   197, 198, 210, 231
Lessing, Gotthold Ephraim, xxi, 12, 18,
   22
linguistic turn, xviii
literary theory, xviii, xx, 4–5, 13, 89, 201,
   205
looking, 9, 14–15, 17, 35, 72, 78, 83–84,
   120, 136, 153, 157, 163, 164, 166,
   167, 170, 173–75, 177–81, 182–84,
   189, 191, 194, 198, 206, 208, 210,
   211–12
Lope de Vega, ix, 143–45, 165, 168

## M

Magritte, René, 14, 22, 24, 224, 235
make-belief, 4, 70, 73, 80, 115
Mannings, David, 70, 84, 87, 90, 91
Marie de Medici. *See* Medici, Marie de
Marin, Louis, xviii, 157, 165, 167, 169,
   170, 225
martyrdom, 150, 160, 162
Mary Magdalene, xx, 25–30, 31, 33–37,
   39–42, 44, 46–47, 49, 50–57, 58, 59,
   60, 74–75, 234
Medici, Marie de, 115, 118–22
*media res*, 73
Merleau-Ponty, Maurice, 192, 196, 199
metalanguage, metalinguistic
   commentary, xx, 3, 76, 145
Mignard, Pierre, 74, 91, 235
moment (in time), xxi, 3, 9, 19, 25, 29, 34,
   37, 40–42, 45, 46–47, 56–57, 70,
   73, 93–131, 132, 134, 135, 153, 160,
   162, 173, 179, 181, 182, 183, 185,
   193, 195, 210, 212
Mondzain, Marie-José, 202, 208–213,
   225–26, 231
Morizot, Jacques, 14, 22, 24, 226
Mozart, Wolfgang Amadeus, 75–76
mysticism, xx, 25, 34–36, 41–42, 55, 159,
   205, 207

## N

Nancy, Jean-Luc, 150, 166, 167, 170, 226
narrative, 18, 23, 26, 31, 37, 39–41, 54,
   56, 73, 93–94, 95–96, 98, 101, 103,
   109, 112, 115–16, 124, 130–31, 141,
   159–60, 175, 179–80, 182, 189, 193,
   195,
negative image, 33, 171–72, 173, 175,
   177–78, 182, 189, 194, 197, 209
*noli me tangere*, vii, 26–27, 30, 37, 43, 46,
   48–54, 56, 60, 233, 240–41
Origen, 58, 60
origin (birth) of language, xxiii, 182,
   209–10, 211, 212

# P

Pacheco, Francesco, x, 148–49, 166, 168
Panofsky, Erwin, 133, 135, 206
passivity, 208, 212
Paul (Saint), 206, 208
pictorial language, xx, 2, 5, 7–8, 9–13, 16, 20, 37, 42, 46, 47, 50–52, 58, 94–95, 101–3, 111–12, 115, 120, 129, 140, 156, 159, 163, 205, 207, 211, 214
Pierce, Charles Sanders, 5, 9, 22, 229
poetry, poetic, xxii, 2, 4, 8–9, 12–13, 20, 40, 54, 80, 102, 104, 107, 112, 115, 124, 141–46, 147–50, 154, 164, 168
Pommier, Édouard, 86, 87, 92, 167
Poussin, Nicolas, vii, viii, xxi, 46–48, 50, 53, 60, 95–98, 100–106, 134, 136, 215, 233
portraiture, xxi–xxii, 8, 21, 23, 67–70, 71–75, 78, 80–86, 87, 88, 89, 92, 107–8, 120–21, 139–164, 165, 166, 167, 168, 169, 215, 217, 221, 226, 228, 235–36
pragmatics, 1, 3–4, 15, 21, 70, 72, 78
prehistory/prehistorians, xxiii, 171–95, 196, 197, 198, 199, 209–12
print, 57, 141, 142, 214–15
propaganda, 212
Protestantism, 47, 65
psychoanalysis, 91, 204, 205–6, 209, 211

# Q

Quesnel, Pasquier, 27–29, 58, 59

# R

reading, xix, xx–xxi, 3–5, 6, 13, 14, 16, 23, 24, 61–65, 70–71, 150, 153, 155–56, 162, 172–76, 177–78, 194, 205, 206, 207, 233, 234, 235, 236, 237, 243, 246
   close reading, 80–82, 83, 89, 90
   reading as an act, 12–13, 16, 61, 63, 66, 71, 72–79, 83, 88, 162
   reading in public, xx, 61, 63–65, 66, 76, 86, 162
   reading in private, xx, 61, 63–67, 69–70, 74, 76, 84–86,

reference, 2, 4, 6–11, 21, 26, 71, 95, 143, 207, 212
Regnault, Félix, x, 171, 173–75, 177–78, 180, 182, 185–86, 189, 194, 196, 197, 198
Rembrandt Harmenszoon van Rijn (Rembrandt), 62, 63, 65
Retz, Cardinal de, 93–94, 132, 134
Reynolds, Joshua, viii, xxi, 68, 70–72, 80–86, 87, 88, 89, 90–91, 92, 235–36
rhetoric, 5, 20, 99, 102, 130, 141, 145, 147–48, 202, 204, 213–15, 231
Ribera, José de, x, 157–59, 166, 169
Richardson, Samuel, 71, 133, 134
Richardson, Jonathan, 133, 135
Richeome, Louis, 47, 58, 60
Royal Academy of Painting, xxi, 82, 95, 100, 105, 107, 112, 124, 131, 132, 134
Rubens, Peter-Paul, ix, 106, 115, 119–20

# S

*Sacra Conversazione*, 66, 89, 233
Saint-Paul, Charles de, 33, 40, 53, 59, 60
Saussure, Ferdinand de, 13
*seeing as*, xxiii, 16, 47, 173–75, 177, 183–84, 187–89, 192–95
self-reference, 14, 18, 34, 104, 143–44
semiotics, xviii, xxiii, 3, 10, 20, 34, 130, 140, 143, 166, 168, 201, 205, 209, 211, 215, 227
showing, xix, 3–4, 16, 23, 73, 101, 120, 124, 210–11, 212
solitude, 61, 66–67, 70, 84, 86
Subleyras, Pierre, viii, 69, 70, 80–86, 87, 89, 90, 92, 236, 242
substitution, 9, 30, 41–42, 103
supper at Emmaus, vii, xx, 25, 29, 31–32, 37–42, 45–46, 54–57, 59, 60, 233, 237, 240

# T

theatricality, 67, 70, 84, 85–86, 100, 103–5, 112, 114, 123, 129, 150, 179, 213, 218, 222

Theotokópoulos, Doménikos (El Greco), x, 151–54, 165, 166, 169, 245

theology, xxi–xxiii, 27, 29, 73, 156, 205, 207–8, 211

    images in theology, xxviii, 29, 50, 73, 91, 204, 207–8

Timanthes of Cythnos, ix, 109–10, 117

time, xxi, 12–14, 18, 21, 41, 63, 67, 94, 95, 99–100, 102–5, 107–9, 118, 123, 124, 129, 130, 134, 135, 148, 183, 189, 193, 194–95, 205, 210, 211, 219

Titian, vii, 50–51, 53, 88, 236

Tower of Babel, 211

Trent, Tridentine, 28–29, 50

*trompe-l'oeil*, 162

# U

*ut pictura poesis*, 94, 147, 163, 165, 168, 219, 230

# V

vanitas, vanity, 84, 156–57, 164

Vega, Lope de, ix, 143–45, 165, 168

veil of Veronica, 57

Velazquez, Diego Rodriguez, 56, 60, 145, 168, 237

Vermeer, Johannes, 12, 16, 24, 63, 86, 89, 216, 237

Vernet, Claude-Joseph, 106, 118, 129–130, 134, 137, 237

visibility, 4–5, 15–18, 23, 43, 45, 46, 52, 54, 123, 127, 130, 141, 145, 153, 156, 157, 163, 173, 188, 193, 202, 203, 207, 211, 213, 215, 217, 218, 219, 223, 224, 225, 226, 227, 229, 231

Vouilloux, Bernard, 22, 23, 229–30

# W

Wenger, Alexandre, 78, 88, 92

Wittgenstein, Ludwig, 3, 22, 23, 218

Wollheim, Richard, 12, 16–17, 22, 24

written language, writing, x, xxii, 1, 3, 5, 8, 11, 12–14, 15, 63, 93, 140–45, 147–48, 150, 156, 157–59, 201, 213